In Search of the Truth

An Exposure of the Conspiracy

Azar Mirza-Beg

2014

In Search of the Truth

An Exposure of the Conspiracy

Azar Mirza-Beg

IN SEARCH OF THE TRUTH is a portrait of our times, society, and religion. The author, a sheikh of a dervish order, reveals to the modern reader for the first time the secret intrigues and conspiracies of Satan that will bring the world inevitably to destruction, unless all spiritually aware people, and Muslims, unite and stand up against the army of forces of evil.

AZAR MIRZA-BEG was born in the Soviet Union in 1951, and spent his youth in search of spiritual knowledge and for Masters who could initiate him into the mystical way. His early interest was with Yoga, which was then replaced by the teachings of Gurdjieff and Sufi studies that finally led him to become a Sufi teacher and the present Master of the Kubrawi order .

He lived the larger part of his life in various regions of the colossal Soviet empire, but with the raising of the Iron Curtain, he moved to Western Europe and resided in Berlin, Paris, and London. Now he lives in Baku, Transcaucasia.

In Search of the Truth
An Exposure of the Conspiracy

Copyright © 2001-2014 by Azar Mirza Beg
All rights reserved

This publication may not be reproduced or disseminated in any form without permission in writing from the publishers.

Published March 1, 2014 by Progressive Press, San Diego, Calif., www.ProgressivePress.com

Createspace edition, ISBN 1-61577-704-0, EAN 978-1-61577-704-4
Length: 89,000 words on 208 pages, 6 x 9 in. List Price: $16.95.

Subjects:
1. Sufi mysticism and autobiography: the author's search for a teacher
2. The decadence of atheistic modernism and Soviet Communism
3. The corruption of nations by intelligence agencies
4. Zionist Jewry: destruction of the Soviet Union, and war on Islam
5. Society perverted by media, Islam twisted by Young Turks and Wahhabis
6. Neo-fascism in Europe

BISAC Subject area codes:

REL090000 RELIGION / Islam / Sufism
POL005000 POLITICAL SCIENCE / Political Ideologies / Communism
POL036000 POLITICAL SCIENCE / Security / Intelligence
HIS037070 HISTORY / Modern / 20th Century
HIS022000 HISTORY / Jewish

IN SEARCH OF THE TRUTH is a portrait of our times, society and religion. The author, a sheikh of a dervish order, reveals to the modern reader for the first time the secret intrigues and conspiracies of Satan that are bringing the world to destruction. It is a call for all spiritually aware people and Muslims to stand united against the army of forces of Evil.

CONTENTS

CHAPTER ONE: THE GUIDES 7
CHAPTER TWO: REINCARNATION 63
CHAPTER THREE: THE HIERARCHY OF THE SCIENCES 73
CHAPTER FOUR: THE ORIGIN OF RELIGION 86
CHAPTER FIVE: PEOPLE vs. SECRET SERVICES 105
CHAPTER SIX: THE TWENTIETH CENTURY'S GREATEST FABRICATION 124
CHAPTER SEVEN: *CONSPIRACY THEORY* 136
CHAPTER EIGHT: WHY THE BBC HATES CHRISTMAS? 163
CHAPTER NINE: BYZANTINE INTRIGUES 178
CHAPTER TEN: NEO-NAZIS, SKINHEADS, AND OTHERS 195
CHAPTER ELEVEN: THE ELITE SPEAKS RUSSIAN 201
APPENDIX I: A DERVISH'S LETTER TO TURKMENBASHI 206

"Say: O you, who are Jews, if you think that you are the favorites of Allah to the exclusion of other people, then invoke death if you are truthful." (Koran, 62:5).[1]

---

[1] This and all other citations from the Koran are in the translation of M.H.Shakir.

CHAPTER ONE:
THE GUIDES

In the name of God, the Merciful, the Compassionate!

It was in my early childhood that I became aware of the significant place religion held in society, when I observed an argument between children. One group insisted that they believed in the existence of God, while the other held the opposite stance, claiming that there is no God. Both sides stood firm in defense of their positions. The fact that the matter of the existence or non-existence of God caused such a heated debate made me begin to understand its significance for mankind. At the same time I wondered, "Which standpoint is correct, and which is false?" I also noticed that some parents taught their children religious ideas, while others held an atheistic position. I wondered why people could not come to an agreement about this matter.

Later in my early youth, I saw that my soul had religious inclinations, and that believing in God was its essential requirement, as well as an intense desire to find the truth behind religious tenets. In the atheistic realities of the Soviet Union, I did not receive any encouragement to follow the career of a clergyman. However, I realized that a religious seminary would allow me to acquire the required knowledge that would solve my problems, and would also help me to understand the mysteries of life and the afterlife.

Even though I was born into a Muslim family, I had no firm convictions about which theological school I wanted to enroll in, Muslim or Christian. Since our house was situated in a Christian and Jewish neighborhood, I was under the influence of the prevailing attitudes of these people, who considered Muslims as an inferior race, as an uncivilized, backward people. This made me share their viewpoint about the inferiority of everything Muslim, even their religion. Besides, Muslim priests in Baku were of the uneducated sort, who had no real religious credentials. These people, from dawn to dusk, hung around mosques and the graves of holy men to earn money. I had no desire to be one of them, a member of this ignoramus class.

Once in a magazine, I saw a picture of an Indian yogi that struck my imagination. I was impressed by the strange postures and exercises of these folk. I decided I had to find a way to travel to India, where I could find yogi sages who would teach me their wisdom. I thought surely this group should know something important, should be in possession of truth, of some secret that made them turn their backs on society and choose to live an ascetic life in caves and woods. A couple of years passed like this, while I constantly cherished the idea of going to India — this mysterious land of adventure and magic.

Then I met Leon. He was a sophisticated intellectual person who made a little business by the illegal selling of religious literature. From him I acquired my first religious books, photocopies of Patanjali's *Yoga Sutras* and the Gospels. Later he switched to another business, collecting Russian icons. A hundred or so valuable icons covered the walls of his apartment. Much later, I learned about his drug addiction. The proceeds from the antiquarian business provided money to support this expensive habit. He told me that he was part of a ring of art smugglers involved in the trafficking of contraband icons abroad. He offered me icons to buy with life-sized figures and images of Christian saints.

"Or I can sell you this one," he said, pointing at an icon as big as a doorframe bearing an image of Christ. It was a huge wooden board, bearing nothing but the head of the Savior. He said, "This icon once graced the entrance of one of the Kremlin's towers, but was removed after the revolution."

I asked, "How can I transport such a huge and heavy board to my home town without attracting the attention of the police? Why don't you offer me the smaller pieces?"

"The smaller ones I smuggle through the border to the West, to Germany. So I don't need these larger icons," he replied.

Leon was the person who introduced me to Sufism. I told him, once, about my interest in Sanskrit, and he found it a ridiculous idea.

He said, "You are Muslim. Rather than learning Sanskrit go and learn Arabic or Persian, which are more related languages to your Turkic, so that you can study your Islamic classic literature."

"But Islam has no philosophy, mysticism or Yogis!" I exclaimed.

"You are wrong," he said. "Muslims also have philosophical literature. I can sell you a book about Gurdjieff. This man was also from the Caucasus, as you are, and he was a Sufi."

"Who are Sufis?" I asked.

Chapter One: The Guides

An English author wrote that Idries Shah did not just describe himself as the highest authority on Sufi matters in the world, but he even claimed to be the Pole, the pivot of the Universe. To this, the least that could be said was that nobody contributed more than Shah to popularize the doctrine of Sufism in literary works around the world. As Shah said, he had done as much as was humanly possible for a writer to promote Sufi ideas. As to the matter of his being the Pole of the world (*Qutb*), there is no documentary evidence that Shah himself made this statement. It could have been that somebody else described him as such. Nevertheless, even if he made this claim, there was nobody to challenge him, since the other contemporary Sufis were pygmy personalities, who could not be taken seriously no matter what they said or did.

Qutb is a Sufi term which can be translated from Arabic as either of the two geographic poles. In Sufi circles, they use this term to describe the highest position in the hierarchy of saints, the leader of the Sufi brotherhood on whom the order of the universe depends.

In Muslim folklore there is a legendary mystic, Mulla Nasrudin, whose anecdotes are widely circulated among the population. This is one of his stories:

Nasrudin is an old man. One day, he is standing outside his village at a crossroads. One traveling dervish stops by him and asks a question. "I am going on a pilgrimage to a holy site, to the mausoleum of a saint. I have lost my way and my compass is broken. Could you tell me which way the pole is?"

Nasrudin sticks his staff into the ground. "Here it is. This is the exact spot where the Pole is!"

The man looks at Nasrudin in a puzzled way, and then retorts angrily. "Prove it!"

"I have already proved it," Nasrudin tells him, "but if you don't believe me, then you can go and travel around the world, circumnavigate the Earth, to find if I am right or wrong."

Present-day Muslims, who are not familiar with Sufi terminology or ideas, understand this anecdote as if this Muslim sage is mocking the pilgrim, and replying in a rude manner. In reality, this Sufi tale was designed to illustrate their idea of the world, their viewpoint, and the specifics of the mystical path. Thus Nasrudin, who is a Sufi Master, stands at a crossroads, at a meeting point for travelers from different places, the usual spot for all men of wisdom in the Eastern fairy tales to give directions to the people. Then, as the dervish, who is an aspiring mystic, stops to ask for directions to a holy site, Nasrudin – himself a holy man, a guide of the mystical path – advises the man to rather stay with him in that place, which is the ultimate holy place on the Earth, to accept him as his teacher.

Thus Nasrudin used this word, the "Pole," not for its geographic meaning, but rather he answered philosophically, using it as a Sufi technical term. Since the Pole is a Perfect Man, a model man, the most advanced human being, the highest representative of God on the Earth, and at the same time, a rank—it is an ultimate goal, an ultimate destination or stage—it is the final point of the aspirations of the farer of the Sufi way. His other statement, "I already proved it," means that he had already proved his credentials as *Qutb* through his work, his life, and his holy being.

Although I lived in England during Idries Shah's last years, I never had a chance to meet him personally. He passed away on November 23, 1996 (may God grant him mercy).

***

Some thirty years ago, a distinguished Indian Yogi, Devananda, moved to the West, and set up Yoga centers in Europe and America to popularize his Yoga school. It seems he was not a mystic himself, but described his teacher, Sivananda—the founder of the school—as a great mystical persona. Devananda, here and there in his book, brings out passages and quotations from the literary works of his guru, in which he described his various mystical experiences, spiritual states, and insights. Sivananda died in India in 1963.

In the sixties, countless thousands of the Western youth traveled to India to look for gurus, wise men, and mystics. India with its exotics, fakirs, and *saddhus* gave them the impression of a place full of holy men. But in reality, today, spirituality in India, as everywhere else, is at its lowest point, so much so that this huge subcontinent could be likened to an immense spiritual desert. However, Sivananda, it seems, proved that the land is not a complete wilderness after all.

Some forty years ago, the Soviet authorities put on trial a Buddhist scholar called Dandaron, who was accused of secretly preaching religious teachings to the Soviet youth while holding the position of an academician. He was of Buryat descent, a Mongol ethnicity whose traditional faith is Buddhist, and was born in the Siberian region on the Chinese border. He authored, to his credit, several scholarly works on Buddhism. Dandaron was a devoted lama, a saintly person. He continued to preach religion all his life, despite everything, whether it was in the confinement of prison or outside. He established a society in which he taught a Tantric Buddhist teaching. The authorities used their standard tactics against him, falsely accusing him of immoral behavior, organizing sexual orgies, and spoiling university students. The prosecutors misinterpreted the sexual symbolism of the Tantric doctrine for actual agitation to sexual immorality. He was imprisoned, along with several of his followers, while others, under the pressure of the police, bore false witness against him.

Ironically, the Soviet clergy, without exception, instead of conducting their direct duties in serving God and religion, were cooperating with the authorities and stood most loyal to the atheistic regime, while Dandaron, whose official position was a propagandist of atheism, heroically worked to disseminate religious knowledge. He spent, in total, some thirty years in Siberian labor camps, and died there while serving his last prison term in 1974.

It would be appropriate to quote here a verse of Nesimi, a sheikh of a Sufi brotherhood who had been accused by a pharisaic clergyman of heresy, and was condemned to execution by flaying:

Whether thou'd cut the zealot's finger he will deny the Truth.
Lo, but this truth lover cries not though they flay him from head to foot.

N.V.Abayev was yet another Buryat, a Buddhist specialist and academician, who made himself famous among the Soviet Orientalists as the foremost authority on Lamaism and *Ch'an* (Zen) Buddhism. He authored several scholarly books on the art of self-cultivation by mind control in the *Ch'an* and Taoist schools, as well as on the martial arts of Asia. In his works, he followed the Soviet regulations by bringing in quotations from Marx, Lenin, and Engels, but otherwise all his writings were very clever: they went much further than the standard works of Orientalists.

Abayev had a very positive opinion of D.T.Suzuki and his works. I never read the books of this Japanese professor, since I found them much too academic and theoretical, unlike the intuitive, experimental approach of mystical authors. In my opinion, Suzuki was just a theoretician of Buddhist doctrine, a Buddhist philosopher who could not instruct his pupils or give guidance on the mystical path and teach its methods. But, since Abayev praised his works, I accept this Japanese professor as a good religious theoretician.

I personally never met Abayev. I heard about him from an acquaintance, whose friend, a devout Buddhist, had a chance to meet him in Ulan-Ude, Abayev's hometown, near Lake Baikal. The renowned academician, despite his outward disguise as a Soviet atheist scientist, admitted in his conversation with this young man to being a man of faith, a true follower of Buddhism. Later he even made another confession to his guest, in that he claimed that he had reached the upper stage of the path, and was on the verge of attaining the last stage of enlightenment. Soon the young devotee left him, promising to keep his secret to protect him from persecution by the secret police. Nevertheless, despite his promise, the young man told his friend about the conversation, who in his turn told the story to me.

Since it is very rare that one is able to meet a true mystic, a true Master, I desired to go to this Buryatia region to see this man. However, since I did not have his house address I postponed the trip, and it never took place. I do not even know for sure if he is still alive or dead. I heard this story more than twenty years ago. At that time he was already a very old man, so probably he is no longer with us.

It can sound strange that a Muslim person should be interested in meeting a Buddhist holy man. To explain this I will say first, that Islam considers the Christian faith, Hinduism and Buddhism also to be heavenly religions, unlike those pseudo-religious, man-made cults, which have no true prophets or heavenly scriptures.

Secondly, the mystical path, according to mystical authorities, is identical for all religions. The difference is only in religious traditions, customs, dogma, and rituals, while the mystical path is the same, since the inner physical laws – the laws of the inner, invisible world – are the same for the followers of different faiths. A Hindu holy man is no different from a holy Muslim. Their inner truth is identical. However, for an ordinary Muslim it would be difficult to accept a Hindu holy man as such, since his Hindu religious doctrine, his discourse, customs, and manners would be very unacceptable to him as a follower of Mohammedan tradition.

However, to a Muslim mystic, Hindu or Buddhist mystics would be no strangers. Thus the true Masters, holy men of different religions, are more related to each other than to the ordinary believers of their own religion, who may appear to them as strangers, as aliens. In fact, any aspiring mystic starts his religious life and study within his own religion's tradition, but after completion of this study of the fundamentals of his particular faith he approaches the next stage, the mystical path which is similar for the adherents of all religions. Thus the Muslim mystic (Sufi), and a Buddhist or Hindu mystic are going along the same mystical path because, despite the fact that various religions outwardly differ from each other, their inner content—their core, their inner dimension—is the same.

People can be followers of different religions, but they are not different as human beings. Since human beings share similar organs, their inner way to God should be the same for all humankind. Nonetheless, for a holy man to be an acceptable person, to be recognized as such, he should address and speak only to his own community or tribe, to the members of his own religion. Otherwise, he will be misunderstood and ignored. The matters of the other world, the invisible world, are not comprehensible to ordinary people, to the world. Thus a true Master, to be acceptable, to be explicit, is going to use the words, metaphors, expressions, and vocabulary of the given religion to be appreciated by his own community.

To finish this passage about Abayev, I will admit that I cannot be sure about the truth of his claims of reaching higher stages of enlightenment—it could have been true or untrue. Nevertheless, the man deserves respect for his scholarly achievements. It is obvious that he was not a cheap charlatan, but a serious man, so his words should be taken seriously. But he was not my spiritual guide or my personal teacher, so I can't say whether he was a good guide of the path or not.

***

In the last century, there lived one more of the Buddha's followers, Chogyam Trungpa, who had claims to the position of a true teacher, to being a true spiritual guide. Born in Tibet, he went to Britain, and then to America, to preach his Tibetan Buddhist doctrine. Today in many parts of Europe, Canada, and America, many of his meditation centers are operating. Although in the West many thousands of Oriental meditation centers can be found, they differ from one another by their names only, while their contents and substance are very similar. These centers, in our modern consumer society, offer custom-made spiritual teachings to suit Western tastes. People who have no religious credentials run these centers. According to them, all religions, in order to be relevant to the needs of modern life, should be reduced to the simple meditation technique to facilitate healing, to cure depression, neurosis, illnesses, and to fight stress. Religious ideas, according to them, are non-essentials that deserve no respect and should go into the garbage bin. It is clear that these meditation centers, along with their instructors, have a special political agenda to disorient people, to make them stay away from places of worship and ultimately from religion.

Although various Buddhist organizations and temples already existed in the West, Trungpa's centers offered something else. They attempted to take a step further, to make a religious institution which was less formalistic and ritualistic and more oriented to mysticism and real personal development. He brought to his centers the practice of solitary retreat, where they built special chambers or cabins so that the chosen candidates could spend a month or two, to assist them to experience mystical insights and heavenly visions. Trungpa's book *Cutting through Spiritual Materialism* proved him to be a very different kind of teacher, somebody who understood the inner, mystical, esoteric contents of religion, unlike other formal representatives of Buddhism who are merely familiar with the letter of religious doctrine. Unlike authors who expand Buddha's teaching in a formal and dogmatic way, he used very modern language with common-day terms and ideas to explain the essence of religion.

Early in my school years, I understood how to tell a good teacher from a poor teacher, a mere imitator. A truly knowledgeable man can use simple, ordinary language to describe the most complicated, scientific ideas, so that even a child would be able to understand him, while the bad teacher would prefer to use technical terms in excess, and an incomprehensible vocabulary to hide his ignorance and lack of understanding. Therefore, it can be said that this Tibetan lama was the only true Buddhist that reached the Western shores. The only one who was offering the real stuff, rather than cheap copies. With his death in 1987, his organization became an empty shell that, gradually and inevitably will lose its distinctive features. It will turn itself into an ordinary religious institution with no live Masters or mystical teachers. An instruction book and a chamber for a solitary retreat is not enough to bring forth a true initiate of the way. A real teacher, a live spiritual instructor, is necessary. Such an instructor should be an all-accomplished Master himself, a mystic who is familiar with the way and all its particulars, making him capable of giving guidance to others. However, no ordinary religious institutions have such kinds of instructors. They are not interested in acquiring them. They are after other things.

Here I feel that some readers may feel confused with my extensive use of the word "mysticism" in connection with Buddhism, Hinduism, and Islam. What I am trying to say is to clarify the point that in all religions, all religious teachers are divided into two clear-cut, distinct categories: ordinary, conventional clergymen on one side, and on the other side advanced human beings, the holy men. This second group is made up of individuals whom I call mystics, since they are not ordinary, regular people, but belong to the category of extraordinary humans who can produce different supernatural phenomena such as reading minds, performing miracles, seeing the future, flying in space and time, and so on. Every religion has its own venerated personalities, saints, or holy men. Although the priesthood accepts the holy men of their own particular religion, still they feel uneasy with them, as they are aware that these individuals are very different, very much unlike themselves, the priests. While they see them as strangers, as people who are made of different material, clerics cannot help but canonize them, to accept them as a part of their religion, since it requires holiness and, possibly, its live representatives.

As I see it, the priesthood regards their saints with suspicion, preferring to see them as dead venerated corpses rather than having to deal with them while they are still alive. Clerics claim that they are the custodians of the word of God, but there are many cases in history when they sent their saints to death. They speak about their respect and love for religion, but it seems that they do not care for the welfare of their saints, of their contemporaries, the individuals whom I would describe as the ultimate representatives of religion and God on the Earth.

Priesthood, clerics, and theologians, being bookish types, know religion from books only. They are better suited to deal adequately with the affairs of this world. Except for the holy books, this crowd would know nothing about religion; even the idea of God would never cross their minds. Thus prophets, holy men, and saints are God's choice to be the ultimate representatives of faith, to be His messengers. Hence, no matter how learned, educated, or respected intellectual clerics are, in the end they never achieve the status of true holy men or saints. Therefore, clerics on the Day of Judgment will be as amazed and horrified as the rest of humanity.

In fact, any religion which has no contemporary saints is a dead religion, or, at least, is at its lowest point of stagnation. In one Chinese book it says, "First there was a true man, and only then there was a true teaching." Thus, no matter how great the holy books are, God sent them to Man, who is the ultimate purpose or meaning of the creation, since without him the universe would be blind, empty, and incomprehensible. Moreover, the utmost human is the Perfect Man of the mystics.

***

Ibn Arabi was one of the greatest Muslim mystics. Born in Spain in 1165, he wrote in one of his books how in Fez, Morocco, he recognized the Pole of the time, the perfect master of the spiritual way, who was trying to hide his high status and identity from the public and the world. Sufis call the leader of their particular order the Pole, while the Pole of the Poles (*Qutb al-Aqtab*) is the Pole of all orders. Unless this type of perfect man reveals himself, the ordinary person has no chance to recognize him by relying on his mind or judgment. Alternatively, one has to himself be like him, like the Pole, an advanced mystic, or at least one's mystical, spiritual status has to be very close to his.

Shah Waliullah of Delhi lived in India in the eighteenth century. He was the most prominent Muslim theologian of his time, and, at the same time, was a Sufi of the highest rank. In one of his works he wrote about the highest stage of the mystical way, saying that he himself was stationed very close to it. Later he achieved this last stage. While reading his writing, a reader can see that this man, with certitude, is describing very advanced mystical stages and states with all their particulars, so that it leaves no doubt that he knows his subject from his own experience. His books and mystical writings are proof of his mystical credentials. To doubt his achievements is similar to doubting the existence of the sun or the moon. While it is impossible to impress an unintelligent person with philosophical speculations in books—because they are not able to understand them or demonstrate any emotions, wonder, or enthusiasm for them—such a person might become very much excited by magical deeds, supernatural powers, and by the acts of primitive sorcery.

My acquaintance with Gurdjieff's literature drew my attention to the Mohammedan East, which may look less of an exotic place in comparison to India, but more promising for finding mystical schools. Time has wiped out the last vestiges of Muslim power from the map of India, and with it, diminished its Islamic strongholds. Today, you can no longer find well-educated circles there that can speak or write in Arabic or Persian, but without the knowledge of these two essential languages the Muslim world will have no culture or civilization. There would be no writers or readers. Therefore, for a Muslim traveler, today's India is an incomprehensible place. Thus the language barrier forced me to make other travel plans, to consider other destinations rather than the Indian subcontinent, not to mention the Iron Curtain, and this narrowed my choice to Soviet Central Asia; that is, the historic Turkistan.

I remember in the summer of 1973, in the open-air mosque of the Khwaja Ahrar monastery in Samarqand, a local woman paid money to a mullah to read a ritual prayer for a member of her kin. After finishing it, the jovial young mullah asked me about the goal of my voyage, whether I was looking for a wife among the local girls.

I replied, "No I am looking for a Sufi master, who will initiate me into the way."

He laughed saying, "Those days when this land had Sufis are gone. You can't find them anywhere around here."

"Maybe at least one or two are left?" I asked.

His firm answer was again no. Then after a little consideration he said, "If you go to neighboring Tajikistan, to the mountains, who knows, maybe you can find somebody there." He later explained his words by saying that in the mountains in Tajikistan there were places where the Soviet realities had not yet reached. Modern times had not yet reached these distant villages there.

At that time I could not get to the mountains of Tajikistan. Nevertheless, I thought that the young mullah gave me important information, and for several years I cherished the idea that one day I would find an opportunity to go there, and possibly find myself a Muslim guru.

Over the next ten years, I made several trips to Turkistan, but I could not find any trace of the Sufi folk there. The Soviet Central Asian republics were as Soviet as any other part of the Union. The atheist disease had reached to its every corner; no part of it remained unaffected. Old city fortifications, mosques, mausoleums, and even *khanakas* (the Sufi study centers) were there, but they stood empty. There was no life inside; they were no longer the magnetic centers of attraction for society, since there was no Muslim society, but only a Marxist society with no traditions, no faith, and no real values.

There was an interesting encounter when I visited the only remaining functioning *madrassah* (a Muslim seminary) in Bukhara to see if there was any chance for me to be permitted to study in it. I met a young man of my age. He was very polite with me, and offered to take me inside the closed premises where an old guard let us in. While we were inside, he, a student of the seminary, gave me a little guided tour.

"You can enroll in this *madrassah* if you can find a mullah to recommend you," he said.

"But it will be a very costly affair for me to move here and study away from my home!" I replied.

To this he answered, "Your parents will help you. If your parents' money does not suffice, then your relatives can come together and help you by gathering funds."

"No, it is not possible," I said. "Your parents and relatives are good Muslims, are positive towards religion. But my parents and relatives are Communist Party members. They are hostile to religion and would not approve, nor understand it."

Later, as we left the *madrassah* and stood outside in the summer evening, I confessed to him about my intention to find a way to defect to the West, to escape from the Soviet Union.

"But this would be an instance of grave state treason. Even if you manage it, your parents will be left behind and it will ruin them. The state will punish them severely," he said.

"Why should I think about them? I can't live in Marxist Russia; I have to go to America, to freedom."

"It is not good," he told me. "They are your father and mother, and you are Muslim. It is a duty for a Muslim to care for his parents, to look after them when they get old."

I did not say anything else, but reflected on the fact that he was a clear-cut, all-round Muslim boy, unlike me. I was different. I cannot follow the rules. If I followed the rules of society, then I would have enrolled in a Communist Party school which bred future Party *apparatchiks*, the state's elite. My old people had their own life, while I had my own. Maybe I am not a good Muslim, but neither am I a good Commie.

Some ten years later, on my next journey to the Bukhara region, I met the man again. He was no longer a seminary student, but a priest (*akhund*) in charge of Khwaja Zainutdin Khanaka, which is nowadays used as a mosque. I reminded him about our encounter ten years before, but he remembered nothing. The people of Bukhara all speak the Tat language, a pidgin form of Persian. So he enquired from me whether I had managed to learn Persian, so we could switch to communicating in Persian, since Russian was neither his nor my native language. He asked me whether I observed all the obligations of *Shariah*, of the sacred law of Islam, and if I was living the Muslim way of life. I stated that I, unlike him, was not interested in the formal study of Islamic sciences, but rather I was a man of the mystical way, of Sufism, the spiritual movement of Islam. To this he said that he is acquainted with some Sufi works, and had read a famous Persian treatise of Al-Hujwiri, *The Revelation of the Veiled*. Besides that, he said that he had managed to master the art of calligraphy, learned Arabic and Persian. He added that there was no match to him in today's Bukhara in the knowledge of Islamic sciences, but still he was no equal to the Muslim scientists that lived in previous centuries.

He said, "I can read their books and understand their language, but I have no mind to write anything myself."

It must be noted here that despite all the changes in Turkistan, a traveler can get a taste of the real East there, a sense of mystery and an atmosphere of spirituality radiating, not just from the grandeur of Islamic historic architecture, but from the manners and behavior of the people as well, unlike in the Caucasus, which was a periphery of the Muslim world. Turkistan at all times, but for the very latest Communist period, was one of the most important spiritual centers of Islam. Still, the plague of Marxism caused much more destruction here than that of Genghis Khan's armies, with the total elimination of the Islamic heritage accumulated in more than a thousand years. As Nasrudin said, it is silly to fight with the elements. Thus historians are making a mistake when they describe the Mongol invasion as representing the mortal threat to Islamic civilization. Mongolic nomads were like a destructive hurricane arriving from the East. Unlike the Mongols, who were driven by the elements, escaping from a famine in the Gobi Desert, Marxist ideology was a poisonous, carefully calculated formula, maliciously prepared with an intent to affect the heart, the soul of society, which is its spirituality, ultimately destroying its religious foundations.

Before Bukhara, I visited Tashkent, a faceless, boring, modern city. I was looking for old manuscripts. Somebody advised me to go to a square in front of the Barakhan Madrassah, where book vendors offered pre-revolutionary religious literature. This small square, or rather small space between a mosque and the *madrassah,* which, at the time, was the only higher education Muslim seminary for the entire USSR, was full of under-cover agents and shady-looking personalities. Nearby a small modern house had been built. The plaque on the wall informed us that this was the Young Communist League's Red Corner, which was a propaganda center. Places like this were usually strategically stationed near to places of worship, so that young atheist militia could police the area to prevent any kind of religious meetings or demonstrations.

As I stood there in the center of the square, I felt most uncomfortable and vulnerable. The place was something like the Bermuda triangle – you can go there and disappear forever, and no trace of you will ever be found. I had a feeling that this place was nothing but a secret police trap to catch strangers like me, since informers and undercover cops stood there on the ready to come upon me in case I took a single wrong step.

I made a few careful enquiries, but it seemed nobody had any books on mysticism, which probably was not a sought-after subject among the seminary students of the *madrassah*. Then I noticed a man in a Kirghiz hat and ethnic clothes who was standing at a distance looking at me, and smiling as if he knew me from somewhere. At first I did not pay him much attention since I took him for a young seminary student. Sometime later when I saw many wrinkles on his neck, I understood that he must be a middle-aged man. He was not a *madrassah* student but was rather the seminary teacher himself. His youngish, fair-skinned face illuminated peace and kindness. All the body language of this man signaled to me an invitation to approach and strike up a conversation with him. His Mongol face definitely had a certain radiance, and in his eyes I saw some kind of recognition of me. I thought, maybe he was a Master of the mystical way who perceived my spiritual aspirations, and expected me to approach him and ask to be accepted as his pupil.

I was in a confused state of mind. On one hand, I wanted to go away from this dangerous place. On the other hand, to find a Sufi Master had been my dream for many years. But I stood there as if paralyzed. I could not make myself approach him as I was afraid to give myself away, to be attacked by the police, by these dogs that were after my flesh and blood.

Sometime later I saw him still there, sitting on his heels on the sandy surface of the square. Although his back was turned to me, I felt as if he still waited and expected me to approach him. I felt very silly. Many contradictory thoughts were crossing my mind. First, that it was my duty to get to him and find out whether he was the man that I was looking for all these years. Secondly, there were many minor considerations such as, should I approach him and then greet him by taking his hands in my two hands and shake it, as everybody else around me was doing? Should I start a conversation in the "imperial" Russian, the language of the Soviet empire, which probably was not the proper thing to do under the circumstances? What language other than Russian could serve us as a Lingua Franca of today's Turkistan? Many Turkic ethnic groups that populate the region speak in their own various dialects. However, I cannot speak any of these properly. Maybe, alternatively, I should speak to him in the dialect of modern Turkey. However, I did not think that he spoke Turkish. I could not make my mind up on anything.

The Kirghiz and his assistant at last stood up. I saw as he spat angrily on the ground in front of himself and went away. I stood there not moving, wondering whether he was angry with me for not taking the initiative to make his acquaintance.

I said to myself, "If he really is a Master, then I have lost my opportunity to meet a true *murshid* (teacher) in this life."

Similarly with him, if he was who I thought he was, he had a good excuse to be very angry with me, because I knew by now that it is a rare chance to meet a true Master in one's lifetime, but it is equally difficult to meet a true disciple. A Master can sit and wait his entire life for the prospect of an encounter with a disciple with the potential to become a Master himself, which in the end may never come to pass. And, now this Kirghiz Master saw me standing in confusion, not being able to find in me the courage to approach him. However, later, in trying to find an excuse or self-justification, I thought that if I had made an acquaintance with him, not just I, but he as well, could have ended up in a Siberian labor camp.

Later, in Bukhara I asked my acquaintance, the *akhund,* if he knew this Kirghiz man, whether he was a Sufi.

"No, he is not a Sufi. He is a professor of theology for Kirghiz seminary students," he said.

I perceived that although he had an Islamic education, he was no different from other ignorant people who think that to be a Sufi one has to wear a distinctive head dress, a patched frock, and belong to a dervish order, rather than have an inner state or spiritual condition. The ordinary people do not see beyond outward appearances. They notice only superficial signs and attributes.

Then he said, "I could direct you to the real Sufis, to a Sufi commune that exists near Dushanbe, in Tajikistan."

He named the Sufi order to which these people belonged. He also told me that their leader, a sheikh, was a holy man. This man, according to him, had magical powers, could perform miracles, and heal illnesses. Besides that, he said, he had tens of thousands of followers.

"What is his name?" I enquired.

"Turajon," he said.

"Can you give me his address?" I asked.

"Yes, I can give it to you. But it is unlikely that you will be allowed to have an audience with him," he said.

Thus I took a flight to Dushanbe, the main city of Tajikistan, this mountainous Soviet region. Tajiks are the only Persian-speaking ethnic group in the whole of Turkistan. The information that I had was of doubtful character. The whole story was making no sense at all. How would the KGB allow all this? The idea sounds extraordinary, as it was going against all the rules and conventions of the Marxist state.

On my way there I was trying to make sense out of all this, but without any success. A Sufi order, a religious organization, functioning freely within the borders of the Soviet Union was an impossible idea. I had a substantial amount of money on me. I was dreaming, thinking that even if the story about Turajon proved to be a phony one, then at least I will be able to find a mountainous village to which the "Soviet way of life had not yet reached."

I remembered my recent conversation with an old devout Muslim in Bukhara. I complained to him about my dissatisfaction with my lot, with our hard times, that I could not properly conduct my religious Sufi activities in our own Muslim lands. To which he said, "No borders can block us from God's grace (*ridha*)." I liked his answer very much. Unlike the region where I came from, in Turkistan many people remained loyal to their faith and their spiritual values, rather than yielding to the Marxist realities of the Soviet Union. Many people there accepted poverty and marginalization, rather than the godless, materialistic way of life in the mainstream of Soviet society.

I was sitting in a seat on a Soviet airplane, reflecting that this old man was right – I can stay in Russia, and it can still be that God's grace will reach me here, after all. A mountain village in Tajikistan looks very much like one in Afghanistan, Iran, or even India. I can buy a cheap house there, and then find a local village girl and marry her. The nature and countryside scenery is similar to everywhere else; the sky is also the same. So what difference does it make? East or west, people everywhere are the same and the Heavens are the same.

Previously I heard about a group of naïve Moscow youth, who came together and purchased ten or so houses in the Caucasus Mountains with the intention of forming a religious commune, to meditate together, and to live a life as pious folk. However, as soon as the authorities learned about this, they prosecuted them and destroyed their dream community.

The small town that I was looking for was situated not very far from Dushanbe. As I arrived there, I had no clear picture in my mind about what I should expect. In the location I saw huge buildings and a new mosque in the process of construction. All the architecture was on a grand scale. Somebody there told me that millions of rubles were spent to build this. It was not clear who provided all that money—let alone to say who allowed it—since it was a well-known fact that in the seventy years of its rule, the Red regime in Russia, the Kremlin, did not ever give a single permission to build any place of worship anywhere in the country.

Some twenty or so old men were sitting in the yard of the mosque. They all had beards. Their whole attire consisted of the most authentic Muslim traditional dress. I thought, was this a masquerade or for real? I really liked the intricate material of a black turban. They told me proudly that the turban was from Afghanistan. I knew that this region was not that far away from the Afghan border. However, the last time any people there were allowed to travel abroad was sixty or so years ago. I knew of course that at that time Soviet troops were already stationed in Afghanistan, conducting a secret, undeclared war against the Mujahedin.

All the people there were very friendly with me, until I asked about their leader, Turajon. They were in shock and disbelief, wondering how I knew about him, and who told me his name. Then they said that it was completely impossible for me to see him. Soon they started to argue loudly among themselves. The language was not familiar to me, but I soon understood that these nice, pious, virtuous-looking old men had intentions of taking me to the authorities, so that the secret police would interrogate me, to find out whether I was a foreign spy or some kind of "enemy." One younger-looking man in modern clothing was defending me, as he was against taking me to the police. Somebody offered me halva, a sweet pastry, to eat. However, I declined the offer since I understood that they wanted to keep me busy eating it, while they sent somebody to make a call to the police. The old man was surprised that I showed no interest in halva, which usually is specially cooked for funeral parties, and considered to possess certain mystical powers that could prolong one's life and improve one's health.

At that stage, I decided to make a run for my life. As I started moving slowly toward the gates, trying not to attract much attention, they were still in the middle of an argument. Once I was outside, behind the wall, I started to run as fast as I could.

In the town square I saw a pickup truck, driven by some young Tajiks. The young men reluctantly gave me a lift to the highway. There I found a bus stop to Dushanbe. I sat in there relieved, thinking that it was all over. However, I was wrong. I saw a white Volga, a Soviet luxury car, passing by in the other direction, which then made a U-turn and turned back and stopped by me. The man inside the car offered me a lift to Dushanbe. It was very unusual for a Soviet citizen to offer you a ride for free, but I was very eager to get away from this "holy" community with their phony guru, so I accepted the offer. Once inside I was relaxed, and carelessly admitted to the man that I was there to find more information about Turajon, this man with miraculous powers. I even showed him the old manuscripts which I had bought on the black market. Suddenly the man started to behave nastily, accusing me of being a Western spy, an illegal art dealer who was stealing the national heritage from the region, and of many other crimes against the Soviet state. He said that he himself was a graduate of the local Institute of Oriental Studies, so he can tell an enemy from a friend, and that I was a "*dushman*" (enemy).

Then he said, "I will take you to the right place (the KGB branch office) with these hot items (manuscripts) in your hands. It is a surefire thing that you will end up in jail for a long time."

I saw a large tree by the road in front of the car. As we got to it, I thought to grab the wheel and turn it around, so as to force him to drive the car straight into the tree…

The Volga was speeding toward the city, while we sat there solemnly in silence. I was not sure where he was taking me until the car stopped by my hotel. I got out and went inside. I was sharing the ground floor room with a stranger. Once inside, I locked the door, opened the windows wide open, and asked the man I was sharing the room with not to open the door without informing me first.

I had a sleepless night, expecting the arrival of secret police officers. By the morning, I understood that the Orientalist in the Volga probably never reported on me. I went early to the airport, and flew out on the first plane. While on board, I was blaming myself for my idiocy in believing the words of that young mullah from Samarqand. For many years, I had cherished the idea of going sometime in the future to Tajikistan, to its mountains, "to the places where the Soviet realities, the Soviet way of life had not yet reached." What a silly thought! What a joke! It is sufficient that the most distant village has a single police officer representing the Soviet state, the godless authorities. Therefore, how could it be that there are villages with people that have never heard about the arrival of the Communist regime? These old bastards can put on any disguise, any religious clothes, but inside they are no different from any other Soviet citizen. Don't they call the Soviet people the "nation of informers?"

Therefore, I assume that this Turajon affair was an intrigue of the KGB in the area near the Afghan border.

Thus with a high decree from the Soviet authorities, it was permitted, as an exceptional case, to allow a "religious commune" to be established there for high state reasons. Thus this pseudo-Sufi brotherhood was nothing but a show, made to impress the official Afghan guests of the Soviet Union. Islamic insurgents, the anti-communist resistance, were fighting a holy war against the Soviet army, so the Kremlin decided to relax its oppression of religion in the area to improve its image in the eyes of the Muslims in Afghanistan. Besides, Russia's spy agency required this kind of religious community in the region under its control as a long-term strategy, to be used as leverage, as a tool in its future intrigues. Moreover, this Turajon was nothing but a KGB man, an agent, and a valuable asset.

Some twenty years later, when I was staying in England, I heard about a civil war that was going on between Muslim insurgents and the current Tajik regime. As a "veteran" of life in the Soviet Union, I do not believe in the possibility of a Muslim insurgency among the local population. How can there be an Islamic revolt in the ex-republics of the Soviet Union? It is an impossible thing, unless it is organized and supported by the authorities. Though the Soviet empire no longer exists, the previous Soviet population still continues to live with their old Soviet mentality, and they are not very resourceful people or the kind of material that can organize themselves and set up an independent movement on their own, unless the idea has been backed by the authorities.

This conviction of mine has a firm rationale. Besides, no religious organization or movement can start by itself, spontaneously, without a person who has the required religious credentials. However, there are no such kinds of people in the republics of the former Soviet Union, since all its clergymen were handpicked people, loyal to the atheist authorities; this clergy was nothing but KGB cadres. The Marxist regime was so brutal toward the people, and especially toward religious people, that it was beyond human capability to preserve one's religious convictions, religious integrity, or a human face intact and uncompromised. My Soviet experience allows me to know for sure that any religious movements in these republics are nothing but pseudo-religious movements, organized on the orders of the authorities of the secular regimes, while the direct control of them is maintained by their state security agencies. Thus all religious activity in these republics is merely a controlled activity, with the strategic goal not to allow religion to come to power and govern.

We can observe similar policies and intrigues in the other parts of the Muslim world, where the State of Israel and global Zionist organizations are financing different pseudo-Islamic militants to prevent the coming forth of a political Islamic movement. The Zionist circles of the West are afraid to see the emergence of political Islamic movements that can come to power by peaceful, democratic means. Therefore, they secretly arm these pseudo-Islamic militants to unbind the hands of the atheist regimes, to give them an excuse to declare war against Islam. Since the Kremlin no longer has the material resources to support these pseudo-Islamic insurgents, be it in the Caucasus or in Central Asia, they are now funded by the Western countries, Europeans and Americans, and Arab Wahhabi states as well. Today, the United States and Israel have officially stated that they have special interests everywhere in the world, including in the Caucasus and in Central Asia, which I prefer to call Turkistan.

The Western Zionist circles do not want to see these republics maintain an independent policy. But they are especially against the possibility that the people there will show a desire to return to their Islamic roots. Thus today, the secular regimes of Turkistan are offering their secret services, the former KGB infrastructure, to their new masters, the Western powers and the Zionist circles, to facilitate Western and Zionist objectives in the region. These nasty organizations, these agencies, thanks to their experience under Soviet rule in fighting faith and spirituality, could prove to be very useful to their new customers.

Later, I heard an indicative report about a person who was a leader of the current Tajik Islamic movement. His name is Turajonzode, which means in Persian a son of Turajon! Can he by any chance be a relative, or maybe even a son of that Turajon, the man of magic? If he is, then his KGB connections would be very obvious. So, the time has come for this "heir apparent" of the "holy family" to pay back his dues to his patrons, to do a little dirty work through instigating people to start "religious" civil wars, which will result in public chaos, destruction, economic devastation, and genocidal acts upon the heads of the Muslim populace.

Some people say that Pharaohs and dictators are, so to say, God's agents, or His punishment sent to try and to chastise them. However, I heard a much better idea coming from a religious authority. It states that tyrants are no guiltier than the people who accept their tyranny.

I very much appreciated one conversation I had with a Nigerian Catholic, a Negro with a gigantic body frame, who on hearing about my country of origin, said that he had heard about the atrocities committed by Stalin. Then he added, "I think that there are no males in Russia."

"Why?" I asked.

"If there was a male, then he would go and kill his oppressor," he said.

I liked what he said very much. It was a sentiment I wondered about all my life. Why had the oppressed Soviet people failed to revolt, to rise up and dethrone the tyrant, since inaction against your oppressor would produce an incentive for the continuation of oppression? Alternatively, to say it in other words, if the people fail to act against injustice, then they themselves are the main cause of this injustice.

I consider the major injustice of modern times and life was my inability to walk along the way of religious knowledge in modern society and the modern world. I blamed the people and society for not allowing me to live a religious life, to pursue my inclinations, to progress along the mystical way, while the modern world is encouraging obscenities, every kind of wickedness and corruption. Even today after the fall of the Marxist regime, in Baku I am not allowed to freely conduct my religious activities, to perform my duties before the Lord. As I look around, I can see that the capitalist oppressors are no better than the Marxist oppressors. I see that the establishment, the previous Soviet rulers, managed to hold their positions, changed old Marxist phony slogans to new Western phony slogans. Thus yesterday's Communists are today's free-market and globalization advocates. The establishment is trying once more to keep believers in a strait jacket, to restrict religion to places of worship, rather than allow it to be a living force, to be an integral part of life and society.

Therefore no matter how I try, I cannot see any improvement in the situation, since people are still jailed for doing their regular, legitimate religious work, while the secret police hounds, acting on the orders of their paranoid tyrannical masters and leaders, still roam the streets looking for new prey, for those activists in their faith. Insight and a discernible look into the matter can help us bring out the true nature of the situation, to understand that today's Masonic powers are no different from yesterday's, since Jew-Masonic ideology or Zionism has nothing to do with one's religious background, whether it is Judaic, Christian, or Islamic. A Zionist is one who subscribes to this ideology or acts as its agent. Moreover, Zionists themselves are nothing but Satan's agents, as their ideology serves his interests in his long fight with Man for his mind and soul.

As a religious person, I do not require modern terminology or definitions meant to confuse and disorient people. Modern terms and ideas can change from time to time to suit the political trend, while religious terms will always remain the same, simple and crystal clear, to serve us as road signs and directions. They will not change until the Day of Judgment, and always will remain genuine, veritable, and contemporary.

I remember how Marxist ideologists wickedly took words from our vocabulary and introduced new, misleading usages to disorient the people, to confuse their minds. They called bad things good things and good things bad. Thus terms such as communism, socialism, capitalism, internationalism, democracy, globalization and human rights are obscure and misleading. I, as a man of insight and as a representative of religion, use our old words and terms to describe happenings, events and various matters of our complex times. Thus these modern terms such as communism, socialism, capitalism, democracy etc., are nothing but satanic murmurings, ideas introduced to this world by godless people, by Jew-Masonic ideologists, by the Jewish think tank, who are the modern day agents of the Devil.

Our old religious terminology makes things simple, easy to understand and easy to qualify. Thus no matter how hard these satanic forces try to make easy things look complicated, we religious guides are here to expose them, to bring the light to the world and to the people.

What went wrong with the world? The twentieth century was the most trying period in the history of humankind, since it upset the old, traditional, customary way of life and overturned the conventional system of values. We can see that the tumultuous last one hundred years created in history a dividing line, a gap, a certain break and void. This new world I would describe as being of a devilish design. It is a conspiracy with an ideology suggesting that humankind should start to write history from a new page, with no memory of its past, of its history, by forgetting its previous experience, its traditions, its wisdom, so that humanity would not know where it came from and where it is going.

Today, satanic agents have set the rules of the game for humanity so we can pretend that, in the new world and new age, Satan and his actions no longer exist. However, if we disagree and state that we know about the existence of Satan and his actions, then they will call us rogues who are breaking the rules they set for us. They are going to call us baddies, "fundamentalists," backward people. However, we will not fall into this trap. We will not allow them to deceive us with these satanic tricks.

I remember how in Soviet times, a few remaining places of worship—churches, mosques, and temples—were allowed to function, but mainly for the Red regime's propaganda purposes, as they served as showpieces for visiting foreigners to demonstrate the existence of religious freedoms in the country. The tourist information bureaus, however, were not allowed to inform Soviet tourists about these places of worship, since it was against the regulations. As I traveled, it was habitual for me to visit the places of worship in every Soviet city. But, even to ask the whereabouts of a functioning church or mosque could make one feel nervous, since every Soviet citizen felt very uncomfortable with this and tried to avoid answering it, as if to say it was equated with revealing vital state secrets, or as if it was a place of ill-repute. But once inside, a rare visitor could find out for himself how hazardous it can be to visit such sites, as the places were full of the secret police and their informers. If a young-looking man by chance visited a place of worship, "worshippers" would surround him asking prying questions.

They usually asked, "Are you a member of the Young Communist League? Are you a member of the Communist Party? It is against the law for such people to visit places of worship. We should report such people to the authorities."

I experienced this especially at mosques, where people asked for my full name and address, without even trying to hide their intention of reporting me to the secret police. Thus the Red regime's main intention was to discourage people, to scare them away from attending places of worship. It seemed that everybody on the premises – cleaners, sweepers, door attendants and managers — worked as informers for the KGB, alongside their direct line of activity. The regime was trying hard to keep the youth away from religion, as it was considered that belief was a matter of bad upbringing, which would die out gradually with the death of older citizens born before the revolution, who never passed through the Soviet education system.

The official Soviet psychiatry system treated believers as mentally disturbed, abnormal people. According to this system, somebody who had a correct education, who finished a Soviet school, cannot be a believer. But if he was, then it meant that he was a mentally ill person, a lunatic, an individual with a defective mentality, who should be put in a psychiatric institution for treatment. There were many officially reported cases where parents who taught their children religious ideas were forced to give up their parental rights. Then their children would be placed in state orphanages to give them an atheist upbringing. At those times, one could get oneself in a Siberian labor camp for the mere possession of the Bible or the Koran. After Stalin died, this practice was relaxed. In Moscow or Leningrad one would not get a sentence, a jail term, for the possession of the holy books, since the authorities were afraid of foreign journalists and bad publicity abroad. But in the provinces, there were many reports about trials of individuals who kept the Bible or the Koran, even if it was permitted by Soviet law.

***

On a Moscow-Baku train, I was sharing a coach compartment with a Muslim man from the Northern Caucasus. As the train passed by a mosque, I enquired whether it was a functioning mosque, or used as a warehouse or a factory in accord with the usual Soviet practice. He related to me the story of this mosque. The authorities were not allowing people to go there for worship. Therefore, it stood empty for a long period. However, the local Muslims continued, secretly, to meet there for worship and prayers. Yet, as soon as the authorities were informed about this, the secret police sent arsonists to set the old historic mosque on fire. Thus this building was no longer suitable for worship, since only the outward stone structure remained undamaged.

Then in answer to my question, he said that in his village, to this very day, there remained a secret Sufi brotherhood. The members of the secret society regularly came together to perform a collective *dhikr* (the remembrance of God). Then he gave me his address and invited me to stay at his place, promising to introduce me to the members of this Sufi brotherhood.

After some time passed, I decided to go there. The first city on my travels was Derbend. I decided to spend a night in this historic city, and on the next day move further to the distant village in the mountains. The city was once a part of Persia, its northernmost city in Transcaucasia, standing on a strategic passageway to the North.

By evening, I decided to attend the Friday Prayer at the local mosque – which is considered the oldest in the Caucasus, built in the eighth century by the Arabs whose victorious troops brought Islam to the region by defeating the armies of idolaters. Since that time, Islam was the dominant religion of the peoples of the Caucasus, right up until the arrival of the Russian invaders. In this region, before the Russian invasion, lived small, insignificant groups of Georgian Christians who were under the Muslim dominion.

This huge old mosque had just a few worshipers. After the completion of the required Muslim prayers we, a group of five or six men, sat on a carpet to read in turn from a large-sized Koran. Sometime later, as I prepared to leave the place, the youngest man of the group introduced himself to me. He said that he himself chose the career of a priest. But when I showed him a small-sized, foreign-made Koran, his face turned pale in color.

"This is a foreign-published, contraband Koran, and so it is illegal to possess it. It is against the law," he said.

He continued, "You bought it on the black market, so this is a crime as well!"

But when he asked where I was staying, I understood that he was going to report me to the secret police. This young aspiring priest knew the rules of the game – he was allowed to hold the position in exchange for loyalty to the Red regime, their atheistic, anti-religious rules and regulations.

Nobody was waiting for me in the hotel, and I went to bed, but could not go to sleep. In the morning, I decided to leave the city and return home, back to Baku, otherwise I could have expected some kind of trouble with the local secret police office. I abandoned my plans to make acquaintance with the members of the secret Sufi brotherhood of the region. But I didn't regret it much, since I assumed from what I heard about them that these people were uneducated types, and their practice of Sufism consisted of a few silly rites and primitive, pseudo-religious dancing and nothing else.

Back in Baku I decided to pay a visit to the office of Sheikh-ul-Islam, the head of the Caucasus Muslim Board. Today I can see that my going to this place was a result of frustration about my inability to study religion, to advance my religious knowledge on my own. Obviously, this was an act of insanity and desperation, since the place was a den of the secret police and their informers. Definitely, I had no friend in there, though quite unrealistically, I dreamed that the head of this institution could turn out to be a nice person, and offer himself to me as my private tutor on spiritual matters.

In the office, a youngish-looking man wearing European clothes greeted me. He was the manager of the mosque and a graduate of the faculty of Oriental studies at the local university. The faculty was well known as it produced agents for the Kremlin, who would be employed to assist and to promote the regime's imperialist, expansionist policies abroad, while their scholastic degrees and positions served to cover up their spying activities.

I do not remember now if he asked me to produce my IDs, which could have been dangerous for me since he could report me to his head office, the KGB. He said that he would introduce me to the Sheikh, but that I must wait. In another room, several men in the Muslim priest's dress were watching TV. The film that drew their keen attention was a Soviet-made film based on a story from the *Arabian Nights*. Later, two men dressed as local clandestine priests joined me in the waiting room, and I witnessed in there a strange and bizarre conversation that took place between them.

One mullah was saying to the other, "I have wasted my life in this religious field, and so far I have gained nothing, and now I am as poor as ever. My hands are empty, but not any longer!"

The other mullah questioned him saying, "So what do you intend to do? Are you intending to abandon this religious job now?"

The first man said, "Yes, now I am clever. No more of this foolishness. Now I am going to be a regular guy. I am going to be a womanizer and live like a dirty man."

The men it seemed were not aware that I understood their language, their Turkic dialect, since these talks were not appropriate for representatives of the clergy, even if they were just uneducated types like them, who conducted their religious activities without getting official permission.

In those times, a few remaining mosques were getting a huge amount of money through collections, allowing the top mullahs and their appointed men to appropriate large funds and to live a luxurious lifestyle. Part of the money usually ended up in the pockets of the KGB chiefs, since in reality the controls were in the hands of this department, without whose approval no priest could be appointed, not even the Sheikh-ul-Islam himself.

These KGB cadres today still continue to hold their positions at the religious offices, continuing to pocket huge sums of money. Thus today, in the same mosque's office they have set up a travel agency organizing tours for the believers to sacred places abroad. This tourist agency, besides bringing them profit, allows the local secret services to keep an eye on the activities of traveling believers abroad.

In this way, the clandestine mullahs felt angry and disappointed, since the top mullahs got all the tasty pieces, while they had to gratify themselves with morsels, to live on the leftovers from the feast.

After they were done watching the film, the Sheikh-ul-Islam entered the room. He was a frail old man. I explained to him the reason for my visit, that I was interested in the study of Islamic tenets and especially Sufism, this Islamic spiritual doctrine.

"Sufism is not Islam. It is a heresy, and it has nothing to do with Islam," he said.

None of my words could make him accept that Sufism is a part of Islam. Probably, he was right to reject this mystical teaching, since, as a cleric, he naturally was specialized in Islamic fundamentals, while this teaching was not a part of it. Thus Sufis accept all Islamic fundamentals and tenets, and consider their mystical teaching as a complementary science to traditional Islam, bringing it to perfection. But the Islamic clergy will forever continue the argument that Islam, as they know it, is complete, perfect, and self-sufficient without Sufi mysticism.

I can't help but agree with the Muslim theologians, that as the Prophet (peace be upon him) brought to the world the new religion of Islam, mysticism was not openly a part of it; it was not a part of the conventional Mohammedan religion. Thus the Prophet laid the generalities of faith, while the mystical ideas remained in the dark, restricted to the Sufi circles. Theologians have no knowledge of mysticism; they are not specialized in this, but neither am I a well-versed man in Muslim theology.

Thus I see Islam as a teaching for the wider public, for the ordinary believers, while the Sufi mystical knowledge is for the people who are on the road of sainthood. I cannot get into a discussion here about the opinions of Islamic theologians about the institute of sainthood, whether they fully accept the idea or not. But the idea is widely accepted in all other religions. The history of Islam also has thousands of examples of the lives of holy people who were venerated by the public, and the absolute majority of them were representatives of the Sufi movement.

Thus if Islam could be likened to a tree, then Sufi holy men would be its fruits. If Islam could be likened to a garden, Sufi saints would be its flowers. What is the use of a tree unless it bears fruit? Or of a garden without its flowers? Similarly, no religion is complete or perfect unless it has its holy men. No religion is complete without its mystical spiritual dimension, since the manuals of mystical teaching allow an individual, a searcher after the Truth, to walk along the way of holy men, along the way of sainthood. Thus a perfect Sufi Master is a holy person, an exemplary man for all Muslims – a living example. Mohammad (peace be upon him) besides being a prophet was a holy man as well. He was the last and final prophet sent to the world. There is no need for a new one. The Sufis say that, while God completed cycle of prophethood with the Prophet, He, out of His Mercy, opened the cycle of sainthood for the world and its people, for them to benefit from it, to keep religion alive and vital.

A year later, I heard that a younger man, a robustly built clergyman, a graduate of the Tashkent Muslim seminary, replaced this old and frail Sheikh-ul-Islam. The thought behind it, as officially declared, was that he as a young and strong man was more suitable for the state to promote its policy abroad, to raise its prestige in the Muslim world. Thus his main function and duty, rather than to strengthen the faith of Muslims in the Caucasus, was to promote a favorable image of the atheist regime among Muslims around the world.

I remember a true story that took place during that period. There was a man who was well known as a person of ill repute, a gambler, an alcoholic, and a womanizer. He somehow found himself a job at a theatre as a singer and comedian. He had good vocal talents. Once an instructor in the KGB noticed him and advised the authorities to give him another position, a job as a mullah. Individuals with beautiful voices are much valued at mosques, and serve at various religious ceremonies. The authorities considered his reputation as a scoundrel as something reassuring, as he had no true religious sentiments, and therefore was a safe person to join religion and promote the interests of the Red regime.

At first, the man was very surprised by the offer, but later he accepted it when the authorities reassured him that, thanks to this new position, his status in Soviet society would rise dramatically, because by working as a mullah he could serve his country even better. He passed a crash course in the basics of Islamic faith, was taught to read prayers in Arabic with beautiful inflections, and was send to Baghdad, Iraq. In that country he managed to impress ordinary Muslim crowds with his beautiful vocals. The local Arabs said, "For many years we were misled by Western propaganda that Russia, the Soviet Union, was an atheist, anti-Islamic regime. But now we see that this Russian Muslim can recite exquisitely from the Holy Koran in excellent Arabic. This means that there is Islam in Russia, and Islam is respected by the authorities."

Later, the Soviet ambassador in Baghdad candidly admitted that this mullah had done more in his brief visit to Iraq to promote the interests of the Kremlin and to improve its image in the region than his embassy had managed to do in many years.

The Soviet regime did everything possible to destroy faith. It used every kind of trickery it could devise to keep people away from religion. Thus no religious books or literature were available to the public. Old Islamic manuscripts and pre-Revolutionary published religious books, when not destroyed, were forcibly taken away from the people and collected in the State Manuscripts Department. The access to these books was permitted only to specially authorized persons and foreign guests.

In those times, I heard about many cases of imprisonment of Muslims who clandestinely taught the Arabic language to the youth. Though any teacher could teach English, French, or German at home without any special permission from the authorities, it was different with Arabic, the language of the Koran. The authorities were against it, since they saw that learning Arabic could be the first step toward the study of Islam.

After my failure to make friends with the Sheikh-ul-Islam, I decided to attend the mosque on Fridays on a regular basis, so that I could learn about Islam by listening to the Friday Sermons. Although attending these prayer gatherings in mosques is compulsory to every Muslim, unfortunately, I could only attend it two times in Baku, under the Communist rule.

There were only two functioning mosques within the town's limits. This time I went to the other mosque, the Ajdar-Beg. In the yard I saw a blind man who was lecturing a couple of people on different aspects of Islamic faith. Everything that he said was all new to me. "But he is a blind man," I wondered. "How could he manage to learn all this?" However, after some consideration I understood that he had probably frequented mosques all his life as an exemplary Muslim, listened to many Friday Prayers, and remembered all he heard. This man's misfortune, his blindness, deprived him from the active worldly life, but allowed him to become a devout Muslim. And he knew a lot about religion, while I with my unimpaired eyesight could not find a way to get religious knowledge! Whose fault was it – that of the atheist Red regime or my own? At the time, I could not answer this question.

Then I went to the mosque's office and spoke to the first mullah I met in there. He happened to be a Shiite cleric, an *akhund*. I expressed to him my desire to attend henceforth all Friday Prayers and he praised my decision.

"But I don't know which group of Muslims I should pray with, with Sunni Tatars or Shiite Azeris, as my father was a Sunni, but my mother is a Shiite," I said.

On hearing this, the *akhund* started to blame the Sunnis and their doctrine, and advised me to mix only with Shiites, who according to him were the followers of the true creed. I took his advice to attend Shiite gatherings, since the majority of Muslims in Baku were Shiites, though I had doubts about it, due to the widely accepted rule that a Muslim should follow his father's faith and creed. Besides this, I would have preferred to mix with the Tatar folk who produced in me the impression of being the spiritually healthier community, as I witnessed that their attendance at the mosque was hugely more numerous. More than this, I saw that they came there just to pray, while a dozen or so Azeris, who on a regular basis attended the Friday Prayer sessions, were doing it out of idleness, and hung around the mosque till the night to make themselves a couple of rubles.

Later that day I heard a beautiful sermon read by this *akhund*. I wondered how such a regular-looking man could deliver such a clever sermon, but later I realized that everything he said was not his own words and thoughts, but translations from Arabic and Persian quotations of past great Islamic religious authorities.

In Baku I heard many times how lay people spoke unflatteringly about mullahs, about their hypocritical behavior and manners. To these words I always replied with the argument that Muslims should listen to what the mullah is saying, as long as these are the words of God, of the Prophet (peace be upon him), or other religious authorities, but shouldn't pay attention to the mullah's behavior in his personal life. It should be kept in mind that Muslim clergymen, by being to some extent religiously educated people, are still ordinary human beings with the weaknesses characteristic of ordinary humans. They are not holy people; they are not saints.

Very recently in Baku, on a TV talk show, a local mullah made a complaint that the modern-day townspeople were demonstrating no respect to him, nor paying homage as is required for representatives of the clergy. He was the standard Soviet-era mullah – poorly educated, ignorant, and of the crooked KGB cadre.

He said, "I am a clergyman, a 'Holy Father,' and for this reason the people should treat me accordingly."

By calling himself a "Holy Father" this stupid man demonstrated his ignorance about Islam. It is clear that he had heard how ethnic Russians, the Orthodox Christians, address their priests in this fashion, and this made him think that this title is appropriate in the case of Muslim priests. It is a fact that all local mullahs know very little, if anything, about Islam, similar to the rest of population. During the Communist era, Muslims of the Caucasus were kept ignorant about the Islamic history of their land, about the world outside of the Soviet Union, about everything but their Soviet realities. In this region anybody who could master a little Russian, the language of ethnic Russians, could pass for a scientific person. The Red regime kept Muslims ignorant about their true identity. Even their self-awareness was based on the information, or rather disinformation, they obtained from Russian language books, newspapers, films and television. Therefore, they made up their minds about the Muslim lifestyle and customs based on watching these films, and reading Soviet books. For example, to this very day, they think that a harem, rather than being the private living quarters of a Muslim house, is a bordello; that a belly dance, rather than being a pre-Islamic pagan dance of the desert Arabs, is a universal dance of all Muslim women. Their idea of Islam and Muslims is a grotesque caricature based on ideas they accumulated by watching films made in Christian countries.

Surely, in Islam, mullahs were never considered as holy men, saintly men, nor were they a consecrated class. They are not saints. In Islam, there were schools of theologians which even challenged the idea of holy people as something un-Islamic, as an alien idea.

I remember an anecdotal incident that took place in the Soviet times. Once, one of my acquaintances said to me, "You know, yesterday I finished reading a Russian language book. It stated that our Muslim prophet is an actual historic figure. Previously I assumed that all these religious stories about prophets are nothing but the fairytales of mullahs. But, since our Soviet author stated this, then it must be true after all... But it contradicts what we were taught in schools."

On my second attendance of the Friday Prayer, the same *akhund* gave another sermon. In this sermon he started to relate the sad and tragic story of the martyrdom of Shiite imams. As he did it, from time to time his voice broke, as his reading changed into wailing, loud crying in a mournful fashion, demonstrating his grief over the fate of the household of Ali (may God be pleased with him), of this saintly man, the leader of all Muslims, who died more than a thousand years ago.

I must say that I very much like this kind of religious art, which is a part of Shiite religious culture and heritage. When I was living in the West, I tried hard and unsuccessfully to find a CD of this wailing session to impress my European and American acquaintances. They could get a certain culture shock from it, as they would find it strange that Muslims can enjoy themselves by listening to wailing, lamenting males.

The *akhund* was doing it in a superb fashion with professionalism and artistry. In the mosque there were no more than five or six male worshipers attending the Friday Prayer. At a certain point I understood that the man was trying hard and using all his talent for my benefit, to impress me, as I was not his regular customer. All the males in there, except me, were crying. But, I tried hard with all my strength not to cry, which was very difficult to do since weeping and laughing are both very contagious emotions.

"No man, no matter how much you try, you can't make me weep in public," I was thinking.

An old man sitting next to me wept with his head bent to the floor, but I noticed that he, from the corner of his eyes, was looking at me to see whether I would drop a tear or not. At the end, the *akhund* understood that his skills were not enough to force me to weep, so he stopped the session. After finishing the show he said, "You must all pay me for my efforts, otherwise why should I waste my time coming here and straining my voice unless I am paid?"

One or two men walked towards him and gave him several rubles, but not me. It was not a clever thing for me to do, since it made the *akhund* very angry with me, and, as I understood later, he decided to punish me for this. I moved toward the exit, and while in the anteroom, I put on my shoes and exchanged Muslim greetings with a recently-arrived African worshiper, a foreign exchange student. As I was doing this, the *akhund* entered the anteroom and exclaimed "aha" triumphantly, as if he had caught me doing something illegal or inappropriate. But, after all, was not talking to foreign citizens a crime by the Soviet standards! He came toward me, pointed his index finger at me and said, "Give me your full name and house address." After he got what he wanted, he went out to his office.

By now, I knew for sure that he had the intent to report me to the KGB, which could consequently bring about, in one way or another, my imprisonment. But I hoped at the time nothing like this would happen and that I would avoid problems with the authorities. I remember how on a previous occasion as I attended the Friday Prayer, local Shiite "worshipers" surrounded me asking for my name and address, so that they could report me to the secret police and get a payment of a couple of rubles for the information.

One old man was especially persistent as he begged me saying, "Don't give your name and address to them, but give it to me, will you please?"

He probably thought that if he got this exclusive information, his report will look more vital and bring him more money from his employers. Later, after I left the mosque, as I got closer to my house, I noticed a young man, one of the "worshipers," shadowing me to ascertain my place of residence. But as I discovered it and faced him, he produced a foxy smile, gave up his "detective operation" and then went away. The Soviet authorities expected the people to report on each other, on their fellow citizens, and they were doing it very eagerly.

At that time I spent a period of several years on travels around the extensive geography of the Soviet Union. Anybody who knew me thought that this kind of lifestyle was evidence of idleness and a lack of direction in life. But very few of them realized that I was not doing it for fun, and that my only objective on these travels was to find ways to escape from the country, to get away from this atheist state, to find freedom. Thus in total I investigated approximately seven thousand kilometers of the border areas of this vast country to find a point of escape, a point where I could cross the border to get away, abroad. But unfortunately, all borders of the Soviet Union were well-protected, no matter if it was from the land, sea, or air.

I remember how once I even considered purchasing a glider with which I could fly over the mountainous area in the South Caucasus to Iran. I found an advert in a Moscow newspaper that offered a hand-made apparatus for sale.

The man on the telephone, in answer to my question said, "Yes, of course it is very dangerous sport. You are going to fly in the air. So, unless you are a trained person, a glider is not for you."

As I am not much of a sportsman, I decided against buying a glider, but, anyway, I could not get close to the border area without attracting the attention of the police, since all areas close to the border were considered forbidden for anyone except for the locals.

But, still, most of my time on my travels away from Baku I spent in Moscow, in this large, spirited, energetic city – a world metropolis. You could see in this city people arriving from any place in the world to see these "fearsome Russians" and their mighty militarist country. You could get there a taste of the big cities of London, Paris, or New York, with all its similarities. The city was full of embassies, which to my mind, could provide me with an opportunity to escape behind the Iron Curtain.

Since I am not a merry person, not an enjoyer, not interested in having a good time, I spend my time usually in an unhappy, melancholic state of mind. But in Moscow, when I was in the most depressed condition I went to the Tatar mosque, the only mosque in town. Attending the Friday Prayer was to me a very uplifting experience, since I was among believers, the Muslim folk. I liked those Tatars very much, who produced an impression of a strong and well-organized people.

The mosque was usually full of believers. It could not accommodate everybody, so a large group of worshipers stood outside in the mosque's yard. Those outside prayed as they were standing, without making the prostrations. I observed that Tatar worshipers produced an impression of being true believers, who gathered there not to make themselves some money, nor out of idleness, but to pray together, and to experience a sense of community. As soon as they finished the prayers, all of them like one left the premises. As they lived in various areas of the city, the mosque was the place where they could come together, to get a sense of belonging and to preserve their Muslim identity. I wished my people to be like them.

Once when I was traveling in Turkistan, I went to see the mausoleum of Sheikh Baha' ud-Din Naqshband (may his secret be sanctified), near Bukhara. He was a fourteenth-century Sufi Master. I found a bus which took me to the village where the saint was buried. The Master was one of the most venerated holy men of Turkistan. Previously the site was a popular place of pilgrimage attracting hordes of admirers from around the world, since followers of his order were widespread around the Muslim world. But at this time, the Red regime did not allow the place to be used for religious purposes, and it stood there in a very dreary state. The authorities were afraid of a public outcry so they did not destroy it, but cunningly allowed it to fall to pieces with the passage of time by not conducting any repair work.

Thus the *khanaka* building, the place where dervishes normally gathered, was crumbling to pieces, and a sign on its walls advised people not to come close to the structure, as it was in an extreme condition of dilapidation and could collapse at any moment. This architectural ensemble was made up of two mosques, a *khanaka* and a graveyard. The gate to the graveyard was locked up, and I asked the guard to open it for me as I wanted to take a picture of the gravestone of the saint. But he would not allow me to, saying that the public were not permitted to see the grave. When I understood that no matter how much I asked, he would not allow me in, I decided at least to take a picture of the *khanaka* building.

"No, no, no, you are not allowed to take pictures over here," he cried. Then he added, "If you take a single shot I will call the police!"

I put away my camera, and as I was very thirsty, I picked up some grapes from a vine hanging down from the wall. But this made him even more unfriendly with me. He did not allow me to taste it, and demanded I leave all I had picked on the ground. After this, I went away, and walked around the village to find any indication of Sufis in the area. It was a hot summer's day, and I saw no living soul there, no villagers. I had longed to visit this place for a couple of years. I expected to confront some kind of mystical encounter or to experience something unusual there.

Then I saw a man who appeared as if from nowhere, going in the direction of an old one-story building. Then he disappeared, and I tried to guess where he went. Maybe he went inside the building, I thought. The structure had a mysterious air about it. Could it be a traditional meeting place for the local mystics, the followers of some contemporary living sheikh, I wondered. The house definitely had the appearance of a cult building though, and not of a mosque. There was a great probability that it was a *khanaka,* a house of dervishes. It was half-buried in the tall grass and had the appearance of abandonment. But could it be that it still secretly functioned as a meeting place for the *Naqshbandis,* the followers of the order of the saint? I stood there for some time, but nobody came out.

Though it was obvious that this place would never regain what it lost – its past glory, its past eminence – still you could feel something magical about the area. I am not a superstitious person, but I definitely felt something. But after all, there was nothing unusual about this, since it was the place where a countless number of mystics and their followers once lived. A traveler there walks on the same ground on which these great men once walked.

Yet in connection with magic and miraculous experiences, it can be said that they are always around us. People simply do not want to see or to notice them. This is a great mystery of life which, for ordinary men, is as if it does not exist, since they ignore it and are very much involved in worldly affairs, their usual everyday living and standard routine. Nevertheless, if a man would demonstrate an actual desire to experience mystery, miracles would be found all around him. The problem is that people simply do not want it; they are not interested.

In the end, I decided to return to my hotel. Much later, many years later, I read somewhere that the followers of this saint still lived in that village and kept the cult alive. Yet I do not believe the report.

Several years later, when I again visited the place, the guard, once more, did not allow me to see the grave. Then, as I stood there by the gate of the graveyard, I saw a middle-aged couple arrive. They were ethnic Russians, non-Muslims from Moscow. I had the impression that they were not a married couple, but that she was an escort, or perhaps his lover. It is a shame that the guard allowed them to enter the gravesite, but not me!

Before entering the gate this man loudly declared, "I was told that this place in previous times was considered as an important pilgrimage site, the sacred place which created the saying, 'Why should one go to Mecca or Medina if he can go to a nearer site such as the tomb of Baha' ud-Din Naqshband!'"

I had already heard several times such statements by different Muslims in Bukhara and Samarqand. I wondered whether this sacrilegious declaration could be an acceptable thing for Muslims, since the Kaaba and the burial site of the Prophet (peace be upon him) were the utmost holy places for pilgrimage. But, strangely enough, I heard that in the past Sufis also made such statements.

However, I must say that I myself will never go to Mecca, or at least I will not do an actual pilgrimage in my bodily form, since this is not for me. My practical life experience has made me understand that it is not clever to mix with a crowd, to stand in crowded places, since there can be a stampede that could kill you. No force on the earth can make me to go to a crowded place, as I am afraid of noise, clatter, and the clamor of a crowd, and a pilgrimage to Mecca requires a very strong physique and endurance. Many people have died while performing this rite in the hot Arabian climate. But I have done my pilgrimage to Sheikh Baha' ud-Din's shrine, even though it was not very successful, as I was somewhat disappointed, since it is not the act of pilgrimage itself that is of much importance, but what one gets from it in the spiritual sense, whether it is beneficial for one's faith.

When the couple left, I asked the guard what was special about them that he allowed them to see the grave.

"I had a call from the regional Communist Party office, urging me to let them in," he said.

This angered me so much that I resolved to go around and jump over the wall of the cemetery, but in the end I decided not to do it, since there were many small bushes everywhere in the graveyard, which were probably full of venomous snakes. Besides, the prospect of an encounter with the Uzbek police was the last thing I would like. They were the most intimidating and fierce type.

Later, I returned to Bukhara, to my hotel. It was in the historic Kukeldash Madrassah, an ancient seminary building, which in Soviet times was used as a tourist hotel. Next to the hotel an attractive ancient building was located, with the portal of the main façade completely covered with richly ornamented, colored mosaic tiles. This building also was a seminary in the good old days, when the area was under Islamic rule. But in the

Soviet period it was used to entertain foreign tourists, as a music and dance scene, as a bar where alcoholic drinks were on offer.

That day I followed a group of German tourists inside the building. The local Culture Ministry had organized a "native culture" entertainment with traditional music, and not-so-traditional belly dancing. The "local beauty" moved her skinny body this way and that way on a makeshift stage, doing what she thought were seductive body movements, while the German tourists sat there with grim-faced expressions, not understanding why they had paid so much money for this tour in which they were subjected to such torturously boring dance and Asian music. They were wondering whether it was supposed to be pleasant entertainment. It seemed that the German idea of amusement and a good time was a very different one from that of the Uzbek Culture Ministry. In those times, throughout the Soviet Union, the Culture Ministries of the Soviet Muslim republics, to suit the secular regime, cunningly accepted this belly dance as a universal Muslim dance, or as an example of Islamic culture.

At last, the Germans, fed up with all of this, stood up and left despite all the protests from the local guide.

She said, "It is local culture. This dance and music is a part of the tourist tour program. Why don't you wait and see the end of the music and dance session?"

As Bukhara, unlike Baku, despite all the Soviet propaganda, was a very conservative Muslim city where dancers like these were considered whores, it is obvious that in this local society she must have come from an ill-reputed family background to accept such a position without compromising herself and her family.

Outside, right in the front of this *madrassah,* stood a bronze monument to Mulla Nasrudin, sitting on his donkey. A local photographer offered to take my picture in the front of the monument and I accepted the offer. Then he told me about an intrigue surrounding the sculpture. He said that a Russian sculptor was invited to do the work. He, to flatter the local authorities, likened Nasrudin's image to that of a local big man. But when I asked him about the identity of this person and his position, the photographer said that he could not reveal his name, since he was afraid to do this. Still I understood that this must be the local Communist Party boss, since there was no bigger position than this. I found it bizarre and absurd that old religious seminaries were sacrilegiously misused, and our mystic Nasrudin's monument was erected to glorify the local Communist boss.

Next to the monument was a pond. Near to this pond my favorite teahouse was located. I liked the place since it was a gathering place of old turbaned men who were reminiscent of the bygone days of old Bukhara, the Islamic Bukhara, once attracting crowds of pilgrims from faraway places in the Muslim world. Across from the pond a *khanaka* building was located. It had been a gathering place for traveling dervishes to use as a prayer and meditation house. Now it also was converted into a museum. The *khanaka* today serves as proof to some people who are trying to distort the history of Islam by claiming that Sufism is not an Islamic movement, while in the heyday of Islam, when it was at the height of its strength and glory, Sufism was an integral part of it and held a prominent position in society.

On another day, I heard an interesting story about a godly person from a traveling businessperson with whom I shared my hotel room. To my question about whether he had heard about the existence of a living holy man in the area, he related a story about one of his relatives who lived and died several years ago in a port city on the eastern shores of the Caspian Sea. This was an old pious man venerated by the populace as a saintly person. At a certain stage, the authorities decided to put him in jail. It was told that the holy man was very careless and cheerful during the court proceedings. More than this, he told his prosecutor that he can put him in jail, but he could not hold him in there because he would escape from jail with the help of Allah. He was sentenced and sent to prison. However the next day, somehow, he managed to escape. This was repeated several times – he was imprisoned, but on the next day he somehow managed to escape. Nobody could find any explanation for how he did it. Probably, he was an able hypnotist or had some kind of magical powers. In the end the authorities, fed up with this, let him go and to live his life as he pleased. He died several years later at his home.

***

Once, during the Soviet era, my mother was summoned to the borough branch of the KGB, which was in the same block of tenement buildings that my family was living in. She had a talk in there with an officer, who told her about their concern in the secret service department, about the case of my numerous attendances at places of worship. He told her that they had received many reports from mosques in various parts of the Soviet Union, which stated that I had attended them. He said that they could not let the matter stay like this. According to him, his superiors had urged him to take action against me, to conduct a criminal investigation to find something unlawful in my conduct, so that they could start legal proceedings against me.

He said, "So far I protected your son against the pressures from my superiors, but henceforth, I will no longer do this. One more such report arriving from a mosque, and I will immediately start a criminal investigation against your son, and will lock your son in jail." But my mother persuaded him not to do anything at this time, promising him firmly that henceforth I would not go near any mosque.

On another occasion, the same officer approached my mother, and told her that a political proclamation against the Soviet state was found on the staircase of our tenement building. This incident made me one of the possible suspects. Therefore, they had to check all the different suspects in the building, and do house searches. Thus he asked her to be at home the next day, so that they could come for a house search. I was in Moscow at the time. This prospect of a house search by the secret police made her very afraid and nervous, so that she immediately collected all my English language religious books into a suitcase and hid them at the neighbors. A local borough police officer and a secret service officer conducted the house search the next day. They could not find anything incriminating me, and went away, to my mother's relief. But as I see it, their story about the proclamation which was found on the stairs was just an excuse to allow them to do these house searches in the private apartments of our building. However, I never found out what their true objective was in conducting this operation.

***

During the Gorbachev era, during the "perestroika" period of reforms, I decided to check on my chances to start my religious activities. I went to the Council for Religious Affairs in Baku, and said to its director that I had an intention of registering a Sufi society.

He said, "We are against it. I'm warning you against pursuing this matter. But if you do, then you will end up in jail."

I understood that he meant the KGB when he said "we," since all similar councils that supervised religious affairs in the Soviet Union came under the direct control of this agency. I started an argument with him. A woman secretary of his was amazed with my courage for speaking in this manner to such a high official.

Then he said, "Anyway, in this town, with this kind of people, you won't be able to find the required twenty men to be your co-founders. No person will dare sign this application." This was an intriguingly candid statement on his side, which later proved to be the truth.

Later I witnessed an interesting scene there. A Russian Orthodox deacon in his full religious garb made his entrance to the room. He had some matter to settle with the director. Then, when his pleas were fulfilled, he moved backwards to the door, while bowing to the director deep to the ground. I lost count, but he made more than ten such obeisances. To the outsider, the scene might appear bizarre and strange. But I knew the position of the Church in Russia, its subordination to the KGB. The career of this deacon was dependent on this official's good will. If the deacon lost favor with him, he would lose his job, his position as a priest. The KGB was the boss; it appointed and discharged priests.

With the arrival of "perestroika," the Kremlin, little by little, started to relax its restrictions on travel abroad. Nevertheless, I still could get no opportunity to leave the country. Once on Moscow's Central Television Channel, I saw a program made by a Soviet TV correspondent about the Indian subcontinent's religions, in which, besides other things, a resort-like camp was depicted, organized by the late Indian guru – Rajneesh (Osho). I heard a little about the history of this sect, about its problems with the U.S. authorities and their consequent deportation from America. I decided to send a letter to their headquarters in Poona, to ask whether they could send me an invitation to stay at their camp. I thought that with such an invitation in my hand, if I was lucky, I could get permission from the Soviet authorities to travel abroad.

A long time passed before I heard from them. The current manager and treasurer of the organization wrote to me saying that he regretted it, but he could not extend an invitation to me since they had just recently issued invitations to two Russians to stay at their camp free of charge. He said that he found it strange that my letter, the first letter he ever received from Russia, arrived that late. It took my letter six months to get to him.

I understood immediately what was behind it. The KGB had a special machine kept in the Central Post Office in Moscow, which allowed it to read any sealed letter coming in and going out of the country. My letter must have attracted their attention. Thus they held it for six months, to allow them to prepare their own agents and send them to this camp, to establish relations with the sect and their managers. After checking everything related with the sect, they found out that it was in possession of several hundred millions in U.S. dollars, collected through devoted followers of Rajneesh. Thus the KGB wanted to see how it could profit from the sect, probably by offering them protection from the American secret services, which had a hostile attitude toward them.

I had an acquaintance in Moscow who, in the Soviet Union, was a top black-market dealer in English-language religious books. He invited me to his house once. He had in his place a huge library of religious literature. Several shelves were full of books concerned with UFOs.

"How many titles are there?" I asked him.

"A thousand," he answered.

I found it strange that so many books on such a rubbishy matter were published. Eventually I heard from him that an enthusiast had bought from him the entire library of a thousand UFO books. I thought that he must have been an insane person to pay five thousand rubles, which was a fortune in those times, for this kind of literature.

This dealer told me about numerous UFO freaks in Moscow who gather every Sunday near a metro station. However, when I said that I wanted to go and see these people he warned me against it, saying, "There are among this crowd more KBG agents than ordinary fanatics."

As I see it, since the KGB treated believers as enemies and regarded combat against religion as its major task, UFOs also were a part of their concern. The agency treated superstitions as a part of religion as well. Thus UFOs probably came under the category of faiths and superstitions. For this reason, they operated a branch dealing with everything connected with UFOs.

Unlike what Hollywood wants us to believe, the secret services around the world, along with governments, are not suppressing any information about mythological UFOs and visiting aliens, but on the contrary, they are manufacturing it and manipulating it to achieve their political objectives. Are not UFOs an atheist agitation and anti-religious propaganda for a Cosmos without God?

The Soviets were not usually so eager to spread rumors, to manufacture information, about matters connected with UFOs. However, on two occasions they acted against their rules. During Gorbachev's reforms period, I observed two instances when the government-controlled mass media started, all as one, to discuss sightings of UFOs in different parts of the Soviet Union. I noticed that both occasions coincided with major political events which were highly sensitive for Gorbachev. Thus the KGB released this phony information, activated their UFO branch agents who witnessed "visitations" as a diversion, as a distraction, to help the head of state overcome his political problems.

Because of my difficulties with getting a formal religious education in theology, as well as in the science of mysticism, I saw that I could not use my spiritual potential fully in the Soviet Union. Thus escaping Russia and going abroad was a major priority in my life. But with the years passing, I saw myself helpless and impotent in getting a way out, which made me feel hopeless and melancholic. But when my despair reached its highest degree I decided to abandon my sentiments, my thoughts of "freedom," "democracy," and "human rights" as vain, worldly ideas lacking any real substance, as the modern day mythology, and to start a real, profound activity by turning my thoughts completely to God, and to aspire for nothing but God.

At those times, a lack of mystical books and Sufi instructors made me invent my own methods, my own mystical technique. I thought, is not the mystical way something very natural, inborn, and intuitive? Thus I invented my own methods, which later proved to be the standard methods that were used in the traditional mystical schools throughout history.

After some time I achieved certain mystical states and various supernatural phenomena. All the Sufi classics usually advise young searchers after the Truth to look for a teacher, for a Guide, and not to start a mystical work on their own without the supervision of an experienced instructor, a true Master. But in modern times the situation is different. There no longer exists an extensive network of Sufi mystical schools, and no true sheikhs. All these are in the past. The authoritative Sufi books say that the world and the Cosmos cannot be preserved without a Perfect Master, a living Perfect Man of the Sufis. It will perish the very moment the last Master dies. However, today, in our evil times, I do not know anything about the existence of such a kind of person. It may be that this kind of individual is living, but in that case he must be hiding his identity from the public, from the world. Who knows? Common sense tells us that if such a man, a perfect Guide, is not available, then a seeker should rely on himself and try to explore the mystical way on his own, by using his intuition, and eventually, by passing a self-initiation to enter the way.

There is an Indian maxim that says, "When a pupil is ready, then there emerges a teacher." The meaning of this proverb is that when an aspiring mystic is ready for the way, there will be no difficulty for him to find a teacher, a Master. Such a teacher can be either in a bodily shape or in the shape of a symbolic teacher, as in the case of Sufi tradition – *al-Khidr*, a spiritual mentor of all self-made Muslim mystics.

Chapter One: The Guides

Studying Sufi classics can be very helpful in getting theoretical knowledge. From reading them one can get something beneficial. They can in no way harm anyone, unlike having the company of phony Sufis or associations with pseudo-masters. Traveling around the world in search of the true teachers can cost a lot of money. It involves much discomfort and many dangers. There are a lot of robbers and highwaymen on the roads, and in the end the searcher will be empty-handed.

As to my early mystical experiences, I have forgotten many things, many details. Therefore, it is advisable for the beginner to put on paper his mystical experiences. I remember that these early mystical states were very real, not a product of the imagination. There was always with me a sense that these were supernatural states which one cannot encounter in the ordinary human condition. In this elevated state of mind, I looked down with an aversion at my carnal self with its fleshly desires, passions, and especially its sexuality, as something low and primitive. I felt myself above all this, content with myself and with my new condition. With this altered state of mind (or being), I was not willing to go down to the level of earthly sensuality, to return back to the ordinary condition.

Furthermore, I have to point out here an important thing. This feeling of aversion for sex was not a moral, conceptual one, nor was it a result of intellectual deduction, but was a consequence of the physical and mental changes that took place in my being. Among other things, I remember when, after the first three days of intense meditations, I went outside to look at people and saw them as very different from myself, as a sleeping crowd. Not that they were really sleeping, but that they, unlike me, were agitated, insanely hectic, and as if possessed by vain thoughts and pursuits. On the other hand, I was extremely and unnaturally calm. But, when I stopped meditating, after several days this condition started to wear off, and gradually I returned to my ordinary state, to the state of worldly people. One should be committed and not to afraid to lose one's ordinary self, one's "personality." Once you jump in the water, you have to swim until you get to the other shore.

***

Once, in Berlin, I attended a certain congress where the representatives of various Eastern religions, and different celebrities came together. It took place in a park under a huge tent that was usually used for circus shows, and the audience was made up of college students.

One by one, the guests were invited to the stage to be introduced and to say something. As they went on and off the stage, it became clear that the audience, these young Germans, held a particular attitude, a patronizing attitude, to the invited religious personas. It was obvious that they regarded all believers and people of religious professions as humans with primitive, underdeveloped minds, while considering themselves, as the humans with skeptical minds, as a smart and a superior kind of human. Besides, their behavior was as if they were saying that they came there only out of politeness anyway, not to listen to serious, tedious sermons, but on the contrary to get some light entertainment.

The most popular man with the audience was a bearded American Jewish professor. As his German was excellent and because he knew Germans very well, understood their mind-set very well, his performance made them love him very much. They clapped hands to his jokes and anecdotes. Otherwise, the most applauded guests were those who kept it very short, who said fewer words. These visitors understood what was expected from them, and they tried hard to suit the public. Thus a famous American female writer (Erica Jong) entered the stage from one side, and then crossed it without stopping, while waving her hand at the audience. They applauded her with the utmost enthusiasm.

Days before this, I went to Berlin's polytechnic college that taught sciences, and saw plenty of similar technologically-minded people there. Then at this congress, I was thinking that probably there was no university in the city where the humanities were taught. It could be that the attitude of students attending the humanities faculties would be different, more sensitive, and less arrogant than this.

Then a youngish-looking man of Indian descent, who inherited the leadership of a pseudo-Sufi society from his father, came to the stage. At the beginning of the last century, his father made himself famous in Western Europe as an Indian musician and a holy man. He got a lot of publicity from the press at the time. But it seems that the role of a holy man was too heavy a burden for his son to carry. He behaved on the stage in a very silly manner, walking as if in a sleep. Then for some time he had difficulty in finding the whereabouts of a microphone. The audience laughed at him, but you cannot blame them for this. In the end, he left the stage to the relief of everybody.

Then a young Buddhist whose parents came from Thailand came to the microphone. He lived and studied in Germany, was a kung-fu instructor, and an aspiring student of Buddhism. But the audience hated him very much, while I liked him. I saw in him a rare exponent, a man with the potential of a Master.

He went on the stage and deliberately behaved so as to make the German audience angry with him. He started to deliver a serious, thoughtful sermon on spiritual matters. But it was not what was expected of him, or anticipated. His earnest tone and words were something that the audience could not stomach. Thus they started to show their dissatisfaction, first in a low voice, and then very loudly. They whistled, jeered at him, and clapped hands to disrupt his speech. Nevertheless, he continued with his speech, without paying them any attention. At a certain point I felt he had managed to make the Germans so angry that they were ready to jump on the stage to beat him, even kill him. There was mayhem going on in the auditorium; everybody except me was screaming at this young monk, beating their feet on the ground, demanding him to shut his mouth and leave the stage.

Germans are usually a very calm and phlegmatic people, and, to my mind, these people never in their lives got that angry and indignant with somebody. These, however, were no longer polite young men. He had somehow managed to bring out the killer instincts in them.

At last he finished and went away, surprisingly alive and unbeaten. I wanted to go behind the stage and shake his hand. I think he gave a wonderful lesson to this audience, a lesson of a lifetime.

Another time in London, I was looking for a suitable place to have a solitary retreat practice. I was looking for religious organizations that could assist me with this. I heard that the Church had many monasteries and unused chapels. But unfortunately I could not find any help in this matter from Christian organizations. Then I learned the address of a Buddhist organization founded by a Tibetan lama, Chogyam Trungpa. I thought that, perhaps, with these people I could find a common language, since I knew that they had solitary retreat centers in America and Canada. Therefore, I thought that if I am lucky, they might have one in England.

I arrived there in the evening and it was not yet open. I met an English woman there in front of the temple. She told me that she is not the type of person who usually attends such places, and that she was there only because of her invalid son. I wondered why she thought that to attend a religious center or a temple is something to be ashamed of.

Her son was in a wheelchair. Later, I saw another man also in a wheelchair. A woman with a German-sounding surname, who managed that place, arrived and started to give short instructions on meditation to four or five people. The two young men in wheelchairs tried hard to imitate her meditation instructions. One of them was in an especially bad physical and mental condition. His head fell to the side and a stream of saliva was running from the corner of his mouth. I wondered why their mothers had brought them here. There should probably be some kind of institution for sick people where medical personnel could better attend their needs. For example, in Muslim mosques, people with a mental deficiency are not allowed to attend public prayers.

Later, I told the manager about my desire to spend some time in a solitary retreat, and inquired whether they had facilities for this and if they would allow me to use them. She responded by saying that she should first interview me, and took me inside a tiny cubicle with two chairs facing each other. There we sat with our knees touching each other, while she asked me prying questions about my personal life. It took five or ten minutes, but it felt much longer than this to me. I was extremely uncomfortable, almost expecting that the door would open at any minute and a German shepherd dog jump in and attack me.

At the end she said, "Yes, we have a cottage for these purposes. But I will never allow you to use it; never will I let you go there, as I don't trust you!"

I found all this very strange. I wondered whether she had the right to interrogate me like this, since I think nobody has a right to interrogate anybody without a good reason. One has to at least be a police officer.

It is very regrettable that this Buddhist organization, which was founded by such a distinguished man, is now controlled by this kind of person. I understood why she stated that she did not trust me, did not believe me. Someone like her, with her mentality, could not understand why a healthy, youngish-looking man would like to spend two months in a solitary retreat, or even an evening in the temple, rather than go clubbing somewhere in town. I saw that with her skills as a religious instructor, she could not attract anybody to this center but miserable invalids and mentally deficient people. Later it got to me that she was not German, but a Jewish woman, as it is usual in London for this Semitic group to control every charity. And it seems that they use these charities for no other purpose, but to promote their Jewish, Zionist interests.

I have to admit here that I am not a natural-born writer, a true man of letters, or a good wordsmith. But what makes my words convincing, meaningful, and effective is my position, the standpoint of a religious person. Thus if the weakest person decides to take a religious stance, then he will come out as a strong and powerful person, since his foundations will be firm, healthy, and sound. Therefore, as I have limited writing skills, a poor command of English, and my pen is not strong enough or as good as I would like, still what makes my writing valuable is that, behind my words, behind the blackness of letters, appears a shining of reality and truth.

There was a Japanese philosophical film called *Rashomon*, in which a man, to find the truth, went to see monks, priests, kings, even angels and gods, but all of them lied to him and he never could manage to find the truth anywhere.

Thus today, if anybody decides to search for the truth, even if he travels around the world, he will surely come back empty-handed. Newspapers, judges, public figures, priests, none of them can quench his thirst for the truth, since in the modern world there are no more true religious leaders, nor true prophets. But a seeker after the Truth can find himself a spiritual mentor, a spiritual Guide, and in the case of Islam a Sufi Master.

In Turkey, the Bektashi dervish order once functioned. As an illustration to my words, I want to bring up here one of my favorite Bektashi anecdotes:

Once upon a time, a poor Bektashi dervish and a merchant traveled together. By the evening, they decided to spend the night in an abandoned house by the roadside. As the merchant fastened his horse, he raised his hands and asked God to look after his animal. The dervish followed suit and fastened his donkey. Then he raised his hands and said, "O Hajji Baba, please look after my donkey!"

The merchant asked him, "Who is this Hajji Baba?"

The dervish said, "He is my late spiritual mentor, my sheikh."

The merchant became angry: "O you infidel, why are you praying to this Hajji Baba, when you can pray to Allah?"

After this, they both went inside and spent the night there. By the morning, when they went outside, they saw that the donkey was grazing peacefully, while the horse had gone. The merchant started to lament and later exclaimed, "How come that I entrusted my animal to God, and it is gone, but this infidel dervish entrusted his animal to Hajji Baba, and it is here and safe?"

To which the dervish answered: "God has many believers like you. How can He manage to look after so many of his believers and their property? But my Hajji Baba has no one but me. Thus he took good care of my animal."

This story tells us that a seeker after the Truth has to look for a Guide, a sheikh, a spiritual mentor, to find the way to God.

George Gurdjieff wrote in his books that he considered Mulla Nasrudin as his Guide, his spiritual teacher, while another Sufi personality, Idries Shah, published many books of anecdotes of this legendary figure. According to the latter, Nasrudin's anecdotes were used in Sufi circles as school texts to teach students the position of Man in society and in the universe. One Russian researcher wrote that sometimes by acting in an irrelevant manner, like a fool, Nasrudin was trying to overturn the habitual concepts of the world, claiming that this world is not the real one, and deserves neither respect nor a serious attitude. Thus it can be said that Nasrudin's tales make him an actual person, a live Master, a live teacher to thousands of aspiring mystics throughout the centuries. For that reason, I will end this chapter about the spiritual guides of the mystical way by bringing together here several anecdotes of Nasrudin.

There was a book of Nasrudin's anecdotes published by the Soviet Academy of Sciences. This book is the largest compendium of Nasrudin's tales published anywhere in the world, and contains more than a thousand anecdotes with its variations translated into Russian from twenty-three languages of different Muslim ethnicities in the Soviet Union. There are stories translated even from the language of the Greeks, who are Christians. No matter how bad the Soviet system was, it at least spent much of its resources on scientific endeavors, and paid good salaries to its scientists – very unlike the current Kremlin rulers that are only interested in plundering the remaining natural resources of the country. This book can serve as a good example for this argument.

As to Nasrudin and his tales, it could be said that by being a Master, educator, and Guide to all humanity, he was at the same time no one's personal instructor, and never followed any particular creed, order, or community. He was open to the whole world benefiting from his wisdom. He was like the sun that shines, giving light, not to anybody in particular, but to everybody and everything without discrimination. Nevertheless, some of his anecdotes have specific mystical, technical qualities and application, while ordinary people could benefit merely from their humorous qualities.

Unfortunately, the Nasrudin play that I wrote in my youth never reached the stage, and in the end even I lost the manuscript itself. But I will bring here some of the anecdotes to demonstrate the wonderful, exceptional qualities of his tales. I will make it seven, since tradition tells us that it was a strict rule in Sufi schools for Nasrudin's storytellers to deliver not less than seven tales at a time, to bring out their full potential.

***

A scholar arrives in a village and asks the whereabouts of Nasrudin. The villagers go to look for him and find him in a field as he is cutting the grass. The scholar introduces himself, and says, "Nasrudin, they say that you are a man of knowledge. I came here to ask you forty questions."

Nasrudin sees that if he answers all forty questions he will never manage to cut all the grass, and his donkey is going to starve all winter. He says, "Tell me all your questions, so that I can see what they are."

The scholar tells, one after another, all forty questions. As he finishes asking questions, Nasrudin rises to his feet, takes his sickle and says, "To all your questions I have one answer – I don't know!"

To try to make an interpretation or explanation of Nasrudin tales can be a defeating task, but in some cases giving a philosophical commentary can help to bring out their higher wisdom or a technical meaning employed at Sufi schools, which is usually missed by the ordinary reader, and would otherwise remain miscomprehended forever.

There is a special way of approaching things, be it a woman, a child, a teacher, a king, or God. This scholar was expecting Nasrudin to solve his problems, to give an answer to forty questions, as if this wise man was his personal tutor, adviser, or his personal encyclopedia. He never offered any money or any gift for the consultation, as if it was a sacred duty of Nasrudin to answer the questions of strangers. Scholars, these bookish people, are not a kin of, or a related people to mystics. Thus the welfare of his donkey was more important to Nasrudin than the welfare of this man, since he had obligations toward his animal which tirelessly served him to the best of its capabilities. But despite of all this, Nasrudin allowed the stranger to reveal his mind and his problems, since the questions themselves can describe the questioner very well. He learned a lot about the scholar, but gave nothing in return but Nasrudin's practical wisdom. Besides, if the scholar would only have asked a few questions, then he probably could have assured himself of a chance to get them answered. Finally, Nasrudin found an appropriate answer to end the audience, and give his donkey and his family an opportunity to survive the year. Yet according to another author, this anecdote speaks to us about the fact that the essence of Sufi teaching (of Sufism) cannot be expressed in words as a collection of views, since it provides no systematic answers to questions.

***

On another occasion, Mulla Nasrudin saw an Armenian priest, who had spread his provisions on a tablecloth on the grass, sitting by the road eating lunch. Nasrudin approached him, sat down, and without uttering a word, helped himself to the food. The clergyman looked at Nasrudin and said, "My friend, according to Muslims, we are infidels. Then why are you eating with me?"

Nasrudin says, "And according to Christians we are infidels. Hence, when two infidels meet, then they are clean to each other."

Here, in this anecdote, Nasrudin is trying to shock people by drawing attention to the absurdity of the respected representatives of two religions having problems in coming to terms with each other, while claiming to be in service to one and the same God.

***

One day Nasrudin lunches with the Mongol ruler, Tamerlane. They were served with an eggplant dish. He, this Asian ruler, decides to put the loyalty of Nasrudin to the test and says, "More than anything I like this eggplant dish."

"It is the same with me, my Lord," Nasrudin replies.

A few minutes later Tamerlane says, "Every time I eat an eggplant dish, I have a stomach ache."

"So do I, my Lord."

"But I must say that these eggplants are a very nourishing meal," says Tamerlane. "Every time I eat them a light comes to my eyes."

"So with me, my Lord," said Nasrudin.

Then the monarch demands a cook to be brought before him, and says to him, "If ever you serve me eggplants, I will order you to be flayed, to be skinned like eggplants. Remember, henceforth – I hate them!"

Nasrudin, as he heard this, pushes the dish away from him. "My Lord, I also hate them!"

"Hey Nasrudin," says Tamerlane. "What kind of man are you? You agree with everything I say about eggplants. What is this?"

To which Nasrudin answers, "This is all a clear matter, my Lord. It cannot be otherwise. It is you who are paying my salary, and I am serving you, not eggplants."

Chapter One: The Guides

In this tale, Nasrudin is behaving as a calculating, cold-blooded, unscrupulous person, while demonstrating a cynicism inappropriate to a holy man. Various instances of patriotism, fighting for good causes that can seem to some people as heroism, to Sufis are nothing but self-defeating sentimentality, emotionalism, and weakness. According to mystics a true hero is he who achieves something on the way, who stands above all the tribulations of life, who preserves, at all times and by all means, his inner truth.

The message of this anecdote is not directed to the world, to the worldly people who are already cynical enough and unscrupulous, but to an aspiring mystic whose duties before God are not in fighting holy wars, or in trying to save humanity from evil forces, but rather in obedience to his spiritual guide and in performing the daily tasks of the mystical path.

***

Nasrudin was invited to a wedding party. By the door there was nobody waiting to meet the guests or to look after their shoes. He was afraid that if he left his new shoes by the door, in accordance with the Muslim custom, and went inside, somebody could steal them. Thus he took out of his pocket a handkerchief, wrapped the shoes in it, and took them along. A guest sitting next to him thought that he kept under his armpit a valuable book, so he asked Nasrudin, "Is it a book?"

"Yes," says Nasrudin, "And a very valuable one. I am afraid to lose it. So wherever I go I take it along."

"Where did you get it from?" the guest asked.

"I got it in a shoemaker's shop." Nasrudin replied.

Mystics assume that ordinary people cannot see holiness or sacred phenomena when they are confronted with them in their daily life, but maybe they can if it is brought to them in the form of the holy books. Nasrudin meant that books are theory while shoes are the practice. That is, the mystical practice is much higher, much more important than theological deliberations.

***

Once at a party Nasrudin was asked to play on a lute. He took the lute in his hands without showing any embarrassment, and started to pluck the strings. As he pressed his finger on the same fret, he continuously plucked strings, but without any effect.

At last, somebody interrupted him. "O Nasrudin, they don't play a lute like this. You should move your fingers so you can produce a melody."

Nasrudin says, "This is how those people who can't play on the lute do it. The ignorant runs his fingers across the fingerboard trying to find the exact fret. But, as soon as I took the lute in my hands, I found the exact fret that I needed and held it there."

This is a highly technical and specialized anecdote which has relevance only to the people of the mystical way. Nasrudin, as a Master, explains that once an aspiring mystic gets initiation, the process, the progress will continue. This is a property of the mystical path. In other words if a pupil would find the end of the thread, then winding down the yarn will be a matter of time. Thus the trick to enter a gateway of the Sufi path is to try to pass, not a formal, but true, sacred initiation, which can only be a self-initiation.

***

One day a man visits Nasrudin. He says, "Nasrudin, I have fallen ill. Nobody can find me a remedy to cure this affliction. Maybe you could help me find a treatment."

"What is your illness?" Nasrudin asks.

"All the hairs on my body and my head are aching," answers the man.

"That is very strange," says Nasrudin. "I have never heard of such an ailment. Well, did you eat something inappropriate lately?"

"I ate ice with bread," is the reply.

"Then your illness is inhuman and your food is inhuman. Better you go to find a veterinarian!"

Here in this tale Nasrudin tries to stress that one should not neglect or ignore the wisdom accumulated by previous generations, the life experience accumulated by parents and ancestors, the common sense and sensibility of the ordinary people. Gurdjieff, on one occasion, said that the mystical work or way should not begin and start on a level lower than the ordinary life. The wisdom of this tale has many applications. It can be used in dieting practices. Some pedantic people try to introduce bizarre dieting practices in their lives, but the wisdom is in following the example of your old men, of your predecessors. Then you can know in advance what to expect, what kind of health problems or illnesses. But if you start to experiment, then you should expect uncustomary things – unusual ailments without any drugs available to cure them.

The tale also has a mystical application. Mystics sometimes call their way an ancient way, a way trodden by others, a well-known way, where all obstacles and dangers are well-explained and described. It is a way that leads somewhere. But all new cults and pseudo-religions that were invented by human intellect are fruitless, leading nowhere but to disappointment, physical or mental illness, or even to death. There is no necessity to introduce any new teachings, new religions. The world has its well-established heavenly religions and the ancient mystical way.

***

One day Nasrudin's villagers surround him and ask him to read them a sermon.

"Leave me alone! I can't read any sermons," he says.

Nevertheless, the villagers keep on urging him to do this. At last, when he is persuaded by them to rise to the pulpit to read a sermon, he asks them, "Do you know?"

"No, we don't know," they answer.

"If you don't know, then there is nothing that I can explain to you," says Nasrudin.

The next time the villagers decide again to find a way to persuade him to read a sermon. When he sees that he cannot avoid it, he rises to the pulpit and says, "Do you know?"

"Yes, we know," the congregation answer hastily.

"If you know already, then there is no need for me to say anything." He then descends and runs away.

The villagers see that this time, as well, they failed. Then they decide that the next time they would devise a better plan. The next time as he rises to the pulpit and he inquires, "Do you know?" a part of the congregation answer, "Yes, we know," while the others would say, "No, we don't know."

Nasrudin sees that they are trying to outwit him, so he says, "In that case, the part who knows should inform the other part."

The tale is trying to explain that it is impossible to talk or to explain anything to people. They are an ignorant crowd that does not know anything about Man and the universe. Unless somebody knows his ABCs, it is a waste of time to try to teach him complicated things. Thus people prefer to stay blind rather than to face reality. And it is a futile thing to try to teach them anything.

God says, "These are they whom Allah guided, therefore follow their guidance" (Koran, 6:90).

CHAPTER TWO:
REINCARNATION

In the summer of 1995, when I still lived in England, I decided one day to visit London's Theosophical Society. That day they were offering two lectures. The first lecture was free of charge, and its theme was reincarnation. I decided to attend this lecture, especially since I was somehow intrigued how they were going to explain this idea of repetitions of lives and everything connected with it. So far all explanations of the reincarnation theory that I had heard were very unsatisfactory and unconvincing, so , I was happy to find somebody ready to discuss the subject.

The room where the discourse took place was small, but big enough to accommodate some ten to fifteen people who were gathered there. They had an old woman for a lecturer. She gave a perfectly standard explanation of the theory, and I heard nothing new or interesting. I started to regret coming there and the waste of time. But then I decided to intervene and enter into the discussion, to bring a fresh look on the subject. I asked the lady for permission to give another view, a different exposition of the idea of reincarnation. It was somehow strange that she found it possible to allow me to take her place on the podium and deliver my thoughts to the small auditorium.

I said that the content of the lecture was identical to all other explanations I had heard or read before. I would like to give my opinion concerning reincarnation, to give its full and complete exposition, that to my mind, were the Buddha himself a participant of the discussion, he would turn down the offer to say something. Rather, he would allow me to explain the subject, saying that this man could give the lecture in his place, as it would be a quite satisfactory one.

The religions of Islam and Christianity both altogether reject the idea of repetitions of lives. The idea is not the part of their religious doctrines. However, some Christian and Muslim heretical sects did entertain the idea. I notice that all European female truth seekers, including Helena Petrovna Blavatsky (the founder of the Theosophical Society), when they are trying to ponder religion and the holy books, they look for some justification of their feminist sentiments and ideas. These women make efforts to prove that both sexes are equal. But unfortunately, they are too obsessed with matters concerning their gender, so that they can never distance themselves from it to be impartial, honest, or objective. In this instance, they assume that the theory of repetitions of lives proves that both sexes are equal, since a male in his next life, can be born as a female. They are very quick and hasty in their desire to see in the reincarnation theory a proof of the equality of sexes, while not showing the slightest interest in trying to find proofs to substantiate the theory. They fail to analyze the theory to see whether it makes any sense, if it is a plausible idea. They are not interested in finding out whether this mostly Oriental doctrine is true or false, but rather look for how they can benefit from it, to what use they can put it to suit their individual tastes, positions, or sentiments. Definitely, they are not true truth seekers.

Early in my life, I came to the realization that all people in this world are divided into two categories or types. One type is the ordinary worldly people, who all their lives are in the pursuit of material things. A person who belongs to this category during his (or her) entire life has no time, even as little as ten minutes, to spend reflecting on matters concerning life and death, eternity, God, and the Creation. There are a billion Buddhists on the Earth who accept the doctrine of reincarnation as a fact, without spending any time on the subject to find out whether this idea is substantial or sensible.

On the other hand, there is a small group of people who are born as genuine truth seekers. This kind of person continuously spends all his time thinking about spiritual, abstract matters. If a person with an average intelligence would devote half an hour daily to meditation on higher matters, there would be no need for the holy books or prophets. But it seems that humanity has no time to spend on such things. So for that very reason, from time to time, God finds it necessary to send His Word and His messengers to the world.

Once, I decided to spare some time to think about the theory of reincarnation, to solve this problem for myself. It took me no more than a half of hour to find all the answers concerning the matter.

Europeans who popularized the Oriental teachings, such as Blavatsky, Alexandra David-Neel, and Herman Hesse, tried in vain to understand these ideas and explain them intellectually, rationally. These teachings remained a mystery which they could not penetrate or comprehend. They themselves admitted it in their writings.

Westerners – as a rationalistic people, as an intellectual race – have difficulty grasping Eastern teachings and religions. On the contrary, Asians are mostly emotional people, an irrational race. For this reason, Europeans find the Eastern teachings something very strange, like exotic fruits unsuitable for their palate. An example of this that can be presented is the Protestants with their rationalistic reforms movement, who managed to take the Catholic Christian faith of the southerners, readjust it, and introduce changes to make it more suitable for the northern European mind.

It must be understood that all heavenly religions first appeared in the East. The holy books, religious scriptures originated in the East, in Asian society. Therefore, when they are taken from the Asian context, and artificially, so to say, transplanted in the European body, it will look like an artificial limb. It obviously will lose its character and meaning. Thus if a sermon read by an Eastern priest in a temple somewhere in Asia, meant for the Asian people and mind, would be repeated word for word in an European auditorium, it would surely be met with misunderstanding. The Eastern priest, when he composed his sermon, kept an Asian audience in mind. He did not mean it for people with a foreign, European mentality.

Therefore, when I heard the speech of the Theosophist lady I saw the same thing, that this exposition or explanation of reincarnation must have been originally told by an Eastern priest to Eastern worshipers. Then a European participant of the congregation memorized it and repeated it, word for word, somewhere in Europe. The words are the same, but its effect on the Western gathering was entirely different. Even worse, here and there in the text of the sermon he added his own interpretations, the European, Western interpretations that managed to alter and corrupt the original message. Thus European propagandists of the Eastern religions are stating that since a male in the next life can be born as a female or as an animal, then it can serve as proof of the equality of all creatures in the eyes of God. They see in it proof of the equality of all humans, male and female, and the equality between humans and animals as well. However, all these ideas are very modern ideas, introduced to the world by Westerners. Feminists and animal rights campaigners all are Europeans. These kinds of ideas are alien to the Asian mentality, and unacceptable to them. The ideas are, basically, anti-religious, since God created everybody and everything unequal. One creature is higher and another lower. This inequality is basic to religion. Only an atheist could pretend that there is no difference between an animal and a human, that they should be treated indiscriminately. But this kind of equation rejects the superiority of soul and spirit over the beastly, over the animal passions and instincts.

Western agitators, Theosophists and others, when they heard about the theory of reincarnation, felt in it something attractive to the Western psyche, something that they could sell easily to the public. They think in this way, that the Christian priest attracts the believers to the Christian faith by promising them Paradise, but this Hindu or Buddhist idea of reincarnation promises an eternal, repeated return to the worldly life, which would be an even more attractive idea — something that could be more marketable to the people, since a lot of people, rather than live in Paradise, would prefer to grab the opportunity to return to a worldly life, the possibility of the repeated return to the earthly life.

An ordinary person, when asked whether he wanted an eternal life on the Earth, would answer positively with great enthusiasm. But a thinking person, an intelligent person, if he considered it properly, would find it a silly desire. Everything in the world is well thought out and reasonable. Likewise, the human life span of some eighty years given by God is the optimal figure, the optimal length of existence possible.

Somebody with a vivid imagination would understand that a life span, let say, of six hundred years, would be unbearable for the human psyche. Life is sweet as long as it is short. Would life continue for hundreds of years, no person, no heart would bear it. There is no doubt that people would start committing suicide long before the end of their time. Therefore a life lasting eighty or so years granted by God to Man is the best for him to live and to fulfill his mission, his ambitions in life and in the world.

Let us now examine the same sermon read in the original cultural background, and see the reaction to it by an Asian congregation, to whom it was initially addressed. The Oriental priest starts his speech with an announcement that he has brought them very good news, that there is reincarnation and repetition of lives, so that in the next life a man can be born again as a female, or even as a dog.

Would this priest deliver his sermon to a Western European audience, this kind of announcement would produce a favorable impression on the people, and they would be very positive about all this. It is quite an acceptable idea, an acceptable prospect for a European male, especially for one who lives in the Northern parts of the continent, to be born again as a female. In this culture, here in England, many males are having sex changes by having surgical operations. Besides, most men in England think that English women have all the fun, that they have much more chance to enjoy themselves than men. Life for British women is happy and comfortable. They would be glad to be women. Similarly, the idea of being born again as a dog would be quite acceptable for most of the British population.

Chapter Two: Reincarnation

The other day I was walking on the road by Hampstead Heath. I was returning from shopping with heavy bags in my hands and my legs were aching. I saw a Mercedes parked there. A woman driver took a dog out of the car and let it run free. The dog was enjoying itself on the lawn. Later the woman called the dog back. Then she wiped the dog clean from the mud with a Turkish towel. Only after this, did she allow it to come inside the car. I understood that she had driven the car to the park, so that her dog could enjoy itself by playing on the grass.

There, watching this scene, I felt envious of this dog, since in my whole life I never had a chance to sit in a Mercedes car. More than that, the dog will be driven home and this attractive woman will probably wash him in a bathtub. Though this creature was born merely as a dog and I as a human, it has more joy and comfort in life than I do.

But the situation with dogs and women in the Orient is very different from England. Dogs in Asia are hungry and uncared for. The prospect of being born again as a dog will hardly sound attractive to Asians. The same can be said about women. No Asian woman would like the idea of having another life as a woman. They find life in their culture and society deprived, miserable, and full of hardship.

As I possess the psyche of an Asian male, I find the idea of being born again as a female something unbearable. All Latin males will share the same sentiments. For the males in these cultures, just thinking about having a sex change causes terrible mental torture. Therefore, I would rather reject the offer of a new life in the female form and face final death, which to me would be a more agreeable prospect. Similarly, I would reject the doctrine of reincarnation as something not religious at all, as something unpleasant and ungodly. I would never accept it as something coming from God. Since He is the Lord, the Compassionate, and the Merciful, He would never do such a cruel thing to his servants, to humans. He would never create life and the world to be something unbearable for its creatures.

They try to reassure me that I can be born again as a woman. To which I would say that if I was born again in the female form, then what would this woman have to do with me? Something, that I call "I" has much to do with my individuality, which is very much connected with the form I bear now, along with my gender, body structure, facial features, and temperament. Thus to be born in another form will mean another bodily shape, another face, and therefore, a different individuality, different mind, different person. It is impossible for me to disconnect myself from the form that I have now, including my gender. I know for sure that would my soul be dressed in another form, then it will be an entirely different individuality, another creature, which would have no resemblance to me in form or mentality. Neither I, nor anybody else, would recognize me in this new form. Nothing could reassure me that this new creature was me.

There is a science called physiognomy, which is the art of judging a human character by the facial features and the body shape. According to this science, all similar faces have the same personality. That is, the personality is connected with bodily shapes and the features of the face. Therefore, all people who look alike belong to the same psychological type; have the same astrology and fate. That means that if anybody would die and then be born again in another body with a different shape, with different facial features, then his whole character would be a new one, of a different kind, with no relation to the previous one, somebody with an entirely different mentality.

The prospect of being born again as another man has zero appeal to me, since I consider myself a lucky man to be born as an individual with religious inclinations, with higher values, with a personality that is a result of a very long development through natural selection. I do not feel the need to return to the world, to a new life as an animal, or as a human with primitive, beastly inclinations, but just want to use this given life to its best in my current body and shape.

In my own case, as a person with religious, spiritual values, with a good prospect to rise to the higher stages of development, to the realm of angels, and to enter Paradise in this given instance of life, why on earth should I desire to go and return back to the lower stages of development, with a low primitive mind? But if they are talking not about psychological individuality, but about something they call soul, something that has nothing to do with my character, then how I can call it my self? In this case, it would be the same for all people and creatures, with no distinctive features. Then it must be an indivisible and single oneness. If we will accept this oneness as something permanent and eternally alive, then it makes all this talk about the repetitions of lives unnecessary and meaningless. It will mean that this single soul exists in everybody, and is never dying, has no distinctive, individualistic features. To most people the idea of existence is connected with their individuality, with their feelings and sentiments, and a kind of indifferent soul lacking any individual features or sentimental attachments would have no value. An ordinary man assumes that his soul has a serial number, and belongs to him forever. But logical reasoning tells us that the only things that can die are forms, bodies, while the soul is something impersonal, lacking any memory. Definitely, it should be something without a serial number, and a date of issue. It should be an eternally existing entity, fully independent from the body, whereas personality traits are something fully dependent on the form, on the body shape, and they die with the body.

It can appear as if the human soul is connected with the body. But in reality it has just a formal, symbolic connection, since the soul at all times remains in the heavenly fold. Likewise, if I were born again in the form of a dog, then how would I recognize myself in it? This is a dog, and this is I. This dog and I are not the same. I always identify myself with my religiousness, and I never saw a religious dog or a dog that is interested in the philosophy. Therefore, this type of reincarnation apology is nothing but nonsense.

So on hearing this reincarnation sermon, the Asian audience will hardly feel happy and positive about all this. Therefore, when the priest continues reading his sermon, and points his finger at the local king, saying that in the next life he can be born as a female, the king will definitely take it as an offence, as an insult.

It might happen that a madman in the temple upon hearing these words, would cry out to the king that he should not stick his nose up in the air any more, since in the next life he could be born as a female. He could even warn the king, saying that if their roads should cross in the future life, then he, the madman would not miss the opportunity, and would grab him in his female form, push him into the bushes and take advantage of him. Everybody in the congregation would laugh at the madman's remarks. Even the women in the audience will hardly feel happy at the prospect of being born again as women in this Asian society.

Then the priest might continue his discourse by telling the king that in the next life he might be born again as a dog. On hearing this, the madman will start to cry out again, and would say to the king that on his way to the temple he met a mongrel, and hit it hard with a stick. Therefore, he should now ask forgiveness from him, in case the dog was a reincarnation of the late king, his father. Everybody will laugh again, and all this will make the monarch even angrier.

Therefore, the monarch would lose his patience with the priest, with his sermon, and respond by saying, "Hey you, priest, when you started your speech, you promised us some good news. But this religious doctrine of yours, this idea of reincarnation, does not sound as something pleasant to me, or as a happy idea. So where is your good news?"

To which the priest will answer that the good news was not the repetition of lives itself, but something else. He will continue, "You all saw that this kind of multiple returns to the world is not a good idea at all, not a good prospect at all. Indeed, it is a very horrible and dreadful idea. The good news is not the repetition of lives, but our religious teaching. The core, the central dogma of our religious teaching is not the idea of reincarnation itself, but rather is the divine teaching, which is the method allowing us to put an end to this cycle of repetitions of lives."

It must be noted here that in the original Hindu and Buddhist texts, they usually call this cycle (or circle) a "vicious circle of repetitions of lives." Therefore, while the Western advocates of the Eastern faiths are offering this idea to the Western public as a sign of hope, the Oriental priests originally introduced this idea to horrify the public, and to draw them to the religion, to their teaching. To complete the subject, I will bring up here an anecdote from another culture, the Muslim one, to illustrate the same ideas:

A priest was once reading a sermon in a mosque. He told the congregation that they should always be grateful to God, under all circumstances. He continued by bringing illustrations, "Say, thank you God, if you were born male, which is much better than being born female. If you are female then say, thank you God for not creating me as an animal, as a dog. If you were born a healthy person, say thank you God for not creating me as a cripple. A cripple should say, thank you God for allowing me to have a life, since it is better than no life at all."

Moreover, a dog or any other animal will not blame his lot for its beastly form, since it has no mind, and hence, no such thought will come to its mind, luckily.

Religious tales and stories were not originally meant for the public – who are always going to miss the point – but for the small group of the inner circle of pupils of mystical schools. Even the most intellectual people, unless they are born truly spiritual types, will misunderstand any religious discourse, since it was not addressed to them; there is nothing appealing in it for their souls and frame of mind. Thus all my life I, as a spiritual type of person, as a mystic, despite all the hardships of my life, misfortunes and misery, could not find an excuse to blame my lot, or accuse God of not being generous with me – since I am a man, a healthy man, and above all He granted me the most valuable thing there is in the world, a truly religious nature, a spiritual soul. As a loving father, He presented me with the most precious item in His treasury – an exalted soul with an inclination for a religious way, a mystical way, the only path that leads to salvation. Does it mean that He was not as merciful and generous to others? They are happy with themselves and with their lot and are not aware of this. They do not know any better.

To continue the line of thought I will say, that in the case of me being born as a woman of the usual type, then I would hardly possess a taste for philosophy or religion, since the physiological particulars of women make them less inclined for philosophizing, as they are down-to-earth creatures with many practical matters to attend to in their daily life. The destiny of a woman is to bear the child, to give birth, and to rear it. She has no time to straighten up her back, to sit up and think about abstract matters.

Once, in a London bookshop in Charing Cross Road, I found on the shelf a book written by an American woman, a pseudo-Sufi, about her solitary retreat experiences. This solitary retreat (in Arabic *khalwa*), lasting for forty days, is a very sacred practice undertaken by mystics for the thousands of years. Being an outsider, she failed. Besides that, because she was a woman she was plagued by her bodily functions. Thus every page I turned to was full of her writings about her problems with menstruation, which did not allow her soul and spirit to leap in the air and fly to the heavenly realms.

I would not blame God for not making me a genius, an extremely talented individual. I am quite content with my average intellectual capabilities, which are an advantage compared to being an utter fool—especially since I understood that average intellectual capabilities are quite enough for a person to be suited to the mystical way, to be successful on it and reach its highest stages, to reach enlightenment. After all, how can we possibly call it an average intellect if it allows its possessor to grasp God's mysteries?

Most religious precepts, proverbs, and fables are very specific, very technical and specialized. Outsiders, ordinary people, cannot understand them. They can never use this wisdom in their practical life, or to apply it to themselves. The experiences of the worldly life and of the mystical way have no parallels or comparisons. Thus the precepts that were intended for the people of the mystical way, of the Sufi Way, have no practical application to the worldly life or to the ordinary psychology.

This particular Muslim anecdote that I brought up above, speaks to a student of the mystical school, who walks on the mystical way, like this: You were born with a very particular nature, particular soul, therefore do value it, and be grateful forever to God who granted it to you. Be grateful that you were born not as an outsider, as a man of dogma, as a formalist, as one of the people of the exoteric forms of religion whose inborn limitations do not allow them to understand or grasp divine knowledge, the mystical teaching. Be thankful that you were born not as a woman, who is normally indifferent to spiritual matters. Be thankful for not being born as an animal, because if you were born as a beast there would be no chance for your salvation.

God says, "And they ask you about the soul. Say: The soul is one of the commands of my Lord, and you are not given aught of knowledge but a little." (Koran, 17:85). Also the Prophet said: "God created the spirits two thousand years before the bodies."

CHAPTER THREE:
THE HIERARCHY OF THE SCIENCES

The twentieth century was the century of the rationalistic man. One can define it also as the age of science and technology. But, unfortunately, this advance of technology had its side effects, as it turned everything in the world upside down. I would characterize it as the age, as the era, of disorder and upside-downiness, as a revolutionary period, which overturned all the previous order of things and put in question the old system of values in human society. The advance of science and technology introduced the capitalist system with its own ways and its own values to the world, and demolished the traditional world order that existed before. The advance of capitalism upset the balance of things in society. The foundations on which Adam's descendants, humankind, stood for thousands of years were destroyed and swept aside.

There is the epic tale of Koroglu among different Turkic-speaking tribes of the Middle East. It is a story about a Muslim brigand who robbed caravans, very much like a Robin Hood figure. He was a chief of highwaymen, who gave a lot of headaches to local rulers, shahs, and sultans. While the population enjoys the epic as a romantic story, it contains also certain passages that possess some clever observations. The last chapter of the poem is about Koroglu in old age:

Once he met in a mountain passage a young man carrying on his shoulder an object unknown to him. He asked him what it was.

The young man answered that it was a rifle, a new European invention, a type of weapon. Koroglu asked him to explain and to demonstrate how it worked. After hearing the young man's explanations, Koroglu deeply sighed in grief, thinking that his times were finished.

He said, "The time of brave and heroic men has ended and a new time has arrived, the time of cowardly and treacherous types."

He was a knightly figure who fought his battles with saber and mace. Now with this type of weapon anybody, even a child, can enter the scene of battle and be victorious.

To explain the changes, it can be said that the advance of science and technology brought capitalists to power, while before, in the previous millennia, the power was in the hands of monarchs and clerics whose rule was based on religious foundations. The capitalist ideology and values are diametrically opposite to those of faith and spirituality. Thus religion and capitalism are mortal enemies to each other. The fight was won by capitalism, and it put an end to the old order of things, where spiritual ideas and values served as the basis upon which human society had stood since its dawn up to modern times. This orderly and harmonious religious structure was demolished.

Once I was doing research into Muslim history. I was puzzled by a question — what made the Turkic tribesmen of Central Asia, in medieval times, so militarily strong and victorious. After a study of numerous historic works, I could not find an answer to this. Later, however, my own reflections on the subject gave me an insight into the matter. The main factor that made these nomadic tribes so strong was their major occupation, which was the breeding of livestock. They were herdsmen. The huge flocks of sheep provided food, while horses provided transport for the army.

In the period of the Baghdad caliphate, the Turkic tribesmen of Central Asia made military raids on this city from time to time. After capturing it, they executed the caliph in power and replaced him with a new one, the man of their choice. Muslim rulers in those times did not keep a regular army, and in Baghdad at a given time, there were only several thousand soldiers guarding the caliph. Thus if the chieftains of the tribes decided to make a raid, they ordered the herdsmen to mount their horses. In this way, in a few days an army two or three hundred thousand strong could be gathered. Even if they would arm themselves merely with wooden spears, such a multitude of horsemen was a tremendous force.

This army of mounted men could reach Baghdad in a week's ride. A caliph could never manage to collect an army to defend him and the city at such short notice. A horse can be compared by modern standards to an armored personnel carrier or a tank. So imagine for a minute, an army made up of three hundred thousand tanks!

Today the Nordic ethnic groups with their advanced technology and military strength have become the dominant race of our times. But the weakness of this race is in its ultimate materialism, in its arrogant attitudes, and in its skeptical mind that regards religion and faith as something that should not be taken into consideration. For them religion is not a science, not something real or actual. Morality for them has no value, nor any use, while their insane, aggressive, and unrestricted industrialization has brought humanity to the brink of self-destruction.

Chapter Three: The Hierarchy of the Sciences

They describe themselves as the intellectual race, but with their reigning position in modern times, with their extreme rationalism, they have done much more harm to the earth than was done in the previous thousands of years of existence of humanity under the rule of the divine religious laws. If the rationalistic mind is something superior, something positive, then why it is so damaging and destructive? It is obvious that rationalism, with its materialistic values, is not the right foundation for human society. It has proved to be nothing but materialistic indulgence and spiritual dumbness.

The Western man is a captive of his passions. His excessive indulgence in serving the needs of his "lower self," his "animal self," makes him ignore God's decrees, while feeling no responsibility for anybody or anything. Are not the godless people who have no fear of Him the most irresponsible types, while the other races – which are described by Westerners as backward and underdeveloped – appear to be more sensible people, living a simpler life in accord and peace with the laws of nature and of God?

The human mind is so complex and multifaceted that it is very difficult to define it, or to make a final judgment of an individual. No matter how strange it may sound, but it seems that the part of the population which is less intellectual is often more useful for the preservation of faith and religion within society than its so-called intellectuals, the "smarter" ones.

Westerners like to talk, at length, about human rights issues, and regard themselves as the representatives of their superior Western civilization. They verbally, aggressively attack the technologically underdeveloped states, the third-world countries, criticizing them for their poor human rights record. But I will state that it is Western capitalism that has deprived humanity of its basic, essential rights. As a human being, I could live happily and contented even without their advanced technology; what makes me unhappy and depressed is that they have deprived me of my basic, natural right to breathe unpolluted air, to drink water which is clean of chemicals and poisons, to eat ecologically clean food.

Let us take the ancient Hindu caste system and consider it. We can see that the high priests introduced this system by no means out of selfishness to suit their whim or caprice, but as a just system that was devised and governed in accord with religious science and wisdom. The ancient people understood that there are different types of people, different categories, and the caste divisions were made to classify people within society, to define and underline the right value system in the community. While modern European psychologists and sociologists do not understand these psychological divisions and classifications, the Hindu caste system scale reflects the realities of human nature, psyche, and typology.

Modern, pseudo-scientific sociological theories are forcing people to abandon their old traditional religious social structures with utopian ideas of technological paradise, while ignoring the nature of things in life and lasting spiritual values.

Thus the Hindu caste system helped for thousands of years to maintain in society a natural order and balance, allowing the spiritual, higher values to prevail, to rule over the bestial and the low. According to Hinduism, the priesthood, the spiritual types, represents the ruling class of humankind, and the lowest class are people with primitive professions, the physical types. But of course this Hindu caste system is a symbolic and formalistic one, rather than following the true divisions along the natural, psychological characteristics of humans – God has already divided people into different typological groups and classes.

In our modern, politically correct times, one should not make any racial remarks. It can be even illegal. Yet one cannot ignore the facts of life that there are races and various categories of humans. And the racial features are not just skin-deep. God created the world as something harmonious, balanced by opposing forces. Therefore, the human races and types serve as balancing factors, complementing each other or creating natural tensions, conflicts, and healthy competition.

There is a Russian proverb that says a fool finds it funny that God placed his ears at the sides of his head. He thinks that one ear on the top of his head would make a much better design. Likewise, an idiot could complain that the Creator should have made humans as the representatives of the same race, so that there would be fewer problems in the world, no racial tensions. But no one can judge and criticize God's plan and design. It can be said that race and racial traits represent one of the fundamental laws of the nature. Without the diversity of races and types, there would be no life, no healthy competition in the world. Every race and personality type has its strong and weak points. An observant person will notice that the black African race is the most physically strong. He will observe, as well, that they are less reflective and more practical types. Thus they are less intellectual and sentimental. Compared to Europeans, Asians are a more emotional and sentimental people, and relatively weak intellectually. The North Europeans are the most rationalistic people, with a certain emotional dumbness.

Chapter Three: The Hierarchy of the Sciences 77

Nevertheless, of course, these characteristics are relative and very general, since every race is in possession of the full rainbow of human types, including intellectual, emotional, and sensual individuals, so that if taken separately, every race, in itself, is fully representative of the human kind.

Japanese are considered as the most European, the most rationalistic people in Asia. However, if you look at their brand of Buddhism, which arrived in Japan from the Asian continent, you will find that it has a very down-to-earth and materialistic quality, unlike its Chinese, Korean, and Indian varieties. Thus the rationalistic racial traits made the Japanese less perceptive and able to grasp the spiritual content of the Buddha's teaching.

Likewise, there is a Persian maxim, which says, "There are two types of Arabs. Beware of both of them! One is a scientific genius and another is totally ignorant." This maxim describes the situation with all Asian Muslims. Their extreme emotionalism is at the expense of rational thinking, while it would not sound a very unbalanced statement to say that the Asian race is much more sensitive to religious ideas than the Nordic, European race. Similarly, it could be said that any given society in the most deprived parts of Asia and Africa, in a rural area ruled by a shaman, would prove to be morally healthier and more spiritually aware than that of Western Europe.

I do not want to be misunderstood, since I am not defending any racist idea or chauvinistic propaganda here. I want to bring up an example to explain myself better. It would not be correct to say that the Arab race brought forth Prophet Mohammad (peace be upon him), but rather that it was Islam that brought forth the Prophet, made the Prophet. In other words, what makes Arabs an important people is their Islamic religion and the Holy Koran; without the religion and the Book, they would remain an insignificant nomadic tribe. What made an historic Arab a great man, a great scientist, was his Islamic faith, not his racial peculiarities.

In addition, it can be said that God created races, but that racism is a human creation. Racist ideas are contrary to religion, and so Islam accepts no racist ideology. Man has to move from his tribal or racial identity to get a productive, religious identity, thus opening up his perspectives.

Patangali was a Hindu mystic. He wrote that there are four types of people and, correspondingly, four forms of religion. According to Hinduism, there is the way of Action (*Karma Yoga*), the way of Devotion (*Bhakti Yoga*), and the way of Gnosis (*Jnana Yoga*). The way of Action is the way or religious method of physical types, requiring strong physical endurance and bodily exercises. The way of Devotion is the religion that is suitable to the emotional types. The way of Gnosis is for the intellectual people or races. It is a philosophical kind of religion. And the highest form, the fourth way is the Royal (*Raja Yoga*) way or method. According to Patanjali, this way is the religion of mystics, of intuitive people, the most noble and superior form of religion.

It must be said that Patanjali himself was a mystic, which is why he described the Royal way, the mystical way, as the most superior. Thus the followers of the way of Action, of the way of Devotion, and the way of Gnosis, in their turn would claim their respective form of religion to be the most superior type. However, the truth is that every kind of person should look for the kind of religion that corresponds to his individual type, the most suitable to his natural peculiarities and capabilities. Therefore, everything is relative. Every form of religion is the best for the type of person that it was designed for.

Everything in the world can be classified and put into categories. There are many sciences, many occupations – some superior, some inferior, some simple, some complicated. There is the science of blacksmithing and the science of sportsmanship, which do not require much brain power. Also, there are sciences which are suitable only for brainy people, brainy types. In other words, there is a certain hierarchy of sciences.

In earlier times, the religious science was considered as the most superior and honorable, as the noblest kind of science. It was considered as the most complex of all sciences, while the other sciences which were considered to require less intelligence stood at a lower rung of the hierarchical scale.

Capitalism brought to the world the ailment of consumerism, with its mass production or production for the masses. Nowadays a product suitable for the masses brings much more profit than products suitable for the elite. Therefore, profits made the inferior, ordinary product of low intelligence more important than a unique product suitable for the highly intelligent people. All this upset the old value system. Now profits are more important than anything else.

The twentieth century, with its consumerist philosophy, introduced a new high class made up of actors, dancers, musicians, magicians, singers, and artists. This class of people are today's elite, the most influential and rich people. Today they are more influential than monarchs. Thus capitalism turned yesterday's street entertainers into the modern day aristocracy. However, in the old times, in the old social structure, these

Chapter Three: The Hierarchy of the Sciences

types of people were the inferior ones, the lowest class. Previously, musicians, dancers and actors had the same status in society as prostitutes.

There was a report made by a nineteen-century journalist about a group of Muslims, fans of a musician. When the musician died the local priest did not allow this man to be buried in a cemetery, arguing that his was an immoral profession and he should not be buried in the cemetery, so as not to desecrate the burial site. Therefore, the devoted fans of the musician buried him in the cemetery at night in a secret ceremony. Today, the burial sites of musicians have, to their fans, the status of holy shrines.

An acquaintance of mine, who had the rare gift of being a philosopher, confided to me that he decided not to follow this vocation, since today it does not pay. So he went into the book-selling business, and made himself a fortune from this trade by selling popular literature. In the old times, clergymen and philosophers had the highest status in society; these professions were the most desirable and the most rewarding.

In sixteenth century Turkistan there lived a holy man, Khwaja Ahrar, a leader of dervishes. He lived in the capital city of Samarqand with three hundred thousand followers around him. He had an army of devoted supporters, while the sultan of Samarqand had just a thousand personal guards in the city. Each dervish or fakir carried a double-bitted axe as the symbol of distinction of the order. Therefore, the sultan was very much afraid of this saint. Besides, the dervishes were collecting alms and were submitting their collections to the holy man. The money went untaxed into his coffers. It is an historic fact that, while the sultan's treasury was empty, the coffers of Sheikh Khwaja Ahrar were filled with gold. He was considered the richest and most powerful man in the whole of Turkistan. Thus, whenever the sultan needed the funds to raise an army for an act of war, he went to the holy man to beg for money.

But today, in the modern capitalist society, the spiritual mentors are standing by the doors of the villas of dancers, musicians and artists – begging for money to conduct their religious work. The situation has changed a lot.

Before, actors, musicians, singers, and artists were considered atheistic, immoral types; they were not accepted in decent society. Now, they are invited by television channels to give talks, to philosophize on life, faith, and religion. They comport themselves as if they were sages, wise men and even prophets. You can find in bookshops plenty of books on the subject of religion and faith written by these bohemian types. In my opinion, pre-capitalist social systems were far more just, fair, and sensible. In those times, in the old social order, every class of people, every category of people was treated according to their true merit and capabilities, according to their true position in the hierarchy of sciences and professions. These value systems were heaven-made, and corresponded to the cosmic hierarchic order.

There is a term – a rare profession that should be recognized as the most honorary and respectable. According to the old social order and its traditional values, the most unique and high status is that of a prophet. The world, at any given time or period, can have only one prophet for each faith. Thus these men – prophets, holy men and saints – should hold the highest and the most honorable position in society. Next to them should stand philosophers, since at any one time, a nation can only have a few philosophers, as this profession requires exceptional brain power and intelligence. It must be said that philosophy is a positive kind of science as long as it serves religion; the materialist philosophers whose positions are not religious, have the wrong foundations, wrong ideologies, based on wrong, unconstructive, harmful outlooks and views. Therefore, the value of a philosophical doctrine depends on its moral and spiritual position; otherwise, it is useless for society.

I remember how I met a Nigerian Muslim businessman. He was the head of the Lions Club in a village. He, while trying to impress me, announced proudly that he could rap. I told him every African can rap, so what was so special about that? He should boast about his business acumen instead. In Africa, tens of millions of rap singers can be found; it is not a big deal. Despite this, in capitalist, consumerist America, rap singers are the top men, while holy men in today's society have the lowest and most miserable status. Certainly, the modern world is under control of the Devil.

Formally, when religious laws and spiritual values governed the world and society, the more intelligence a profession required the more respectable it was. Today the opposite is true. The less intelligence a profession requires, the higher standing in society will be allotted to it. It is very silly. The ancients were more sensible than our modern people. They considered the so-called creative people – dancers, actors, musicians, singers as low-brow people, the people of a low-intelligence class, and treated them accordingly. They treated them as rubbish.

According to the true value system, the highest form of science is religion. In Arabic, a word for science is *ilm*. According to the old Arabic usage, the word was used only for one form of science, for theology. Other sciences were called the practical sciences. The ancients considered the highest, the noblest form of knowledge to be religious knowledge, the

Chapter Three: The Hierarchy of the Sciences

religious sciences. Thus, mystics describe their mystical science as the science of sciences, while one ancient mystic has said that of all knowledge the most important is self-knowledge.

According to the true categorization, if we draw a scale or a ladder illustrating the hierarchy of the sciences in the correct relation to its depth of intelligence and honor, then the people of the entertainment professions are going to hold the lowest level or rank, because the degree of intelligence their crafts require is less.

The lowest rung or rank is going to be held by dancers and sportsmen; you do not need any brains to run or to jump. If we held a jumping competition, monkeys would be the champions. No creature can jump better and higher than a monkey. But a monkey has little intelligence.

The next rung is going to be held by musicians, singers, composers of music and actors. The kind of information you can transmit by a dance is only very limited. Through music, one can communicate a little more information, but it is still quite limited. Sculptors and artists would hold a higher position, since these professions require slightly more intelligence. The next rank will be that of the poets. The next will be that of writers.

Let us draw a picture of a standing man, and then, so as to illustrate the position or standing of each science or profession; we will use his figure as a scale – his feet as the lowest and the head as the highest level. We would put dancers and sportsmen at the heels of the figure, actors and musicians we would place at the ankles, and artists at the shin.

Western authors usually depict classical Greek sculptors as geniuses. This can make some people think that this craft requires a lot of intelligence. But it is a common misconception. During my study at an art school, all of my class except for me was made up of village boys. They had been enrolled in the school by chance; none of them were very talented. However, later I was amazed to see how these ignorant boys learned to model the human bust in a single week. Therefore, it could be said that anybody can be taught modeling, to be a sculptor, in a very short time.

One day Mulla Nasrudin went to a market. He saw a large group of people gathered around a man and laughing like madmen. Nasrudin asked a butcher what this jamboree was all about.

The butcher explained that the man was entertaining the crowd by his ability to break wind noisily at will. People were paying him money to do it. They found it very amusing, and the man made a good income out of it, providing nicely for his family.

Nasrudin, on hearing it, stated philosophically, "If one can earn one's living in this life and world by farting, then this life and this world are no more valuable than farts!"

There is a Hollywood actor who can make faces like no one. He is the king of grimacing. He has made himself hundreds of millions of dollars by using this talent. However, of course, he could never beat a chimpanzee with its ability to grimace and make funny faces.

The poets will hold the position at the knees. The next would be writers, whom we will place at the hips of the figure. Scientists and technologists will hold the position at the waist. Philosophers we will put at the chest. Although philosophy is a very complex and highly intellectual science, their understanding of the world is inferior to that of theologians. Theologians will hold the position at the level of the head of the figure. The position of mystics I would put above the head of the figure, since their knowledge of the world and the universe is much higher than any human being. The ancient hierarchy of sciences and the categories of men is correct and the just one. But modern life and its ruling ideologies made this system of valuation obsolete.

Some historians and sociologists shed tears about how unjust the previous social systems were, how priests in those epochs mistreated poor actors, jugglers, and musicians. But in reality, it was a very fair world with a correct value system. To describe the modern psyche, and the attitudes in Western society, it can be said that the holy and God are no more part of it.

Besides all this, it must be mentioned here that no matter how superior one's mastery is in any given field or profession, it will not allow him to break out of the limitations of his category, to rise to the higher rank or rung. So a painter can be a genius, a distinguished artist, but still, his class, his category makes him hold a low position in the scale.

In Eastern Africa there lives a tribe whose craftsmen produce woodcut sculptures of a superior quality. These artisans are uneducated tribesmen, and they are selling their works to tourists at low prices to make their living. The ingenuity and expressiveness of the carved creations are superior to anything produced anywhere else in the world. Their works are superior to that of the Greeks. Thus the creativity talent in itself is nothing, and we should not consider it as a valuable gift, but as a trifle. The low status of all creative professions is rooted in the fact that these arts are produced for mundane, prosaic purposes. This is futile and vain creativity. At the same time there are many examples of poetry written by mystics, which is no longer the product of people of a low category, since this poetry was created by Masters, spiritually advanced individuals, and the subject matter is of a high degree. In these instances, spiritually advanced individuals use art – poetry, drawing, sculpting – as a vehicle to convey complex religious ideas. They are not standard poets, artists, or sculptors, but Masters whose actual profession and status is the religious one, the top status possible for a man.

Even artistically superb religious art produced by artists who are ordinary human beings would be of low category; it is inferior because their intelligence and understanding of the world and religion stands on a low level.

Similarly, there are religious, canonical forms of art – for example, icons – in which an ordinary artisan produced a religious form of art fully obeying the orders of priests, whom in this case, we should consider as the actual producers and authors of these art objects. Thus the artist's personal contribution in it is his artisanship.

There are religious sculptures and pictures of a schematic kind, of relatively low artistic quality, but nevertheless they could be described as the highest possible examples of art, since its symbolic imagery reflects a complicated religious philosophy often incomprehensible for the ordinary observer.

In the ancient world, unlike today, all the fine arts were religious and spiritual. Art works served as ritualistic artifacts in religious worship. Temples, churches and monasteries were the main examples of ancient and medieval architecture.

In the temples of the Orient, there stood multitudes of statues of the Hindu and Buddhist pantheon of gods. Churches were decorated with iconostases and altar paintings. Their walls were covered with frescoes on biblical subjects.

This state of affairs continued for a very long time. Much later, in Europe, there came changes – an era of Renaissance. In that period, the fine arts gradually started to get out of the control of the Church, and no more wished to follow its canons, its dictates. Painters, by inertia, continued to draw pictures on the traditional biblical themes, but now they began bringing into their works something new – different meanings and different contents. They brought to it their limited, subjective, prosaic understanding of these themes.

It was obvious that the people got tired and bored by the fine art which only praised everything religious and spiritual. Now they expected that it should speak about themselves, reflecting their daily activities and life, showing men just like them – worldly, down-to-earth types.

Gradually, the new ruling class – the bourgeoisie – entered the stage and came to power. They started to push aside the priests and noblemen. Now the bourgeoisie became the side from which orders came. They had their own tastes and preferences, their own values and ideology – materialistic values, bourgeois ideology.

In this way, a painter of that period could paint a picture entitled *The Holy Family*, but depicting these holy persons in the likeness of important contemporary figures, of his probable patrons. It no more showed the Holy Family, the holy men, but rather secular, worldly men.

Dutch and Flemish old masters started to draw scenes of bordello life, whose clientele were the members of bourgeoisie. They painted (with superb artistry, one should admit) public watering places, taverns and other events in daily life.

There also appeared a new genre in the history of painting – the still life. In it, they started to show in close-up the materialistic, mundane values of worldly, secular people – foodstuffs, liquors, smoking paraphernalia. Fine art became a servant of the bourgeoisie, began to serve the new ruling ideology.

A contemporary American artist of Lithuanian descent once collected all his works and moved to Lithuania, which was then a part of the Soviet Union. His decision surprised everybody. He explained his actions by saying he was fed up with America, with its mercantile and covetous attitudes. He donated all his works of art, his paintings, to the state of Lithuania, his newly acquired motherland. According to him, in America, his creative works were met by a cool and cautious attitude.

On the central Soviet TV channel, they showed a documentary about his artistic creativity. I remembered one of his works. Its title was *Cats*. In this picture he showed cats, cats in evening dresses and with bow-ties, who came to see a spectacle: the rock opera *Cats*. Obviously, this kind of art, this approach, and menu would not suit the tastes of the "fat cats" of the bourgeois society; it would not be palatable. The bourgeoisie would be more likely to accept the "sexual revolution." This is the only revolution that would be acceptable to them. Moreover, they would offer it as the most progressive development of the new age.

In addition, I remember an article in a Soviet newspaper that I read in my youth. It told a true story of a French artist, our contemporary. Once, he

Chapter Three: The Hierarchy of the Sciences

walked on a Parisian street, in a low mood, with somber thoughts about the fact that he could not display his work at an art exhibition.

Suddenly, he noticed in front of himself, on a pavement, some dog's excrement. Instantly he got an idea. He wrapped his find in a handkerchief, and ran back to his studio, where he dried up this manure in the oven. Then he put it on a saucer and went to the exhibition. The organizers of the exhibition accepted his artistic work under the title *Dog's Dung on a Saucer,* and put it on display for visitors.

I brought out this particular story here as a morality play. There is something symbolic in it. Now it can be said that the secular art of our dark times with this particular example of avant-garde creativity has reached its apogee, its highest point, when the substance of this art and its form merged and matched each other.

The cities of Western Europe are dotted with museums of modern art, where are exhibited samples of abstract, avant-garde art, and so-called installations. These objects often consist of bathtubs and toilet sinks, as well as various silly mechanisms which are moving, rotating, grating and rumbling.

I see that fine art has made a long journey. In the beginning, it was religious, spiritual and sublime. Later, it became secular, atheistic and worldly. And in the end, in our times, it became meaningless, absurd and nonsensical.

Sigmund Freud, the founder of the pseudo-scientific teaching of psychoanalysis, had many idiotic and crazy ideas, but one of his statements I will mention here as an example for its comic quality. He wrote that he knew how to spot a genius painter in childhood. He said that if a child takes a twig and inspects the contents of his excrement with it, it means that when he grows up, he will become a great painter. Thus despite what art critics and auctioneers are saying, the paintings of the European Old Masters are no more valuable than excrement, since they are the creations of worldly and secular minds. The reader, for more expanded explanations of the levels of art and men, should consult P. D. Ouspensky's book about Gurdjieff's teaching.

In addition, I can say that this hierarchy of humans is similar to the universal hierarchy; that is, the hierarchy of everything in the Ray of Creation. In other words, in the universe there is matter that comes first, second and so on, matter that is high and low. Thus a just social structure is correlated to the cosmic structure of the universe. It is, as above, so below.

God has said, "And whoever is blind in this, he shall (also) be blind in the hereafter; and more erring from the way" (Koran, 17:72).

CHAPTER FOUR:
THE ORIGIN OF RELIGION

The Prophet Muhammad (may the blessings of God be upon him and his family) said, that there always was Islam. Non-Arabs can find this statement peculiar and perplexing. Today they are using this word – Islam – to distinguish the religion of Muslims from the other faiths. But when the Prophet originally used this term he only meant faith, which is the Arabic meaning of the word. Therefore, the meaning of this statement is that there were always faiths and religions in the world. He meant that religion was not his invention, nor was he the first prophet that was sent to the world.

All religious doctrines are unanimous concerning the start of religion. They all connect the appearance of faith with the coming of humans. As soon as Man put his foot on the ground and the human presence started on Earth, there appeared the worship of God. There are different theories by modern scientists about the date of appearance of the human race on Earth. Some are giving figures as twenty thousand years. Others, as two hundred thousand years and the latest theories are saying that it is closer to two million years. But if you ask them how old religion is, they are going to date its emergence to the more recent times. Nevertheless, no matter what the natural scientists are saying, the religious authorities are always going to say that the emergence of the human race in the world is simultaneous with the birth of religion and the worship of God.

Sound thinking will tell us that only when a man starts to be conscious or aware about his being a distinct creature from animals, will he be called a human being. After this realization, the next thing that will come to his mind will be religion, religious ideas. With the awareness of his humanness comes a sense of non-identification (in Arabic – *tajrid*), alienation from the animal world and from the beastly values. Then, with human values, there comes another perspective: the realm of angels (with its values), the next stage or the next evolutionary level. With the realm of angels comes another perspective (with its values), another evolutionary level: the realm of God. Thus the thoughts about angels brought forth the idea of God. Therefore, it can be said that the ideas of angels and God existed, at all times, in the human nature or form. Thus the idea of human perfection, or the possibility of this perfection, always potentially existed within the human form.

Chapter Four: The Origin of Religion

As a believer, I am not interested in starting a dispute with atheistic scientists about the history of the development of religious thought, which is not an essential issue to the people of faith. The essential matter is to understand that a seed of faith always existed. How and where in man can this spiritual seed can be detected? Why, this awareness of being a distinct creature from animals is the very seed which produces religion.

To explain the birth of religion with the arrival to Earth of a rational, thinking creature as Man cannot fully explain the subject since, by itself, thinking will not necessarily bring a person to the religious way. God created the world as something with four distinct directions or sides. All creatures as well were divided among themselves according to class, type and race. There is left, right, front and back. In Islamic philosophy, the four conditions or qualities in the world are defined as – movement, immobility, uniting and separation. These distinctions represent four forces which are the fundamental law of nature, bearing in it everything, every potentiality of growth and evolution.

After the extensive observation of animals, people concluded that they have temperamental categories similar to those of humans. My view on this is that the four bodily humors, their distinctive qualities in animals, are the powers which bore human potentiality, the human possibility, or the human germ. An illustration of this is in the well-known observations of ancient naturalists who discovered and described the peculiarities of the different temperaments and tendencies in humans. They observed that some temperaments, relative to others, are more reflective and thoughtful. They also observed that some temperaments, relative to others, are more emotional or sensual. All this proves that the four divisions in the animal kind bore in itself potentiality for the evolution or development, for its realization in the human form or kind, in the thinking creature.

British naturalist Charles Darwin introduced to modern science his new ideas of the evolution and development of the species. But these ideas were well known to the ancients and were well described in Sufi literature. In the ancient world, this knowledge was a part of their religion, an essential part of their religious teaching. Today, atheistic ideologists are claiming that the modern scientific discoveries of the evolutionary theory are upsetting the religious explanations of the Creation and the emergence of life on Earth. But these are false claims. Similarly, some Orientalists are trying to explain it as the rudimentary endeavors of ancient religious authors. However, in reality, these ideas were not a scientific byproduct of religious thought, but maybe the very heart of all religious teachings.

Muslim mystics described it in their works as a descent of the soul from the higher heavenly fold to the earth, by passing through different forms and stages of Creation – mineral, plant, animal, and finally, the human stage. They then described evolution as starting its ascent to heaven from the human form to the angelic one, and then returning to God.

It would be wrong to ascribe religious feelings to reason and the mind only. Man is usually defined, unlike animals, as a speaking creature. With their thinking faculty men can isolate themselves from their bodily functions and passions; distance themselves, to some degree, from all this. Nevertheless, the intellect itself does not have its own values or preferences. It is an instrument to help Man to elaborate, to reason and to make assessments.

Modern scientists depict the ancients as ignorant people, who, mistakenly, took the heart or the chest as the seat of the mind, rather than the head or the brain. Yet the ancients knew very well that it is the brain which does the thinking. However, there was another reason why they considered the human heart as the center of thinking.

Modern science and psychology is still in the dark about the human psyche. Their idea of the human mind is simplistic and immature. They do not have the whole picture. I would say that thousands of years ago sages, men of wisdom knew everything about the human soul and the mind, and modern psychologists have never managed to give any new insight into human mentality. All the good ideas of the modern psychologists are borrowed from the ancient manuscripts.

Modern experts, however, are not aware that it is the heart which is the command center of the human being, as it is the organ of desire and decision-making. For this very reason, the ancients considered the chest as the seat of the mind and the soul. The intellect just follows the decisions made by the heart. Thus it is the heart which is the master of the human being, not the thinking faculty.

All that I have written so far in this chapter is just an opening, as my intention was to explain the origin and purpose of religion. One of the most common misconceptions about religion is that it is meant for all humanity. It is true and not true at the same time. Mystics will tell that there exist two types of religion. One is the real one, the religion of the mystics, the esoteric, secret religion. The second one is a symbolic, exoteric religion of the masses, of the ordinary people. This second kind is the form of religion that is widely known to the public. All people know what the second kind of religion is. But, today, very few people know about the existence of the first kind, the esoteric kind.

Mystics say that the esoteric religion, a true form of religion, the original form, was never intended for humanity in general, but for the chosen few. There is an old Buddhist text that tells a story of the Buddha's retreat:

After spending two months meditating in seclusion, the Buddha, Prince Siddhartha Gautama, achieved the final enlightenment. When he was approached by God asking him to go and preach the doctrine to the world he declined to do so, saying, "This doctrine is profound, difficult to understand, unattainable by reasoning, and suitable only for the wise. The people of the world, on the other hand, are not suitable to comprehend it. Why should I proclaim it? To whom shall I preach it?"

To that God said, "If on the earth there are just a few suitable individuals to comprehend the teaching, go and teach it to them."

Thus, no matter how incomprehensible it is, still God wants it to be in the world. It can be that there is in the world at a given time, no single person existing that is suitable to understand the teaching. In that case, the doctrine would still be in the world, would be remembered by the people, or kept in books, so when a person is born with the potential to learn, he can learn it indirectly. Thus the realities of religious teaching are like this. Sometimes in history it happens that even though there are true teachers, no true pupils are available anywhere in the world to learn from them. This is the true situation with religion. Do you remember what the Gospels teach? How Jesus Christ said that the gates of Hell are of enormous size, but the door to Paradise is narrow. What this means is that the majority of people will go to Hell, and very few to Paradise. Therefore, this shows that the original plan of God was to create the masses as destined to go to Hell rather than Heaven.

A Chinese researcher was writing that before the Chinese invasion, when Tibet was an independent state, the majority of the population was driven, either by devotion or hunger, to join Buddhist monasteries, so that there was a danger of the disappearance of the whole nation due to a lack of population growth. Surely, God did not create the world as a big monastery for all humanity, but rather they were to live a worldly life, the ordinary human life. Instead, He intended the world to be a big brothel.

Once I heard an atheist lecturer who said that if there is such a thing as God, then why does He not show himself to the world, to reassure the people about his real existence, which could bring the godless people to religion. But this silly man does not realize that God cannot make all people as creatures similar to that of prophets and angels, since this would bring life, the world, to its end. If the whole of humanity, as one, starts to see God, it will be Doomsday.

Once, in the Soviet period, I was at a Muslim funeral gathering in Baku. Besides a Muslim clergyman, a professor of atheism (there was such a profession in Communist Russia) was there as well. The latter, with the intention of humiliating the mullah, started to boast about his rare ability to convince. He stated how he could easily convince his students at university of the futility and uselessness of religion and faith. He said how he, after a single lecture, could skillfully persuade a student to abandon his religious sentiments.

To which the annoyed mullah said, "You are a professor of atheism in an atheist state. Therefore, how can students not to agree with you? To get good marks, students have to pretend that they are unbelievers; if not they will fail the examinations. But this gathering is not a university. We are not your students, and you can never manage to convince anybody that the atheistic position is more correct than the religious one. Thus as a priest, I will tell people that religion is a true thing, a true science. What will you tell them? You will say that you are an atheist, an unbeliever, and your science teaches that there is no God. To which the people will ask you, what is your specialization? What do you know? They will say that you are telling them that there is no God, that God is nothing, something not existing, and that your science is a science of something that is non-existing. Doesn't it sound ridiculous? You are saying that your knowledge is about non-existing things, so what do you know? They will say that they would rather listen to this man, the mullah who said that there is religion and that it is a true science about God. Thus his knowledge is about something that really exists."

This mullah was right when he said that atheism is not a science, but it is an attitude. There is no such science as atheism. After the fall of Communist regime, this professor continued to hold his position at the university, but now he is reading lectures on religion. Now, he is probably going to boast to his friends about how easily he can turn an atheist into a believer.

It was mentioned earlier in the chapter that there are two forms of religion – exoteric, conventional religion, which is familiar to the ordinary people, and the esoteric religion, or mysticism. Mystics will state that there is conventional Christianity and conventional Islam on one side, and esoteric Christianity and esoteric Islam on the other. At first glance this

Chapter Four: The Origin of Religion

idea seems very simple, an easy matter to understand. But in reality, to understand and accept this idea is a major difficulty. For some people, it takes years to understand it; for others, even a whole life is not enough. During the entire history of humanity this matter has remained an unfathomable idea. The majority of people are always going to think that only one form of religion exists, the conventional form. The reason for this is in the herd mentality. The herd instinct is very strong in people. They think like this: how can an entire society hold a false conviction? It is impossible that all the people are foolish and making a mistake. They think the majority opinion can never be wrong.

Christians know their religion, but they are not aware that there is something different as well – esoteric Christianity. The majority of Muslims would not accept anything but conventional Islam. Thus to understand the concept of there being two forms of religion is a major breakthrough in understanding religion. It would be the first major step towards the perception of what religion really is.

For this reason, in the mystical literature, they use the word "true" very often, and consider it a key word in the understanding of many religious ideas. They write "true religion," "true teacher," "true teaching," etc. While conventional religion is interested mostly in rituals and the concern of its theologians is with discursive reasoning, esoteric people are interested in mystical experiences and insight. While ordinary believers and priests are quite satisfied with the study of sacred texts, mystics want to experience for themselves what prophets had seen, to see the visions they experienced. Mystics want to see for themselves the light that Moses saw. There is a religious expression "seeing the light," and they usually understand it as a figure of speech. However, mystics explain it literally and they strive to see the sacred lights within themselves. In the past, mysticism was sometimes described as a "science of sacred lights."

It was not accidental that I referred to Christianity and Islam in order to explain the idea of exotericism and esotericism, because they represent very good examples of this. In Hinduism and Buddhism such a division of religion into two distinct branches or categories is not so clear-cut and obvious. These two religions are of a mixed kind, in which dogmatic and mystical religious texts are very much mixed together, where either form is regarded and accepted as conventional, canonical, by all the mass of believers. They have a different history and tradition to that of the Middle Eastern religions. Buddhist and Hindu canonical religious books are full of mystical passages. Both Hindus and Buddhists were never shy to express mystical ideas. The *Yoga Sutra* of Patanjali is purely a mystical text, and it is a part of conventional Hinduism.

However, despite this, Hinduism and Budhism have two parts as well – the conventional and the secret part. There is a definite line between ordinary Buddhist and Hindu believers, along with their priests, who have only a formal, limited comprehension of religion, and others: the true believers, the individuals having a real knowledge of religion through their mystical experiences and insights.

In addition, it must be said that despite all the apparent differences between the various religions, there is no difference between Buddhist, Hindu, or Muslim mysticism. Mysticism is everywhere the same. More than this, the essential part of religion in the various religions has no seeming differences, except for accidental things with only relative value.

The canonical Buddhist religious doctrine, as its integral part, has the mystical teaching of the Eightfold Path, which is the way to the realization of the Buddha-nature, which to its adherents is the highest stage of the human perfection. The conventional Hindu religious dogma also has a teaching of the mystical way, which is divided into gradual stages of spiritual advancement. Similarly, Islam has Sufi mystical teaching that speaks about the Way (*Tarika*) with its stages of human development, which is the path of holiness.

However, the Church and its Christian religious doctrine do not possess any idea of the mystical way with its gradations; modern Christians have no acquaintance with the stages and particulars of the mystical way. I have no doubt that the original religion of Jesus had the knowledge of the mystical way. Alas, without this sacred mystical science, the Christian religion, as it is taught today, is imperfect, since the most vital, essential part of religion is missing!

Let us take Christianity as an example and compare the belief system of ordinary Christians and the belief of mystics. Both parties would consider the New Testament as a true holy text. But to ordinary believers, to the Church, the contents of their faith is the belief in the true coming of Jesus Christ, while to mystics it would not be an essential matter. Thus if for ordinary Christians believing in the actual coming of Christ is something fundamental for their faith, it would not be so for the esoteric Christians. Mystics after reading the Gospels will see in it a true religious teaching, or rather an indication of it. Nevertheless, to them the story of Jesus is nothing but a story line, not the content of true Christian teaching. This name, the Christian Faith was given to the religion later. The early

Christians called themselves differently, as "Gnostics," which means the people of knowledge.

I am not saying that I do not believe in this story, in the real existence of Jesus Christ. I believe that there was such person, Jesus (peace be upon him) who was a preacher and a prophet. But as a mystic, it is not the essence of my faith. Any mystic after reading the New Testament will recognize its authors as people with esoteric knowledge. But mystics would see that the books did not contain a complete teaching, but rather signs, traces, and evidence of it. Thus the original teaching of Christ was left outside the known Christian texts. The true Christian teaching, the esoteric Christian teaching, is not based on the life story of Jesus, but is something else.

Let me expand here a possible explanation on how the Gospels might have been written. Religious teachers, since time immemorial, were always looking for a suitable means to expand their teachings. But they saw that it was difficult to attract the people's attention to complex philosophical or theological subjects. For this reason they used more down to earth, popular forms of literature and art, as vehicles to conduct religious ideas. They used sayings, anecdotes, poems, and fairytales to convey their knowledge. So let us imagine that the person who wrote the first gospel book, after his failure to sell any copy of his philosophical or theological works, stopped at the Messiah story. Let us imagine that he was walking in a market place, and saw there a huge gathering where an uneducated storyteller had managed to attract a huge crowd of listeners to his tale of Jesus. This man immediately saw the great potential of this story. So when he went home he decided to use this popular narrative as a storyline to expand the esoteric teaching.

I have to mention here that Islam affirms both the Old and New Testaments as holy books. In the Koran, Jesus (Isa) is repeatedly described as a prophet. But as we know, the Gospels are ascribed to four authors, the Four Evangelists, while Muhammad was not the author of the holy book of Muslims, but was an Islamic prophet who recited the revelations made to him by God (Allah). The authors of the Gospels never stated that they witnessed all the events of the story themselves. Therefore, unlike the Koran, which is adopted by Muslims as a heavenly book, where every line and word is the word of God, the Gospels are different. Then why does the Holy Koran accept these books as heavenly? The answer to this is in the fact that they contain numerous words and statements of Christ. Thus it can be said that God spoke through his prophet, through Christ, and these lines make the books holy, heavenly scriptures.

I would describe the Evangelists as true mystics, as people who belonged to the ancient mystical schools. They related the story of Jesus to us, using an abundance of various mystical ideas and concepts. They are speaking about it in a very familiar and well-informed manner, knowledgeably. Their comprehension of Jesus' words and mind are much superior to that of Christian priests and theologians, who always are going to misunderstand and misinterpret it. The former could perceive and recognize the mystical dimension of the Christian teaching, while the latter knew only its form and shape. Modern historians trace the origin of Christianity to the Gnostics, the early Christians of Egypt. Some, but not all, Gnostic texts contain the Jesus Christ figure. Later, the Church Fathers chose the books containing the stories of Jesus, and started to offer them as the only true texts. The Church later conducted a bloody war against these sects and liquidated them while burning their manuscripts. The Church was very efficient and effective in its fight against the original Christian sects, and none of them survived.

Some authors say that the Gnostic sects escaped the persecution of the Church and moved to the remote areas of the Middle East, and finally branched into Islam, its mystical sects. But I cannot say whether this theory is true or false. In addition, I want to mention here that Buddhism and Hinduism are not lesser religions than Christianity, even though the story of Jesus Christ is not a part of their religious doctrines.

In Islam, on the other hand, the mystical stream has always run at all times, alongside the conventional form of the religion. The Muslim priesthood was never efficient enough to fully destroy the mystical movement. Therefore, as I see it, modern Christianity is without its esoteric part, and an exoteric teaching is not a complete religion. The vital part is missing. For this reason, Christianity, throughout its two thousand years of existence, could not produce any spiritual book on par with the New Testament, and never will, since it no longer has the mystical stream. This stream has long since dried up. Therefore, it can be said that it is completely sterile.

Nevertheless I have to admit here that everything that has been stated above, to a certain extent, was done for the sake of debate, as a rhetorical device. Actually, the figure of Jesus Christ is very important in the teaching of esoteric Christianity as a concept of a perfect teacher, as a Master, as an iconic picture-perfect man, as a model for imitation. According to Sufis, he is the Perfect Man (in Arabic – Al-Insan al-Kamil) who represents the highest rung of the human perfection.

Chapter Four: The Origin of Religion

But of course, if God found it necessary, He could send a teacher, a guide to the Christians, to revive the true teaching. However, the problem with the arrival of a teacher to revive the Christian faith is that the tradition has long been lost. Unlike Christianity, Islam has hundreds and thousands of mystical and spiritual books produced up until the latest times, besides its holy book (the Koran). Similarly, Buddhists have hundreds of thousands spiritual texts. The same can be said about Hinduism. Thus today, these three religions – Islam, Hinduism and Buddhism – can be considered live, vital religions. And what makes them so is their mystical streams. As soon as these streams dry up, these religions could be considered dead and barren religions as well.

Thus at first, faith was practiced among a small group of wise men as a secret teaching. Later that group, to preserve the teaching forever, for the next generations, decided to spread it among the general public, among the population, so it would not be lost, and the continuity of the transmission of knowledge would be preserved. This type of faith, the true religion will always remain a preserve of the special kind of people (the chosen people) with the unique qualities to follow the way. Later when religion went public, it fell into the hands of the other type of people, the other category of people, the pharisaical types, the people of dogma and formality.

Clerics can be very clever, brainy, articulate, eloquent people, with a fantastic memory and writing and oratory skills. In their own way, they are very helpful to religion by strengthening the formal, conventional side of faith. These people usually dislike – hate – mystics for being rivals and competitors. They see in mysticism a threat to the priesthood and to conventional religious institutions. This hatred and fear stems from the inability to understand supernatural phenomena, supernatural knowledge, and revelation.

When a mystic speaks about his mystical states, insights, experiences and visions, a theologian feels uneasy with all this, since he himself has never experienced them due to his rationalistic frame of mind. It may sound strange, but in reality theologians, if they were honest, if they would behave true to their principles and natural instincts, should reject the holy books for containing ideas that make no sense and are incomprehensible to the mind and reason. Various miracles, incredible tales, supernatural events of religion, should appear to them, to their frame of mind, as things that cannot be rationalized or explained intellectually. Their reasonable mind and nature tends to reject everything incomprehensible, but their position as priests makes them accept all the fantastic, impossible sounding ideas of the holy texts. Therefore the clergy, by being an intellectual type of people, feel helpless when having to rationalize or to understand miraculous stories told in the books, but they hide all their doubts deeply in their hearts. For this reason, mystics say that humanity will forever remain in doubt about many religious ideas. But it must be mentioned here that the majority of people are the honest believers who accept wholeheartedly everything that priests tell them. The problem with the theologians is that they are a rationalistic kind of people, and so are prone to doubt everything, to analyze and to rationalize everything, since doubting is an essential quality of the mind.

In previous times, in the East, people venerated mystics and considered them as holy men, since they performed miracles and demonstrated supernatural talents. They claimed that they had revelations similar to those of prophets, had premonitions, ecstasies and mystical states that earned them this holy status. Some of them even claimed that their books, mystical books, were produced in heaven and were revealed to them in dreams while asleep.

But clerics cannot compete with the mystics in this area, so when mystics time and again boast about their heavenly visions, travels in time and space, encounters with different angels, priests feel uncomfortable, helpless, and powerless. As holy men came forward and claimed that their faith was strengthened as a consequence of their visions, which revealed that the fantastic sounding ideas in the holy books are all the truth, clerics cannot make the same claim, and continue to rely on their discursive mind and intellectual rationalizations. But the intellect and reason will always remain impotent compared to supernatural phenomena.

This is an anecdote about Mulla Nasrudin illustrating the lasting conflict between priests and mystics:

Nasrudin received a lot of respect and veneration as a holy man. A theologian who was jealous of him decided to challenge him and to beat him in his own field.

"I ascend to the heaven every night," he says.

Mulla Nasrudin pretends as if he believes him: "Did you ever reach the fourth heaven?"

"Yes, many times!" says the theologian very proudly.

Nasrudin continues to pretend as if he trusts his claim, "During your ascent did you feel that something soft was touching your lips?"

The theologian does not understand that Nasrudin wants to trick him into something.

"Yes, yes..."

Nasrudin winks to the congregation, "This was the tail of my donkey when I was flying in the fifth heaven."

Surely, it is undeniable that the clerics with their efforts to preserve religious tradition help the faith. They understand the needs of the ordinary believers. They speak the language of the people. Thus it would be not correct to say that because there is the superior kind of religion – the religion of mystics – that the conventional form of religion is all wrong and unnecessary. Religion is important for the world to preserve the health of humanity, without which people will start to degrade, and finally destroy themselves. Religion and faith help human kind preserve its human qualities.

Similarly, the holy books are indispensable for ordinary people, but not for the mystics who from birth carry their religion in their hearts. While the conventional, traditional religion gives general guidelines to the ordinary believers, the mystical texts provide a particular, individual guidance to mystical types for the advanced study of religion.

The Soviet Union comes to my mind, where the churches, mosques, and temples were empty. Under the rule of the atheist rulers it was difficult to find a single believer. Therefore today, statements like "men require religion, they cannot live without faith" do not sound very convincing. They lived well even without faith, while today, the new leadership has difficulty herding people back to the churches and mosques. They meet hard resistance. People lived for seventy years without faith, and there is no longer any place for religion in their lives. It appears that a religious habit of praying and performing rituals of worship, molded in childhood, culminates into a life-long habit and necessity in grown-ups.

There were some Sufis who made public declarations calling religious dogma unnecessary, a useless superficiality. However, the absolute majority of Sufis deplored them and their conduct, and described them as harmful people with lunatic behavior.

I would liken the exoteric Islam (*Sharia*) to a foundation, and the esoteric Islam (*Tarika*) to a house. One form is dependent on the other. Another comparison can be made in which conventional religion could be likened to a plan of a building, and mysticism to the building itself. Sufis call the ordinary form of religion an abstract, symbolic religion, and their own type of religion as the real one, the substantial one. Therefore, a mystic should not waste his time in worries about the preservation of the mass forms of faith, since even if the whole world abandons religion, the activities of a single mystic would preserve the world from destruction.

Islam states that Allah will not demand from Man that he carry a burden of religious obligations heavier than he can bear. In other words, it means that God requires from the ordinary believers that they follow steadfastly all the religious duties of the conventional religion prescribed to them, of the exoteric religion. For Muslims it is the *Sharia* rulings, and for the Christians the commandments of Christ. These rules are something that is within their strength and capacities. Nothing more than this is required from them, while the duties and requirements of the mystical way, of the esoteric religion, would be too heavy a burden for them to handle or to carry, something that is beyond their natural capacity.

On the contrary, God requires from the man who has a gift for mysticism, with a mind capable of comprehending esoteric science, not to limit his religious duties to the obligations of conventional religion, but to venture, to go along the mystical way. It is his obligation before God, who gave him this talent to carry the additional burden of the mystical way.

No doubt the ordinary people are quite content, happy, and satisfied with their fate and destiny; they enthusiastically follow the general conventions of religion by fulfilling the general ordinances of religion; while the mystical types, if their religious life were limited to the study of the conventional religious sciences, would remain unhappy and unsatisfied. For this kind of individual, the only fulfillment in life is in joining the mystical school, to be the follower of esoteric religion, the most honorable and noble form of religion. And those individuals who fulfill all the obligations of the wayfarer, and get to the end of the road, will be the happiest of them all.

Without religion and faith, humanity could be likened to a crowd of mentally defective creatures, no longer humans, but creatures similar to beasts. It would be a blind humanity. But if among them there would be a single mystic, then, together with him, humanity would no longer be blind. Now because of him, they will be a clever, seeing, and spiritual humanity. The faith occupying his heart would be enough to make the whole of humanity religious. In that case he would be the spiritual ingredient of the world. He would be humanity's thinking mind and seeing eyes. Thus in such a situation there would be no deficiency in the spiritual state of affairs of the world.

Chapter Four: The Origin of Religion

A young man who feels the call of faith may leave his home in search of the truth, of the true teaching, but then later realize that the teaching is something that is inverted inside, in his own heart, in his own self. So to find it he has to enter himself. An experienced seeker will realize eventually that there is no true spirituality, or the Truth, outside of himself.

When I was young and lived in Communist Russia, I could not find philosophical or religious books, since they were forbidden literature. Thus I imagined, fantasized, about the possible contents of these books. I was trying to imagine the things and ideas that sages, the men of wisdom, would write in these books. Later after the fall of the Iron Curtain, when I went to the West and read the books, I found that my fantasies, my ideas, were identical to their ideas and to the actual contents of the written books. Therefore, I understood that the idea of God and religion are in the mystic's heart. Therefore, if we imagine that religious teaching somehow disappeared from the face of the earth, in that case a natural born mystic would be able, single-handedly, to reinvent it anew, since faith is something that comes from within.

But in practice it is hardly possible for a single person to find the way and get to the end of it in a single life, because life is very short, and the mystical way is very long and full of misleading byways. Thus it is very unlikely that a person can get to the end of the road, get to the highest stage, in a single lifetime without a guide. But in the case of him not managing to get to the end of the road, then his disciple, with his instructions, would get to his level while he was still young and strong, and then manage on his own to get even further, to the finish. In this way, an instructor, a teacher, is not something absolutely indispensable, but he can make a disciple's passage on the way much faster.

Some people might say that it is not fair that God was not merciful enough in not making every human suitable for the mystical way, for the true religion. But this statement is not correct, since there would be no merit in the mystical way and religious heroism if it were the domain of everybody. Saints and wise men are valued because they are such a rare species. If everybody was a saint then there would be no special merit in being a saint. It would be something ordinary, something worthless.

For a long period of time I tried to find out the answer to the question of what quality it is that makes a man a truly spiritual person, somebody suitable for the mystical way – whether to be a mystic one should belong to a special typological kind? What is the decisive factor? Authorities on spiritual matters claim that unless someone is born a particular type, he is not suitable for the mystical way.

Similarly, I tried to find an answer to the question, "What is intelligence?" Nobody so far has come out with a sensible answer. Later I concluded that there is no single organ or center of intelligence, nor is there a single quality making a person intelligent. There are not one but numerous characteristics of an individual which collectively are the contributing factors to it. A similar situation is a person's spirituality. There is no particular organ, center, or main characteristic which makes a person a mystical type. But actually there are several personal factors, individual tendencies, which together make the right ingredient.

The Soviet Academy of Sciences once published a book of Tamil tales. Tamils are the original tribe that populated the Indian subcontinent before the arrival of Aryan tribes. Some of these tales must be very old, several thousand years old. One particular tale was a very special one, in which I found an answer to my question or suspicions. Some people consider tales as a primitive form of literature, but is not the Bible a compilation of different tales?

The tale said that once upon a time there lived a young man. One day he caught a beautiful bird. The bird appealed to him with a human voice, and begged to save its life. The young man let it to go free. In thanks, the bird presented him with one of its feathers. The feather had a very special magical quality. If one held it to one's eyes, the world could be seen in its true state.

This young man lived with his mother and father. When he looked at them through the feather, he saw that his father was a dog and his mother a cat. But as he looked at himself he saw that he was a human. He said to himself, "If my father is a dog and my mother a cat, then why I should live with them?" Therefore, he decided to leave his home.

Outside the house he saw his neighbor. When he looked through the feather, he saw that the neighbor was a dog. Then he went around the village and was not able to find a human being, so he left the village. He traveled for a very long time, went to many cities, but was not able to find a single human being.

At last he got to one city when it was late in the evening. He was sitting by the door of a shoemaker's shop. And the shoemaker invited the stranger into his home as an overnight guest. The shoemaker had a wife. The young man looked through the feather at his hosts and saw that both of them were dogs. When a girl entered the room, the shoemaker introduced her to him as his daughter. The young man looked at her and saw that she was a human. He showed her the magical power of the feather. He explained to

Chapter Four: The Origin of Religion

her the situation, and they left the town looking for the land where they could find humans.

This tale perfectly explains the sentiments of a mystic in the world, where he feels himself as a stranger, as a lonely person who can never find a kindred soul. It is the language used in mystical books, where they describe general humanity as no different from animals. However in this politically correct age, calling humanity a gathering of animals is no longer an acceptable thing. But the statement is not an exaggeration or a literary hyperbole, but a very scientific and measured one.

Some thirty years ago a fashionable author, an anthropologist, produced bestsellers under the titles of *The Human Zoo* and *The Naked Ape*, in which he stated that after serious studies he came to the conclusion that there is not much difference between the behavior of humans and apes. There is nothing new in this idea. It is a very old religious concept that humans are afflicted with beastly passions and desires. Even the family values that people often pride themselves in, as being very humane and highly moral, can be found in the animal world. It is an undeniable fact that humans are only different in appearance from animals, and their instincts, passions, and physiological drives are similar to that of wild animals.

Therefore, for a young truth seeker, there is no sense in having an interest or any concern for worldly affairs, as it is nothing but a rat race. Thus the true spiritual ideas have nothing to do with the affairs of this world. Jesus said, "Suppose ye that I came to give peace on earth? I tell you, Nay; but rather division... the father shall be divided against the son and the son against the father; the mother against the daughter..."

Jesus meant by this that a mystic should forever turn his back to the world, while one Sufi author made an extremist statement when he said that no matter what calamities and disasters are confronting the Muslim world, if somebody cares for it, then he is not a true Sufi, a true mystic.

But along with all this, it must be said that this very fight against the temptations and the manifestations of the animal self brings a mystic to his personal salvation.

One more time, I want to bring to the attention of the reader that originally the true religion was the preserve of a small group of mystics. Their teaching was a secret teaching. Later they decided to reveal their secret teaching and knowledge to the world, so that the idea of God and religion would be a part of the world. After that, any individual with mystical potential could find his true place in life and pursue his destiny, to realize that there are values higher than worldly values.

History has demonstrated that as soon as the secret teaching of mystics became a part of the public domain, there appeared imposters, a class of priests that took control of religion and started a fight against the mystics who originally introduced religion to the world. The Church liquidated the Early Christians, the Gnostics; similarly in Persia in the sixteenth century, Sufis helped Shiites come to power and make their Shia doctrine the state religion. Later, as the Shiite clergy strengthened their position, they started repressions against Sufis, the people of the esoteric religion.

If the mystics of Islam, the Sufis, were its holy men, then who are these numerous Christian holy men, saints that are canonized by the Church? As I see it, these persons never belonged to any mystical school, and unlike the Early Christians were not initiated into the mystical path, nor were they versed in mysticism. Therefore, they should merely be categorized as saintly, virtuous, pious men that are in abundance in every religion. They were blameless, nice, God-fearing individuals, but they were not in the possession of the holy, secret knowledge of the mystics. This secret science was a closed book for them. They had no knowledge of the esoteric, concealed teaching of Jesus Christ, of the esoteric, mystical dimension of Christian teaching. However, it could have been that some of these individuals had inner, dormant mystical potential, but, unfortunately, it was never actualized or developed in them, because they had no information about the existence of the mystical doctrine of the Early Christians, which was long since lost and forgotten. Christendom, like every other religion, has its righteous, spotless, saintly men, but they do not belong to the same category as, let us say, Sufis, the mystics of Islam. Though the Church accepted them as the saints, officially canonized them, it should still be counted as an artificial and formal act, not a genuine holiness as is understood and defined by mystics, by the people of esoteric religion.

Once more, I want to underline the fact that mysticism is an essential and vital part of religion, and that without a healthy mystical teaching no religion is perfect or complete. The important role that religion played in the history of humanity must also be mentioned here. Religion was a kind of measure, a yardstick of history. Take the period of ancient religions, the period of the Old Testament. It was a brutal time. I would call it a physical, sensual era with its barbarous, harsh laws. It was the era of sensual people. Then the new religions of the Buddha, Jesus, and Muhammad arrived with their humanistic, emotional message, with more humane religious practices and laws. It was the era of emotional people. Then there came the Reformists with their intellectual Protestant message. It started the era of reason, the era of the rational man. Thus every new form of religion marked the start of the new era. Religion always had a profound effect on society and the direction it took. Where would the world be without religion and faith?

One acquaintance of mine, who had a very rationalistic and skeptical frame of mind, once approached me with a question.

"What is the meaning of life?"

"Life has no meaning whatsoever," I said.

He smiled and said, "This is the same as my conclusion. So far I could not find any meaning to it either!"

That is the sentiments of atheists. I answered him like this only to suit him, because I knew that he would not accept my religious point of view. God and religion make life meaningful. But if there were no religion and spirituality, then life would make no sense and be meaningless.

Different religious doctrines outwardly appear contradictory to each other. However to go along the straight path, people have to advance along the way of their particular faith, since the ways outside of religion lead nowhere. This is especially so if their religion is a heavenly religion.

God says: "Surely those who disbelieve from among the followers of the Book and the polytheists shall be in the fire of hell, abiding therein; they are the worst of men" (Koran, 98:6).

CHAPTER FIVE:
PEOPLE vs. SECRET SERVICES

Recently on a Moscow television channel, on a talk show, they held a public debate about a monument to Felix Dzerzhinsky, the founder of the KGB (the State Security Committee), concerning whether the statue should be returned back and erected in the front of its Moscow headquarters. This tall, bronze statue for many years graced one of the main squares of the Soviet capital. But after the fall of the Communist regime, it was decided to remove this monument which served as a symbol of the notorious organization. At present, Communists again dominate the Russian parliament, and therefore, are proposing to restore the old Soviet symbols, as well as the statue of the secret service chief. Thus the participants of the debate were trying to speak either in favor or against the proposal.

When the Bolsheviks came to power in Russia, they started the Red Terror (as they themselves described it) against the population, against those who did not share their materialistic values. Historians say that their persecutions cost the people more than twenty million lives. The Bolsheviks used genocidal methods to wipe out the ruling classes, social groups, and certain undesirable ethnic groups. Historians say that, on the orders of Joseph Stalin, six million Ukrainian peasants were deliberately exterminated by an artificially created famine. The Baltic republics' Christian ethnicities also lost thousands of lives in mass executions and Siberian labor camps. The nuns in a Russian Orthodox monastery in Moscow were executed by motor gunfire. Numerous Christian and Muslim priests were savagely, publicly mutilated and so on.

But the most oppressed were the Muslims. Each and every Muslim ethnic group was exposed to ethnic cleansing programs, genocidal policies of the regime. Millions of them were sent to their death in the Siberian permafrost fields. The only guilt these ethnicities had, in the eyes of the Marxists, was their being representatives of Islam. Atheist Marxists considered the faith as a philosophy incompatible with their materialistic ideology, and therefore treated it as a dangerous viewpoint to be totally eliminated.

Bukhara, a city in the Central Asia, was considered one of the world's leading religious study centers of Islam. A large part of its population was made up of theologians and religious students. The Communists concluded that to destroy Islam in Russia, it was necessary to wipe out its entire clergy. They set the target, and in several days all the theologians and their students, thirty thousand people, were rounded up by soldiers and taken away. Nobody returned alive. Their fate to this day is unknown. The relatives of these people, when they tried to contact the authorities to find out the whereabouts of their relations, never returned home. Therefore, people stopped asking questions and seeking relatives.

In 1952, the year before his death, Stalin gave an order for the deportation to Siberia of hundreds of thousands of Muslims who were native inhabitants of Georgia. The authorities never even tried to make an excuse, to use a pretext, for their actions, never explained what these people were guilty of.

For all these reasons, the Russian liberals and the veteran dissidents were against the restoration of the monument, giving the reason that the KGB was the major tool of the regime that committed these atrocities, while the communists and patriotic Russians who cherished imperialistic sentiments, stood firmly in favor of strengthening the status of the secret services and of the improvement of its image. On that television show a veteran dissident lady who had spent some time in a KGB prison, mockingly proposed to erect the statue along with a fountain that would send up a stream of red colored water, symbolizing the bloodletting conducted by the service, while a silly man with an esthetic frame of mind supported the monument as a form of art. Then he added that after all Dzerzhinsky was a human and so his character was probably not made up of merely dark features; it could be that he had some light features as well.

Another liberal protested that the monument was proposed for restoration, not for its artistic values, but as a political act to rehabilitate the image of the service, to help restore the self-esteem and pride of its officers. He said that nobody can forbid the secret service men to keep the image of Dzerzhinsky in their offices or in their homes, but putting the statue in the central square is a political notion. The idea behind it was to show the public that the secret service was still there, still strong and in control.

Several years ago, the service had carried out a cosmetic face-lifting operation, changing its name to the Federal Security Service (the FSB). While the new chiefs condemn their previously committed crimes under the rule of Dzerzhinsky, they now are shamelessly willing to rebuild the monument. It must be mentioned that the Soviet security service, during its history, changed the name of the institution many times, while its methods and its ideology remained the same.

Chapter Five: People vs. Secret Services

Thus the opinions were widely divided, and some MPs stood firm for the restoration of the public image and position of the security services in Russian society. Yet another man brought up a clever argument, that in modern times the situation within the state and society is such that the secret service can no longer serve its purpose and objectives to benefit society, to secure peace and order. On the contrary, the security service can be defined as an evil force, as an organization that conducts harmful activities within the state, serving itself only, its own interests, to the effect that no institution within the state can function properly. They control the courts, elections, parliament, government, police, military, economy, ideology, and the Church, while different interest groups use this all-powerful organization, its huge machinery, to manipulate society as it suits them.

He continued his speech, "It is a good idea to ban the secret services altogether. But if this is impossible, then at least their functions should be limited, and they should be put under the control of the Ministry of Home Affairs so that all their actions and operations will be limited to that permitted by the law."

I agree with everything this man said, and will try to argue his thoughts further. For example, no matter how strong any given country is militarily, it can lose any war if its intelligence agencies choose to see their military lose it, if that serves the departmental interests of these agencies.

The rationale behind the intrinsic hatred and hostility of the secret services towards their compatriots is in the fact that they wish to see their institution as the most powerful within society. For this reason, they always want to restrict the strength of the military forces, to weaken the governmental structures of their own country. The bosses of these agencies understand that if they allow the state to get rid of all its enemies, to become very strong, powerful, and secure, then at a certain point, doubts will arise about the necessity of these institutions, so that their funds will be cut, or they will be closed down altogether as something no longer necessary, as something useless.

In my opinion, during the last century the powerful U.S. State security agencies were nothing but public enemy number one, as they tried continuously to help the enemy build its military forces, by supplying them with top-secret information about the latest military technology and know-how. Consider the fact that all major leaks of top-secret military information were made within the department of the CIA, and were a cause of tremendous damage to the American army! To my mind, all these leaks of information on the American side were nothing but deliberate scams with the object of strengthening the Soviet Army, and through this facilitate another spiral of the military build-up.

Thus the military circles, the arms makers, in the pursuit of profits, are always going to use the intelligence services to create the required conditions for increasing military spending. Isn't it in the nature of capitalism for a bunch of arms manufacturers to manipulate politically, using their connections in the intelligence services to help them find ways to boost the arms race, to help them increase their profits? The military commanders, generals, are not ideologists, and so it is up to the intelligence agencies to draw up the image of the enemy, to define who the enemy is, and to provide the justification for the use of military force. Thus, today, most of the wars in the world are designed and planned in advance deep in the vaults of the intelligence agencies of the modern super powers, in the states with strong lobbies of the arms manufactures. They export the wars, revolutions, coups d'état, to different parts of the world to support the Western economy, and above all, the arms industry.

Take the Vietnam War. The United States lost the war; Americans had many casualties and wounded, but American arms manufacturers won by making huge profits. In those times, an American B-52 bomber manufacturer proudly declared that he could replace any lost, shot down bomber with a new one in a short time. Thus as the American nation grieved for every lost bomber (and its pilot) that was shot down by the Vietcong, the bomber's manufacturer celebrated another military order with a bottle of champagne.

The collapse of the Soviet Union is a good example proving the absolute absurdity of the secret services as an institution providing the state's security. The KGB was established by the Bolsheviks to help fight the enemies of the revolution, of the Communist regime. The organization did this by carrying out unseen atrocities, a multitude of crimes committed against its own people – the population of the Soviet Union. As I see it, much later, after the seventy years of the existence of this organization, its chief awakened to a terrible truth. He came to the realization that the KGB had overdone it. They had frightened the Soviet people to the extent that they had lost any interest in fighting against the system. Thus the KGB managed to destroy, to neutralize, all the enemies of the regime within the country, so that this institution of repression and intimidation became no longer necessary.

Thus, in frenzy, the chiefs of the KGB started to organize groups of opposition to the Communist regime by supplying them with the necessary logistics. They started to encourage some individuals to become dissidents, to imitate anti-state activity while reassuring them that they were under the KGB's protection. In this way plenty of dissident groups started their activity, while getting the support and assistance of the KGB.

Later when Gorbachev, on his own whim, decided to destroy and dismantle the Communist system, he used the KGB as his main tool or instrument in this endeavor. It is clear that without the crucial assistance of the KGB he could never have accomplished this tremendous task.

No matter what Western propaganda says, the Soviet Union was a very powerful political and military empire, so that except for Gorbachev with his reform movement and the willing co-operation of the KGB, the regime could have lasted for a long time. Western Kremlinologists claimed that Soviet military technology was in a state of decay. However in reality, it was during the rule of Gorbachev and the consequent governments that Russia's military might came into the state of decay that it is in now.

When Gorbachev started systematically demolishing the Communist empire, the KGB, rather than preventing it, participated in it and joined this anti-state activity. The Soviet secret service's officers were very busy at the time, treacherously helping him to destroy the Red regime. Thus the West should be thankful to the KGB and its chiefs for the fall of the Communism, without whose crucial support Gorbachev would never have succeeded. Isn't this funny and ridiculous?

As I see it, the enmity and antagonism within the Soviet secret service started long before the arrival of Gorbachev. Corruption and bribery were wide-spread among its personnel. Agents tried to compensate their meager salaries by trying to make money on the side.

I can give an example. One of my acquaintances, a black market dealer, had a transaction with a KGB officer who tried to sell him smuggled Swedish pornographic videos that he had bought on his business trip in Western Europe. The agent was forced to conduct this kind of illicit activity to make an additional profit to compensate for his insufficient wages. At the time, he was assigned to do bodyguard duty for the daughter of the U.S. presidential candidate (Gary Hart). She was making a tourist trip around the Soviet Union, and he had to provide the security. He confessed that he was very upset about this assignment as it promised no side profits or incentives.

Thus it was long before Gorbachev came to power that the KGB contingent, in its totality, was psychologically ready to sell the Communist system to the enemy, to whoever was ready to pay for it. All this treachery had already started and continued for years, and the arrival of Gorbachev just accelerated the tendency. The KGB contingent came to the realization that there was much more profit for them in the capitalist system than in the communist one. Therefore, they betrayed the system, and turned on the green light to Gorbachev's reforms that brought down the Marxist regime and its ideology, to be replaced by the capitalist system. And they never regretted the decision, since all the manpower of the KGB hugely benefited from all this in the form of illegal profits that they got during the reforms period. While under the communists they could hardly make ends meet on their poor wages, now many officers of the secret services have gained from the privatization deals of the state-controlled industry.

The state of affairs in Russia today is a dead-end situation, in which the powerful institutions such as the government, the judiciary, the police, the Defense Ministry, as well as the FSB, came together and divided the nation's assets among themselves, among different clans, and are running the country as a Mafia business.

At the end of this TV debate, the clever man addressed the ardent supporters of the secret services, and asked them if it would not be better for them, personally, to live and work in the country without the existence of these agencies – wouldn't they feel better and happier being people who were now masters of their lives? This last argument disarmed them and made them smile at the prospect, imagining the peace and calm that could settle in the country, where the law ruled and not the secret services.

It became clear to every viewer that the participants of the talk show (politicians, army generals, intellectuals and industrialists), who enthusiastically supported the secret services were doing it not out of love, but rather out of fear. The dread and terror they felt toward the secret services made them its unwilling supporters. However, deep in their hearts, they wished the secret service, the FSB, would go to hell.

I agree with everything this man said in the show. I had a long and painful experience living under the atheist Marxist regime. I always cherished seeing the collapse of the regime. Along with it, I expected to see the demolition of the huge monstrous structure of the KGB. Unfortunately, the secret services of the Soviet Union survived under other names, retaining all its personnel, its old methods and tactics. The treachery of the KGB to the previous regime, which they supposedly should have protected, went unnoticed. Nobody asked questions. The KGB never explained its role in this capitalist revolution.

The FSB retained its HQ in the center of Moscow, while in Baku the HQ of the secret service moved to another building, to the mammoth, most

Chapter Five: People vs. Secret Services 111

protected structure in town, to demonstrate to the public its ruling position in society and the state. But I anticipated seeing something like what happened in East Germany, where the mob stormed its secret service headquarters, and put its archives on fire, which brought about the effective collapse of the organization. Unfortunately, now its place has been taken by the united Germany's secret services.

But when the Russian masses attempted to do the same thing, they merely managed to remove the statue of Dzerzhinsky, the "Iron Felix," while the attempt to storm the main office itself was cut short by the intervention of the president, Yeltsin. He arrived at the square in person to persuade the crowd to spare the KGB, since according to him, it was a vital institution for the motherland, vital to its survival. To my mind, it was the Kremlin's Western advisers who urged him to go to the square and save the KGB, and these in their turn were acting on orders (or pleas) from the Western intelligence services, who were concerned for their Russian counterparts and wanted to help them keep their jobs, so that it would allow them to secure their own positions. There can be no doubt that the possible closure of the Eastern European secret services scared the intelligence officers in the West, because this tendency eventually could bring about the necessity of closures in the Western intelligence agencies. However, later events proved that their worries were unnecessary.

It would be wrong to think that the Western opposite numbers of the KGB were any better, less maligning and harmful to the public, to society. The prosperous Western countries are very different places, with different circumstances compared to Russia, whose population is trying to survive under harsh and miserable living conditions.

I remember my first morning in London, when I, in my own amateur way, was trying to study and admire English architecture. When I was walking in the Mayfair area of town, a house caught my attention. As I walked along this building I stopped abruptly, with a strange feeling that something was wrong with it, with its architecture. I stood there for some time, thinking what had made me feel this way. What was wrong with this building?

The ground floor of the building was all blind walls, without any windows or doors, but over it was built a visor-like roof stretching over the sidewalk. There was no sensible explanation for the design – there were no windows to cover from the sun or rain. In addition, this nine-foot wide structure had some barbed wire to protect the windows of the next floor. Then I noticed an English bobby who was looking at me with suspicion. Therefore I continued walking. As I turned around the corner of the building, I could not see any door or entrance leading inside. That puzzled me even more. How were people getting in and out of the house?

It was several years later that I found out from newspapers that the house was the headquarters of MI6, the British intelligence service. Its whereabouts was the best-kept secret in town, and only when they moved to a new location on the southern bank of the Thames was the secrecy removed. The new house, a very imposing white structure, unlike the standard boring British government buildings, is very impressive. It rises up over the river as if it were the flagship of British architecture. Probably the idea behind this choice of location in Central London was carefully planned to demonstrate the importance of the institution, its vital role to British interests abroad.

However, every citizen knew the whereabouts of the KGB's HQ in Moscow. It stood high and wide in one of the city's main squares to inspire awe and horror among the public. The officers of the organization acted openly inside the Soviet Union, so that every citizen was made aware of their activities, for the purpose of intimidating the population. In the West, however, the masses, the working class, know nothing about the activities of the secret service within the state. Everything is done to produce the false impression that in the Western world the secret services are there to protect peace and order. The negative role of these agencies in public life is clear only to intellectuals, to the intelligentsia, who due to their interests and work are affected by it in one way or another.

I know that the intelligence agencies in Germany, Italy, the United Kingdom, and other Western countries, during the Cold War period secretly controlled and supervised various extreme left and right groups within their own states. Thus the secret services often use the method of getting their own agents into a radical political group. Later these moles would persuade the group members to switch to armed resistance and violence, to lead them away from political activity to terrorist methods, and as a result, discredit them in the public eye. An American writer, Upton Sinclair, described this method well in one of his novels, *100%: The Story of a Patriot*.

If a researcher decided to describe and bring out the facts about different crimes committed by the secret services against their own people, it would take up many volumes. Take for example the well-known case of the suspicious death of the Roman Pope. Many researchers in their books wrote that CIA agents poisoned him because of his leftist leanings. While a Turkish assassin shot Pope John Paul II, it was never revealed what was behind this, who directed this terrorist act. The only fact that was made public was that the assassin was a member of the Turkish "Grey Wolves" organization. But was this not an ultra-nationalist group organized in Turkey by its intelligence agencies to terrorize left-wing political activists? Was it not the CIA who advised their Turkish colleagues to set up this organization of hooligans and thugs? The idea behind it was to help the Turkish state, a NATO member state, protect itself against the rise of communism. These "wolves" harassed and terrorized left-wing activists in the colleges and, in many cases, even assassinated personalities in the Turkish political scene. Thus it appears that Western democracy, to protect itself against any revolutions, requires help from hooligans, criminal elements, and even from the Mafia.

I do not know the workings of the secret services from inside. I never worked there, so I do not know all the crimes committed by these agencies. However, the minute information that has reached me has made me understand that they are totally evil organizations.

While staying in Moscow's hotels, I witnessed how the KGB supplied them with an army of prostitutes (including under-age girls), who spied on the foreign businessmen. These prostitutes were heavily involved in illegal hard currency speculations...

Another fact I know is that this organization recruited their servicemen, to some extent, from young men who were raised in orphanages with unknown parents. The idea behind this was to supply the KGB with officers who had no ethnic or religious allegiances, so that they would be loyal exclusively to the organization that made them and that gave them work and a position.

I met many KGB officers who had a queer sexual orientation – homosexuals, sadists, and child abusers. I have an idea that the secret services preferred to recruit such types, as well as alcoholics and drug users, because the spy bosses considered these types the most loyal officers on whom they could rely. These people with their various vices would make the most faithful officers, as long as their employers closed their eyes to their immoral private life. The KGB liked to recruit their employees from individuals on whom it had compromising materials, whom they could then control.

There was a high-ranking British intelligence officer, a traitor, who worked for the Russians. Later, he defected and escaped to the Soviet Union. His case was very well known and much publicized by the press. In 1970, I heard this story about him. A woman acquaintance of mine told me that a woman of bad repute visited this man's apartment in Moscow. A

KGB officer had asked her to pay a visit to an "important man," an English defector, at his place. The prostitute later told about a strange thing that happened to her there. The Englishman was interested in spanking rather than sex. He handed her a whip and asked her to beat him with it. The prostitute found it very bizarre, since this practice was not known in Russia.

I do not know whether his bosses in Britain recruited him to the intelligence agency knowingly, because they knew about his abnormal tastes, but it is a well-known fact with psychologists and psychiatrists that homosexuals and people with abnormal sexual orientations prefer to look for a career in the secret services. They explain it as the desire of an abnormal mind to be in opposition to the public, to the public mores. The work in the secret services probably allows them to be above the people, above society, and even to work against it. To work for the establishment against the people is an exciting thing, but it seems that to be a spy for the enemy, to be a traitor, serves as an additional excitement and provides more kicks.

During the Soviet period, every city, every borough, had its secret service office. One of them was near to our house in Baku. The office was always full of drunken people. These alcoholics were used by the agency for small tasks, if there would be a need to arrest, to beat, to intimidate, or even to murder somebody. Drunkards were always present, always at the ready in this office. Their bosses considered these alcoholics very trustworthy types, on the condition that the vodka supplies were provided. But to my mind, alcoholics are good enough for beating tasks, but not for killings. Psychologically, drug addicts are more ready to murder somebody in exchange for a supply of drugs, rather than the ordinary drunkards.

The KGB had the best professionals in town – the most attractive prostitutes, the best thieves, best computer hackers, best mind readers etc.

Once I heard a story of a convicted forger who was imprisoned for his involvement in a counterfeit money production. The KGB officers visited him in prison. They told him how the agency was impressed by his forgery skills. They offered him a deal that if he agreed to work for the agency and produce for them counterfeit hard currency and false documents he could go free. Surely, he accepted the offer.

I am not an academic researcher into the activities of intelligence agencies, but I have the correct picture about who they are. My knowledge of their workings is based on publicly available material and my life experience, the stories that I have heard from people who were closely connected to these agencies. Besides, all the KGB officers I have met in my life were very talkative people, who liked to boast about their work.

Several former officers of the KGB who defected to the West published books on the activities of the organization. These huge, expensive looking books are meant to impress naïve Western readers, and are nothing but empty shells, full of nonsense and rubbish information. The new bosses of these traitors sponsored these publications, urging them to write this nonsense to not compromise their Russian counterparts with public revelations of the evil nature of the organization and its criminal methods. If they allowed the authors to write a serious work, the truth about the intelligence agencies, it would compromise them and damage the phony propaganda of the spy agencies' heroic image that they have created for public opinion. Thus to write a good book about intelligence agencies it is not essential to be an insider. Somebody who is not a part of the agencies has a better chance to do good research into their activities.

Many years ago, I met a male nurse who told me this story which he heard from a mullah. The local authorities in Baku appointed this Muslim priest to be a guide to a visiting Iranian clergyman. Then the local KGB branch received reports that the Iranian was too active in his religious propaganda work among the local Soviet citizens. This was a matter of concern for the atheistic authorities. An order came for the KGB to respond appropriately.

The KGB officers approached the local mullah and informed him that it was decided to punish the Iranian clergyman, and by this to send a message to Islamic Iran to stop sending its religious envoys to the Caucasus. It was decided that the punishment would take the form of an assassination, which should look like a road accident to avoid a diplomatic row. The local mullah's role was to take the Iranian outside after the mosque service, and to make him stand by the curb on the street, while he himself stood one step behind him. Thus the car of killers hit the Iranian and killed him. The local mullah later told how he was impressed by the professionalism of the KGB driver, who managed to hit the Iranian but leave him alive and unscathed.

On another occasion, an acquaintance of mine told me a story he had heard from an officer of the KGB at a party. The drunken officer confided to him that he had returned to Baku from Iran a few days before, where he was on a secret assignment. He went to the Iranian admiralty, to an office, and told the secretary that he had to see her boss so-and-so, the admiral. The secretary let him into the room. This admiral was working for the

Soviets. After passing the admiral a secret message from the Kremlin, the agent returned.

A few days later, he revealed this top-secret information to his drinking partner, my acquaintance, who in turn related it to me. Thus, for a month or two, I also knew that an admiral in the Iranian military fleet was working for the Russians; that he was a Russian spy. But this funny story had a tragic ending, since a month or two later I heard on the news that the Iranian authorities had uncovered a traitor, an admiral who was suspected to be a Soviet spy, and executed him.

For many decades, the Soviets kept a huge army of spies and paid agents in Iran. During World War II, the Soviet army invaded the northern parts of the country. After several years of occupation they withdrew the troops, but left behind a communist separatist republic in its northern provinces. Stalin had a plan to gradually incorporate this separatist republic into the Soviet Union. Besides all this, the Kremlin had yet another plan, a secret agreement with Kurdish nationalists of Marxist orientation. According to this plan, in the Western parts of the newly incorporated territories, it was intended to create a Kurdish autonomous region, or a republic. Consequently, it aimed to extend the territories of this Kurdish Marxist republic to the lands of Iraq and Turkey, which are partially populated by ethnic Kurds. However, the Marxist regime in this Iranian province collapsed, which caused the hundreds thousands of Communist sympathizers to run and take refuge in different parts of the Soviet Union.

The locals in Baku named these refugees "democrats." Consequently, the KGB recruited agents among these "democrats" for various spy assignments in Iran. In Baku, these political refugees were living in several housing blocks. Whenever anybody was sent to Iran on a secret mission, everybody, including small children, got the news. This leaking of information happened in this way – a husband told his wife and the children overheard it, and later told the other children in the block that their daddy was on a cross-border spying assignment. This kind of thing occurred very often, and it amused everybody in the neighborhood very much.

Today, a large group of Iranian communists have obtained refugee status in Sweden, France, and England. The Kremlin no longer has the money or desire to support these Marxist groups, so now the Western intelligence agencies are supporting them, urging them to continue their subversive activities against Iran. Thus ideological differences are not an essential matter in this relationship.

Chapter Five: People vs. Secret Services

Some thirty years ago there was tension between the newly established Islamic Republic of Iran and the United States. There was the threat of an invasion of the country by the Americans. Thus the Soviets, on their own side of the border with Iran, started a massive military buildup. Thousands of Russian tanks were stationed at the border. The Russians considered the possibility of dividing Iran between themselves and the Americans. Russians once more were ready to establish a Marxist republic in the northern provinces of Iran. The KGB put all its agents in Iran on alert. Even its agents in Western Europe, Iranian refugees, were invited to the Soviet Union to be ready for the invasion and the consequent Marxist revolt.

I was living in Baku in those times. One day in the public library, I saw a young, fragile man who was a French citizen. He told me that he was the son of a professional Iranian Marxist revolutionary. His father, an ethnic Jew, was working for many years in close cooperation with the KGB. But now his son had been invited by the Russians to work at the local radio station for the Persian language program. He said it was expected that, very soon, the Islamic regime would fall, and then, after this happened, he was going to move there, as the Soviets had promised him a prominent position in the future Socialist republic of Iran. But when I called him Moscow's spy it scared him, and he ran away from me with the speed of a short distance sprinter. Fortunately neither side, neither the Soviets nor the Americans, dared to start the invasion. Nothing happened.

In the modern world there is a continuous struggle going on; there are open and hidden wars going on. These wars are staged by the powerful Western "democracies," by the "civilized" world, against the underdeveloped third-world countries. The Western imperialist states are always having "special interests" in different parts of the world, and they are permanently designing and staging open and hidden wars. Besides ultramodern armaments, they have huge intelligence agencies ready to start a hidden warfare in the form of plotting coups, sabotages, terrorist acts, or political assassinations.

There is one favored method employed by the intelligence agencies of the Western states, which is to encourage a "friendly" terrorist group to invade an embassy, so that later it could lead to political destabilization, damage diplomatic relations, or even be used as an excuse to start direct military action.

In my lifetime, I have observed a dozen operations of this type, designed by Western intelligence agencies in different parts of the world. During the early stages of the Soviet occupation of Afghanistan, there was an assault by a small group of Afghan militants on the U.S. Embassy in Kabul. An Afghan group, in protest against the Soviet invasion, conducted this seizure. But it was the U.S intelligence agency that arranged this attack on its own embassy, with an object to destabilize the pro-Soviet regime. The Americans were convinced that the Russians, who at the time controlled Afghanistan, would not dare attack the U.S. Embassy to release the diplomatic staff, out of fear for the life of the U.S. ambassador, so as not to enrage Washington. Thus they thought that the hostage intrigue would put the Red regime in Afghanistan under an enormous strain, and so facilitate its collapse.

Russian soldiers surrounded the embassy. The U.S. government asked the Kremlin to show restraint and to try to fulfill the demands of the hostage takers, which were nothing less but the return of the Soviet army back to Russia. Yet the KGB major who was in charge of the troops thought differently. He understood that all this was the U.S. intelligence agency's intrigue, and that in this confrontation, in this fracas between two spy agencies, he could not be allowed to lose the match. Therefore, he ordered the troops to charge with full force, and to not spare the life of anybody, including that of the U.S. ambassador, to send a message to the Americans not to play games with the Russians.

The American government usually behaves so that it can start a war against any state that mistreats U.S. citizens. However in this case, the cold-blooded killing of the U.S. ambassador in Kabul went without any consequence; the White House kept silent and was reluctant to go into open confrontation with Moscow. Alternatively, it was maybe out of a sense of guilt.

There was another Western intelligence agency operation, but this time in Tehran during the reign of Shah Mohammad Reza Pahlavi. In this instance, members of the Mojahedin-e Khalk movement invaded the U.S. Embassy and took the American ambassador and other embassy personnel as hostages. Western intelligence agencies had, now and then, supported this leftist militant group to do acts of sabotage and terrorist activities in Iran. This carefully planned intrigue intended to help to topple the Shah's regime, which at the time had lost favor with the West. America's *Time* magazine and other periodicals were filled with the smiling face of the U.S. ambassador, who it seemed, was very relaxed and cheerful despite the fact that he was a hostage.

The United States State Department had, naturally, informed the ambassador in advance about the planned hostage taking, about its objectives. He in turn informed the embassy staff that everything was under control and urged them to keep calm. Thus the diplomats were giving interviews to Western TV reporters, and behaved in a buoyant mood. However, the scheme ended with no result and the Shah's regime continued to stay in power for some time.

Two similar kinds of embassy hostage-taking intrigues occurred in London. I saw documentaries made by British journalists about the events, which were two excellent examples of investigative journalism. In the first case, it was an attack by Libyan dissidents on their embassy in Central London. It seems that Western political strategists were looking for an excuse for a military intervention in Libya. Thus their intelligence agencies planned a scheme in which an Arab dissident group supported by them would conduct an assault on the embassy, which would lead to grave incidents and shootings, to help damage diplomatic relationships with Libya.

During this siege, somebody shot and killed an English policewoman. The British authorities blamed this on the embassy staff, claiming that a Libyan diplomat took the shot. All these events brought about the closure of the Libyan diplomatic mission, and the expulsion of the entire diplomatic personnel of this Arab state.

But later, the grieving father decided to put the official version of the events to the test, and find the culprit who shot his daughter, the policewoman. This documentary film proved the official story was a falsification. The film's authors found out that the angle and trajectory of the shot demonstrated that the bullet came from another direction rather than from the embassy building. A specialist criminologist said that the murderer could have managed to produce this shot from the only tall building in the square standing next to the embassy. Later, the film's investigators found out that the upper floor of the building, which was the only suitable place for the murderer, was an apartment rented by a non-existent American company. The proprietor of the house said that just a few days prior to the shooting incident, several military-looking Americans rented the apartment, while a gentleman who was a neighbor saw the Americans running down the stairs right after the shooting. They never came back, nor could be found anywhere. Thus the British filmmakers concluded that these people were working for the CIA, and that they were the actual murderers. The father of the victim accepted the version of the film's investigators as the only possibility.

In another incident, an Iranian dissident group attacked the Iranian embassy in London and took Iranian diplomats as hostages. This was an intrigue carefully planned by the British intelligence agency. The idea behind it was to harm relationships between Britain and Iran, so that as an outcome this Islamic state would be entirely politically isolated.

I saw a documentary about this hostage drama, in which the English filmmakers also believed it to be an embassy attack that was designed by the British secret service. The film effectively managed to convince every viewer of the deceit and lies of the official story.

Despite the pleas of the Iranian government for the British authorities to show restraint, to provide the safety of the diplomats, the building was attacked by the British special forces – the SAS – in the most savage fashion, so that some people were wounded, others were shot and killed, including diplomats. The entire interior of the embassy compound was burned down and destroyed by grenades thrown by the SAS men.

The big question in the official version was how the leader of the terrorist group managed to escape through three security cordons. The makers of the documentary concluded that the escaped head of the group was a British intelligence agency mole in this dissident organization, and he was the sole man among the militants who knew what was behind the assault. He was never found. Because of this killing of Iranian diplomats, political relations between the two states were in bad shape for many years. So the goal was achieved.

During my stay in London, I witnessed a more recent siege, this time on the Greek Embassy. A group of Kurdish militants invaded the embassy and took just one diplomat hostage, while they put forward political demands before the Turkish government. The choice of the embassy was significant. The relationship between Turkey and Greece was very cold, antagonistic. Then, if that was the case, what sense would it make for Kurdish militants to attack the Greek rather than the Turkish embassy? The Turkish government for years accused Greeks of harboring and training Kurdish separatists on their soil, who were staging a guerilla war against the Turkish army. Thus the idea behind invading a friendly, cooperating embassy was to stage a spectacle, a political show.

The Greek Embassy is situated in London's most fashionable area, on Kensington High Street. This neighborhood is usually frequented by thousands of tourists. The London police cordoned the entire area, but the strategy and agenda of the police was unusual and bizarre. They, rather than blocking the approaches to the embassy to restrict the activities of Kurds, allowed them to willingly participate in this huge political show.

The British scriptwriters of this political extravaganza decided that this small group of Kurds who invaded the embassy was not an impressive enough bunch of actors. That is why the police opened the police lines to let in more Kurds, to add more spice and color to the scene. They allowed many busloads of Kurdish political activists to pass the police lines and to join the militants. A huge number of Kurdish people arrived and stationed themselves around the embassy.

This siege, or rather circus, lasted for three days. All the British TV channels were showing live transmissions of the events from the area. Kurdish men, women, and children in folk dresses sang and danced around many campfires in the alleys, while British television provided full coverage of the events.

The inhabitants of this posh part of London were complaining that they had problems passing through the police lines, to get in and out of their homes, while Kurdish people were free to move around. Thus the Kensington area of London, with the cooperation of the authorities, was turned, for several days, into a little Kurdistan.

At the end of this symbolic embassy siege, the only hostage at the embassy, the Greek diplomat, came out of the compound arm in arm with his Kurdish captors, speaking to the cameras cheerfully about how happy he was about the incident and how he had made friends with the militants.

This show was staged to help the British put political pressure on the Turkish state, which, ironically, is a strategic partner of the West, a NATO member state. All Western states as well as Russia, for many years have supported the Kurdish Worker's Party (the PKK) and other Kurdish separatist groupings, to stage a guerrilla war against the Turks. They supported them, secretly financed them, to keep this Muslim state under constant pressure. This meaningless war took tens of thousands of lives. The Soviets were interested in establishing a new Marxist state in the Middle East, while the West supports and provides funding to the Kurdish insurgents to stage a perpetual war against Turkey, to damage its economy and the livelihood of its population.

The Kurdish revolt provides the West with political leverage to put pressure on Turkey, and keep the situation in the Middle East volatile. It seems at this stage that the West is not interested in the creation of a Kurdish state, because it would break the partnership of Turkey in NATO, and put an end to its Western orientation. But for now, the Western policy is to keep the Kurdish separatist movement warm until the right time comes. It seems to me that according to them the right time will come when the Muslim people of Turkey decide to return to their Islamic roots, and choose to establish a theocratic Islamic state. As soon as Turkey embraces

Islam, it would serve as a signal to the West to play the Kurdish card, to press forward with the formation of a Kurdish state. This new state, as they see it, would be a new strategic ally of the West. Then the West will give its blessings for the Kurds to start further separatist wars in neighboring countries.

Today, Western Europe is full of Kurdish refugees. They have their own political television channels. I visited the Kurdish TV station office in the most exclusive area of London, not very far from Piccadilly Circus. The Turkish government describes the PKK as bloodthirsty terrorists, but the office I saw was full of pretty secretaries and fashionably-dressed personnel. Who was paying for all this? Why, the British of course – its intelligence agency, thanks to the taxpayers money.

Northern London has a huge Turkish and Kurdish population. I saw there streets many miles long with walls covered with PKK posters and graffiti. There are countless numbers of offices of Kurdish militants stationed there. The British are rich enough and generous enough to provide Kurds with these offices. The Marxist ideology of the militants is of no importance to the British, who will encourage Kurdish separatists to stage wars against the Muslim countries of the Middle East. I saw that these posters covered the front windows of all banks in the area. Who is paying for these thousands of color posters? Why don't the police intervene and stop these groups from covering the walls and windows illegally with anti-Turkish posters? Usually the British police are very efficient in keeping law and order in town, while in this case they showed a very liberal attitude. It is clear that the police are impotent to intervene, since the more powerful organization – the secret service – gave permission for the activities of Kurds in Britain.

I, personally, had an unpleasant experience with a Kurdish society. While I was staying in the Hampstead area, I decided to go to the eastern part of London to see a society, a charity which claimed to be a religious one. The charity bore the name of an Ottoman mystic. London's tube fare is too high, so I decided to go there on foot. It took me eleven hours to walk there and to get back home. During my six years of stay in this city I never drank or ate out to save money. Thus by the time I got home I was very hungry and exhausted. Later, I understood what a waste of time and energy it was.

I got to the office and started asking questions about their religious activities. But they told me that it was a political organization. Actually it was the PKK Marxist group. Because of my being a Turkic-speaker, they first wanted to find out whether I loved or hated Turks. They said that anybody who is an enemy of the Turks is their friend, and anybody who loves the Turks is their enemy. Some ten or so Kurds surrounded me and started to interrogate me for an hour. At one stage, they put the question to me whether there was any chance for Communism to be restored in Russia. My answer to it was no. This answer upset them very much, because the fall of the Communist regime in Russia damaged their position, so it forced them to seek for a new, alternative ideological base. Thus now they are using pseudo-religious and nationalistic slogans to make their cause look more attractive to people.

It was a very unpleasant conversation and they stopped just short of making death threats to me. But finally I managed to leave the place. All the way back home I was checking repeatedly whether any one of them followed me. A lesson to be learned from this incident is that it is a waste of time to try to find truth and faith anywhere but inside one's own self.

CHAPTER SIX:
THE TWENTIETH CENTURY'S GREATEST FABRICATION

This chapter, initially, was an article that I wrote in London several years ago. At that time I decided to write a short essay about the state of affairs of the Muslim population of the USSR, a literary work that Muslim men could use by attaching it to their application when applying for the refugee status. I lost the article, but now I will try to reconstruct it from memory, at least partially, and write it anew.

I've heard many complaints from people emigrating from Russia that Jewish people receive asylum status very easily, and without any problems. In fact, in the West, the authorities do not doubt a grievance made by a Jew about his (or her) mistreatment in Russia. But if a Muslim makes a similar complaint about his mistreatment in the Soviet Union, the Western immigration authorities do not tend to accept this, stating that they have no data in their possession to confirm the persecution of Muslims in Russia. Public libraries in Western Europe are full of books about the persecution of Jews in Russia, but you can never find a single book or piece of information about the persecution of Muslims. Armenians can be added to this preferred set of peoples. The Western position is to accept Jews and Armenians as the only ethnic groups in the Soviet Union who were mistreated by the Communist regime.

In reality, Jews and Armenians were the only citizens that were *not* mistreated as ethnic groups by the Communist authorities. During the Communist rule, many millions of people were executed or sent to labor camps. If there were Jews or Armenians among them, they were prosecuted for various reasons, but not for the reason of their ethnic identity. The Bolshevik revolution did a lot of harm to all the ethnic groups populating Russia, to all *but* the Jews and Armenians. In fact, these ethnic groups were the only beneficiaries of the Bolshevik revolution. This revolution brought a terrible plight to millions of Muslims, through the mass killings and genocidal policies of the Kremlin. But the Western politicians and historians do not want to know anything about it, Jews and Armenians being considered by Western authorities as the most favored groups for asylum, as the people who were victims of the Communist system.

Chapter Six: The Twentieth Century's Greatest Fabrication

Both Jews and Armenians are foreign arrivals in Russia. When the Russians invaded the Caucasus, the Tsar invited Armenians from the entire Middle East to come and live under his rule in the area, while Russian Jews are mostly of Polish origin. Both these groups at the dawn of the revolution were landless strangers, nationalities with no land to their names who were on the lowest rung of the social ladder. Both Christians and Muslims looked upon the Jews with suspicion. Both of these peoples were very unhappy about the situation, about their position in the Russian Empire, especially since both groups, by mentality, are extremely ambitious. Jews could not expect to get to the high positions in Tsarist state institutions, even less so Armenians.

Thus from the point of view of Jews and Armenians, the Russian Empire, the Russian monarchic state, was an obstacle for them in improving their social standing within society. For this reason, Jews and Armenians were heavily involved in underground anti-state activities. They initiated the formation of various revolutionary secret societies, and were the most represented groups in these insurgent organizations. The Tsar's secret police reported to the authorities about this underground activity, and about the fact that the majority of these secret societies, its contingent, was made of Jews and Armenians.

At that time, the Marxist ideology with its internationalist, anti-monarchic, materialistic, and anti-religious ideas came as very handy to the Jews. Was not Karl Marx himself a Jew? He was born to a Jewish family that converted to Christianity. As a young man, he first tried writing religious literary works. But later, being a very ambitious person, he decided to abandon religion altogether, and to join politics. Conversion to Christianity did not make him a Christian, and he always continued to see the world with the eyes of a Jew. Living on the wrong side of the tracks made him very angry at the order of things, where the Jewish folk could not get to the higher, controlling positions in society. He desired to see the old world order replaced by a new world order, in which the possibilities of Jews would be unlimited by any boundaries. These motivations and sentiments resulted in the Marxist ideology.

Thus the Jews looked at the establishment, which was made up of rich, landowning aristocrats, as their enemies, as the obstacle to Jewish success and prosperity. On one side, there stood the ruling Christian royalty, the illustrious noble families, and on the other side were the Jewish underclass, this small minority of strangers and foreigners which belonged to an antagonistic faith. Thus the only way for the Jews to improve their status within society was to make the monarchic rule clear the way for them.

A monarch was always seen as the supreme representative of a nation. More than this, a Tsar was the supreme representative of the Russian Orthodox Christians. Thus the Jews knew that a mere collapse of the monarchy would not solve all their problems, since nationality and Russian nationalism would remain. However, Marxist, Bolshevik ideas were very suitable. The idea of internationalism enforced by the law could suppress any germ of nationalism; it could gradually wipe out all ethnic features in people. In the new world order, every ethnicity would be equal (at least on paper).

According to the Jews, religion and faith should also go. The Jewish ambition saw in religion another obstacle, an age-long barrier for it fulfilling itself in every society, in every state. The Jews understood that as long as there was faith and religion, they were going to remain a religious minority. This realization turned them into the archenemies of religion they are, so that world Jewry continuously uses all their wit and cunning minds towards achieving this much anticipated goal, the goal of the total and final elimination of everything sacred and holy in human society. The evidence for this wicked activity we can see by observing the political and social processes of the last centuries of world history.

Some naïve historians could disagree with this, and bring forward the various instances of representatives of other ethnicities participating in different revolutionary societies, such as Russians and others, even several Muslims. But as I see it these were merely disoriented and misled people, while the brain and soul of these revolutionary, iconoclastic, insurgent activities was always the Jewish people.

Russians were very proud of their Great Russian Empire. The Tsar was the head of all Russians and the head of the Orthodox Christian world. For a Russian to turn his back on his Orthodox creed was the same as to lose his national identity. How could a Russian accept the idea of destroying his Orthodox monarchic state? It would make no sense at all. At the same time, I have heard about a few cases when Muslim individuals joined the Bolsheviks. These several individuals were all the children of rich and noble families. It is obvious that these people were just rich idiots, psychologically unstable, easily influenced men. Otherwise, it is not possible to explain why these rich Muslim aristocrats would turn their backs on their faith and class. Therefore in the cases when Russians and Muslims joined the Bolshevik movement, it should be dismissed as something irregular and nonsensical. With the Jews and Armenians, however, it was not accidental or whimsical, but something very logical, a well thought out position. The Bolshevik revolution brought these deprived

Chapter Six: The Twentieth Century's Greatest Fabrication 127

minorities to key positions in Soviet society; it brought them to the Kremlin. After the revolution, these ethnic groups, for their tremendous contribution to the Soviet regime, were granted favors: Jews with an autonomous district in the Russian Far East, the Armenians with their own republic.

With the collapse of Russian monarchic rule, Armenian revolutionaries attempted to build their national home, to create their statehood in the Caucasus. At that time, well-organized, heavily armed Armenian revolutionary brigades started a campaign of systematic extermination of the local Muslim population.

In 1918 and 1920, the city of Baku, where a large number of Armenians lived, suffered two incidents of mass slaughter of Muslims carried out by this Christian ethnic group. In a few days of carnage conducted by Armenians, fifteen thousand Muslims civilians were massacred in one case; thirty thousand in another. All these mass killings were accompanied by plunder and pillaging. At that time in Transcaucasia, there was not left one town or village that had not suffered at the hands of Armenian revolutionary gangs. These atrocities and crimes committed by Armenians held the local Muslims in fear and horror.

Today in the Armenian Republic, the leader and commander of these Armenian nationalist gangs is officially honored as the national hero of the Armenian nation. As is well known, the Armenian nationalist gangs used a flag with the skull and crossbones as their ensign. Historians and witnesses of these events report the fact that in towns and villages where these revolutionary cutthroats operated, they left behind an innumerable number of Muslim women with their breasts cut out. According to the cold-blooded calculations and estimations of the Armenian nationalists, these women no longer represented any danger to them, since they were in no position to breast feed and bring up children, to raise a new generation of Muslims.

In 1920, as the Red Army invaded Transcaucasia, Armenian nationalist brigades joined forces with them and together attacked the city of Shamakha. They destroyed and burned down the city, slaughtering its entire population under the pretext that they refused to recognize the Bolshevik rule.

In that period, freight trains were arriving in Paris filled to capacity with valuable Persian carpets that were robbed from Muslims by Armenians. Later, they were sold at Paris' antiquarian shops.

According to historians, during the couple of years after the fall of Tsarist rule, gangs of Armenian nationalists and Bolsheviks killed many hundreds of thousands of Muslims in Transcaucasia, mainly civilians. These Armenian nationalists, by accomplishing their ethnic cleansing programs, managed to establish for themselves the Armenian Socialist Republic on the territories, which under the rule of the Tsars were populated mainly by Muslims, by Turkic-speakers. For the benefit of the reader, I would state here that when the Caucasus was invaded and conquered by the armies of the Russian Tsar, the territories that make up the Armenian Republic today were almost entirely populated by Muslims.

During the early years of Soviet rule, German was the most taught foreign language in schools. Ashkenazi Jews took the German language teachers' jobs. Later, when inspectors checked schools, they found that many Jewish teachers, instead of teaching German, were teaching Yiddish, a pidgin German spoken by the European Jews. The education authorities expelled these teachers from the schools. Many Jews protested against his, claiming that it was an act of anti-Semitism, while surely they lost their jobs merely for the reason of not being qualified to teach literary German.

Both Jews and Armenians were widely employed in the Soviet secret services. Since these two groups were minorities, they were considered very suitable by these agencies to spy on the representatives of the other ethnic groups. Both these ethnic groups were the mind and brain behind various intrigues against the Muslim population in Communist Russia, such as genocidal policies, ethnic cleansing programs, deportations and so on. The reason for this was the ignorance of ethnic Russians, their lack of knowledge about the history, culture, and religion of Muslims. Since Asian Jews and Armenians for centuries lived among Muslims, they knew them very well. This knowledge made them specialists, the Kremlin's strategists on matters concerning the Muslims. Thus the Western historians' and Western mass media's laments about the harassments of Jews and Armenians in the Soviet Union are nothing but hypocrisy.

The Jews and Armenians of the Soviet Union were the most prosperous ethnic groups in the entire country. They made up the majority of the professional people. Almost any Soviet Jew had a higher education diploma. In this socialist country all underground millionaires were Jews.

The most prosperous republic in the USSR was the tiny Armenian republic which had no natural resources. All its raw resources were imported from the Muslim Soviet republics. In one of the rare social researches conducted in the Soviet Union, they found that the population of the Armenian Soviet republic was the most prosperous in the country,

Chapter Six: The Twentieth Century's Greatest Fabrication 129

followed by other Christian republics. The research was based on the statistics of the number of private automobiles per capita in each of the fifteen republics of the Soviet Union, as an indicator of prosperity. However, the Muslim populated republics were at the bottom of the list, despite the fact that they supplied the Communist regime and country with most of its oil, gas, gold, and other natural resources. The Kremlin's strategists, who were as a rule the Jews and Armenians, artificially planned all this disparity. Therefore, despite its phony internationalist slogans, the Kremlin, during the Communist rule, conducted racist, anti-Muslim policies, and treated them as second-class citizens.

When World War II broke out, in its early period Muslims complained about the unusually high loss of life among Muslim soldiers in the Soviet army. Muslim boys were writing to their parents about the situation on the front. They were writing that their officers deliberately created a high casualty rate among Muslims. There were claims that the army commanders equipped Muslim soldiers with wooden imitations of rifles and made them attack Germans ahead of non-Muslim soldiers. The Muslim soldiers with these "rifles" were forced to charge on the German troops. But as they were confronted by heavy German gunfire, they ran back, and while doing this they were shot by their own Soviet troops. So they were used as cannon fodder, or as a buffer in the front of non-Muslim soldiers.

Muslim parents and relatives complained to the authorities that a mere visual observation proved that something was wrong at the front line. They noticed that in the mixed villages, the casualties among Muslim recruits were many times higher than those of Christian villagers. Later, after an investigation, the Kremlin blamed these practices on racist officers and distanced itself from all this as if it was not its own policy. Surely, during the war against the Germans, the Kremlin was involved in yet another war, a war against its own Muslim population.

In an outstanding and unprecedented case, Stalin, under pressure from the Muslim population, allowed the Muslims of Transcaucasia to organize its own army unit. It was made up of two to three hundred thousand soldiers. The Muslim unit was stationed in the Crimea. It was put under a commander who was a confidant and friend of Stalin. Despite the fact that the Soviet army had no chance to keep the peninsula in the advance of the German army, the commander demanded that the unit stand to the last soldier in the defense of it. He himself, with an excuse, left for Moscow. The Germans destroyed this entire unit.

The Kremlin never regretted the loss of these troops, because this Muslim unit was an "eyesore", and its liquidation was its ultimate objective. The Soviet authorities never again gave permission for the formation of similar units. By the way, it should be mentioned here that the commander in charge of the Muslim unit was a Jew. Despite the fact that the entire division under his command was lost, he was honored for good service to the state and the Communist cause.

At the end of this war, Joseph Stalin accused the Crimean Tatars and many different Muslim ethnic groups of the Caucasus of sympathizing with the German occupants. He used this false accusation as an excuse to send hundreds of thousands of Muslims from these regions to the Siberian permafrost fields to die and perish.

While Muslims, as an indigenous population of the Soviet Union, suffered attacks on their lives, their cultures and religion, were subjected to many ethnic cleansing campaigns, the Jews and Armenians enjoyed a special status, a privileged position under the Red regime.

After the victory of the Bolshevik revolution, the Soviet authorities declared all the capital cities of Muslim republics to be internationalist cities, and they were populated by non-Muslim settlers, due to special incentives created for their migration to these areas. The authorities made it so that all jobs were available only to these settlers, by depriving Muslims from finding jobs or settling in these cities. Thus while Muslims lived in poverty and worked as serfs in the countryside, non-Muslims lived under artificially created higher standards of life.

Much later, at a certain point, the Western high priests of the Zionist movement decided to dump the Communist regime in Russia. They came to the conclusion that the Jews had benefited as much as possible from Marxism, and they no longer needed this ideology. Another reason why Zionists of the West and Israel decided to dump the Communist system in Russia was its anti-Israeli stance. The Soviets supported the Palestinians and Arabs in their resistance to Israel. The Kremlin was doing it not out of love for Arabs or Muslims, but because of political, military, and economical reasons. It was the Cold War period. There was a confrontation between the capitalist West and the Communist Bloc countries. Since Western European states and the United States supported, politically and militarily, the State of Israel, the Soviet Union could not help but support the Arabs, to supply them with Soviet-made weapons. The Israelis were unhappy with this situation. They wanted to remove Russia from the political stage as a superpower, to shift the balance of power in the Middle East in favor of the Israelis.

Chapter Six: The Twentieth Century's Greatest Fabrication   131

The Western Zionist strategists were reflecting on how it would be possible to dismantle the mighty Soviet Communist regime. And the answer came: "But why, we have our own people in Russia, in the Kremlin, in the Soviet Defense Ministry, in the KGB, and in the Ministry of Interior Affairs!" Thus the decision was to use "their Jewish brothers and sisters," their Jewish connections, to help bring down the Soviet Communist empire. Surely the Jews are the most organized and united people in the world. They like to help and assist each other. Although I do not know the details, somehow the Western Zionist leaders managed to persuade the Russian Jews to commit treachery toward their Russian homeland, and defect to the Western capitalists. This betrayal of the Soviet Jews, this process, could be detected and observed in the mass immigration wave. The Soviet laws did not recognize the right of its citizens to emigrate abroad, Jews included. Soviet propaganda and ideology forced its population to believe that they lived in the best part of the world, in the best political system, under the best economic circumstances. The Communist Party and its leaders convinced the Soviet people that the USSR was the best place under the sun. Therefore, to let the Jews or anybody else go was to destroy this myth, the fable about the Communist paradise. To let Soviet citizens emigrate, to leave this Socialist paradise, would mean admitting it was not the case.

Thus the formula to destroy the Soviet Union was found. But how could the West persuade the Soviet leadership to take this suicidal step? Later, they found the bargaining chip. The massive American military build-up was putting the Soviet economy under a certain strain. To build up its military force, to keep its army on par with NATO, the Kremlin was in desperate need of Western electronics. The United States restricted the sale of sophisticated electronic equipment and other strategic goods to the Soviets, to prevent them using it in their military programs. But at this time, the United States in top secret negotiations, managed to persuade the Kremlin to make this historically grave decision, to let the Jews go in exchange for permission to buy strategic technology in the West.

Besides the Jews, Armenians also were a part of the deal. In the following years, hundreds of thousands of Jews left the Soviet Union. Some of them went to Israel; others went to Western Europe and the United States. The American welcome of the Jews was unprecedented. The arriving Jews were granted free houses, each worth twenty-five thousand dollars. By today's prices, these properties would cost two hundred and fifty thousand dollars.

Old Jews who had worked for forty years to build Communist Russia, on arrival in capitalist America received U.S. pensions. Doctors received medical jobs, even though their Soviet practice and experience was not suitable for American medical institutions, and despite their poor English. Today, if somebody arrived in the United States from Russia he would never be allowed to set up a medical practice. But in those times it was different.

At the height of the immigration of these Soviet Jews, an American reporter made a documentary about Russian Jewish immigrants. I do not know her name, but I remember that she was an attractive blonde. In this documentary she treated the facts very honestly and her opinion was a very balanced one. But at one point, this reporter made the conclusive remark that the Soviet Jewish immigrants arriving in America, in her opinion, were not escaping from any kind of oppression, but were doing it solely for economic reasons.

This film shown on an American TV channel was in drastic discord with the Western propaganda. Zionist organizations decided to punish her, and by doing so, send a message to other reporters who dared to utter a word damaging the Jewish cause. So she was assassinated. Although the American police admitted that they suspected Jewish militant groups in this murder, they arrested no one.

Also, during the peak of the Jewish immigration wave, several Jewish political activists were arrested in Moscow. But, unlike Muslims and other oppressed people of the Soviet Union, they were prosecuted not for their ethnic, racial, or religious identity, but because of their anti-state activities in the agitation of the Soviet Jews to emigrate. At those times nobody dared to be involved in any anti-state political actions. However, these Jewish activists were getting strong support and assistance from Zionist organizations in the West. They freely visited the U.S. Embassy in Moscow to take instructions. Besides that, they had good communications with the Israeli representative in the Dutch embassy, which represented Israeli interests in Russia.

During that period, a huge number of foreigners, in the disguise of regular tourists, visited the Soviet Union. They were all emissaries of overseas Zionist organizations. The "tourists" were supplied with a list of addresses of Soviet Jews whom they saw in their apartments, offered them both moral and material support, and agitated and encouraged them to move to Israel, to return to their "historic motherland."

In those times, I decided, one day, to go to the square in front of the Moscow synagogue, to watch the people who every Saturday regularly

Chapter Six: The Twentieth Century's Greatest Fabrication 133

gathered there after the end of the religious service, when the doors of the temple were closed. The people that used to assemble there were Jewish political activists, as well as Soviet citizens who planned to immigrate to the West or to the State of Israel. That day, as I stood there at the curb of the pavement facing the synagogue, my eyes caught the sight of a young man with a short military haircut wearing a parka jacket. He approached the gathering with quick steps, and made his way into the crowd. The men who knew him and waited for him immediately surrounded him. With quick, adroit movements, he started to take out of the multiple pockets of his sports jacket small squares of bent papers, and distributed them among the men that took him into the circle. After the last square of paper changed hands and was safely hidden inside pockets, he speedily moved away from the crowd and went out of sight. I turned my head to a man that stood by my side, asking him who that young man in the grey parka jacket was. He answered that he was an employee of the U.S. Embassy. I guessed immediately that the American was a marine who worked as a guard in the embassy. I understood that he came to the synagogue to distribute leaflets with the political activity instructions among the local Jews.

The massive emigration of Jews changed the atmosphere and mood in the Soviet Union. Now there was a crack in the wall; in the Iron Curtain a door was opened from inside the Communist prison. The myth of the Communist paradise started to fade away. The Soviet people started to think and ask questions. Questions like, why are the Jews leaving for capitalist countries, where, according to the Communist Party's propaganda, the working class is oppressed and exploited? It looked even stranger to the underprivileged non-Jews to see that the successful Jewish people were departing, leaving behind their high positions, luxurious apartments, and the high lifestyle. Thus people started to doubt the official propaganda, and started to understand that living standards in the West must be much higher than in the Soviet Union, so this was the reason the Jews who prospered under the Soviet regime were leaving.

During the rule of Gorbachev, he relied very much on Jewish and Armenian advisers, with whom he surrounded himself, to bring down the Soviet Union. Thus in the twentieth century the Jews, and to a minor extent the Armenians, destroyed the Russian empire two times: the first time it was the Tsarist, and the second time the Soviet. For sure, Armenians are not as significant a people in world politics as the Jews. They merely caught the wave created by the Jews, and benefited themselves by joining, opportunistically, the favorable conditions.

In 1971, I worked in a film studio in Baku. A KGB officer worked at our office, and from time to time he told stories to us, the office staff, boasting about his exploits as a secret agent. Once he confided to us that in Baku and in other parts of the Caucasus, there operated an Armenian secret organization. He said that the KGB knew all the activists in this organization by their names. In addition, he said that this nationalist secret organization united more than a million ethnic Armenians. However, he never explained why the authorities tolerated the clandestine activities of this secret organization, since any unauthorized society or organization would normally be prosecuted in the Soviet Union. He continued by relating to us that when, in the previous year, the head of the state, Leonid Brezhnev, visited Baku, the KGB put thousands of the activists of this secret society in jail, since there was a danger of his assassination. They kept these people in jail for the duration of Brezhnev's stay, and released them after his departure.

If that was the case, why did the KGB pretend that they knew nothing about the existence of this illegal organization? The explanation of this is in the fact that Armenian nationalists had a secret pact with the Kremlin to assist them in the total ethnic cleansing of the Muslim populated areas of Transcaucasia, which eventually would be populated by Armenians. However, after a passage of time, some nationalists started to lose their patience. They started to accuse Moscow of deception, of making false promises. Therefore, they began to make threats of terrorist acts and assassinations of the Soviet leaders. Thus there was a bomb explosion in Moscow's metro, with a large number of causalities. Three Armenian nationalists were caught and prosecuted in a secret court proceeding. The fact that Armenians were behind the attack was kept secret from the public, not to compromise the image of this privileged ethnic group.

For what reason did the Soviet authorities tolerate the clandestine activities of the Armenian nationalists? The reason was that the Kremlin's policies in Transcaucasia required a strong Armenian nationalist organization to use against the local Muslims, in case they started to demand independence from Russia. But for the time being these groups were on the back burner, being kept warm with promises. Much later, Gorbachev, when he decided to dismantle the Soviet Union, used this Armenian secret organization to create disturbances among different ethnic groups, and to stage a civil war in the Caucasus, to shatter the foundations of the regime.

The fall of Marxism in Russia did not weaken the positions of Jews in society; on the contrary, they reconstructed their positions and secured for themselves places in the government, in industry, in parliament, in the

Chapter Six: The Twentieth Century's Greatest Fabrication 135

banking system, in the police, and in the mass media. They are controlling these institutions.

I read a newspaper article with excerpts from a book written by a former head of the personal security of Yeltsin. This man himself previously worked in the KGB. He, in his book, brought out a list of the most senior Russian politicians that were Jewish. From his materials, one can make up one's mind that any well-known name in today's Russian political scene is Jewish. He wrote that some of these people forged the data in their passports and birth certificates to hide their ethnic identity. In other cases when they were of mixed blood, they chose to put in their identity papers the nationality of the non-Jewish parent.

In the same way, today all Russian TV channels are under the control of the Jews. And the contents of the programs, naturally, are Zionistic. The news programs are anti-Arab, anti-Muslim, anti-Christian, and anti-religious. These channels promote pornography, gambling, obscenities, rumors, and in general, they cultivate immorality – a particular mentality within society that is answering the interests of Zionists. It seems the program makers of these channels overwhelmingly prefer to recruit Jews as actors, dancers, and singers. In films, in reality shows, and in commercials, they prefer to use Jewish boys and girls so as to allow them to make money, to get rich and famous. Thus these television channels are Russian in name only.

A Russian TV viewer can see how the political commentators in their programs glorify the Israeli army and its success in fighting the Arabs. They advise the Russian generals to adopt the Israeli army model to improve the Russian military force. They are trying to set the minds of ethnic Russians into thinking that the next wars Russia will fight will not be with "democratic" and "friendly" Western powers, but with the "uncivilized," "barbarous" Muslims. These Jewish-controlled channels secured the prestigious foreign correspondent positions exclusively for Jews. These positions allow them to guarantee the Zionist contents of their reports. Thus anybody who is familiar with the modern Russian Federation can see that Zionists control it completely.

I detected some Jews in the top positions of the Russian Orthodox Church. Even the spokesperson for the Church is a Jew. Thus Zionists are now trying to take control of the Russian Church.

God Most High says: "O children of Israel! ... And do not mix up the truth with the falsehood, nor hide the truth while you know (it)" (Koran, 2:40-42).

CHAPTER SEVEN:
CONSPIRACY THEORY

Conspiracy Theory is a Hollywood film with Mel Gibson as its protagonist, in which he plays a man who is obsessed with thoughts about different "conspiracy theories." The very choice of actor, who is usually depicted in movies as a character with mental problems, and the whole mood of the film was to make the audience think that individuals who believe in the existence of "conspiracy theories" are mentally unstable people, that these "theories" are products of an insane mind.

Not just in this film, but in whole of the Western mass media there exists a certain attitude, a tendency to depict people who come forward with ideas about various conspiracies, intrigues, and secret plots as mentally disturbed individuals, as lunatics. I think the Western mass media use this method of employing a smear campaign against anybody who comes up with a new "theory" as a preventive medicine, as an antidote. In other words, the mass media is afraid to see different individuals come out and make revelations and exposures.

I like to detect and to expose various evil conspiracies, secret plots, and schemes. Contrary to what the press wants to make us think, individuals who believe in the possibility of conspiracies make up a clever class. In the eyes of an animal or a mentally deficient person, the universe and life have no logical explanation. They do not see any meaning in the events of life; they cannot draw analogies or see any design or logical consequences in the happenings around them. On the contrary, a clever, intelligent individual, as he looks around and looks at the world, detects different occurrences and their outcomes, causes, and effects. To this kind of person, the events of life are not a combination of different, meaningless, unconnected accidents, but are part of a certain design or plan. This person can look around and see in everything a certain line, a connection.

Likewise, a shallow, materialistic type of person sees the universe and the Creation as the result of chaos and disorder; the clever person, as he looks at the world, sees how everything in life is interconnected and continues to exist according to a certain pattern and universal plan. The materialistic mind is always in a state of confusion and misunderstanding, while a thoughtful person, as he looks at the events of life, rejects all incidents that make no sense, and concentrates his mind on reasonable things that make sense.

Chapter Seven: Conspiracy Theory

As I looked in this way at the things of this life and the world, I observed a lot of smaller intrigues, plots, and conspiracies. As the years have passed, I have managed to collect in my mind certain data which has consequently made me conclude that all these small intrigues and plots are a part of a larger conspiracy, which is the major conspiracy of the modern time. This is the Zionist conspiracy.

In my childhood and youth my parents never made any anti-Semitic remarks, nor in my Muslim upbringing did I hear anybody say anything negative about the Jews. But early in my life I noticed that the local Christians – Armenians, Russians, and Ukrainians – hated the Jewish people for some reasons unknown to me. At that time, I explained it to myself that it was the result of historical tensions between Christian and Judaic faiths.

In Baku, my acquaintances were mostly made up of Armenians and Jews. The reason for this was the cosmopolitan tastes and interests of these people. I had a desire to see the world, different places, different nationalities and races; desired to travel around the world. The Jews and Armenians had cosmopolitan attitudes and stood out among the Soviet masses as strangers and foreigners who were always ready to move to another part of the world, while other Soviet citizens, it seemed, were poorly informed about life abroad, and were content with the boring Soviet realities and deeply attached to the soil. But it was much later, at an older age, after my travels to Western Europe, that I understood there actually existed a Jewish global domination conspiracy. I concluded that the Zionists modeled the modern world, its political and social shape.

Theodor Herzl founded Zionism as a political movement at the end of nineteenth century. As I see it, the Jews came to prominence only in the twentieth century. Although some European Jews even before this were very rich, the political and social situation was not so that they could have much influence in any country or society in which they lived. But in the twentieth century everything changed – the Jews came out of the blue and, in a relatively short stretch of time, took over whole world. There were large, powerful empires, but these Jews took over the controls and swept them aside.

When I lived in Western Europe, I observed how the Jews in this part of the world controlled politics, the economy, the judiciary, the banking system, the press, television, the motion picture industry, and the arts. Later I realized that they were asserting control even over the Muslim countries. Very few Muslim countries – namely Syria, Lebanon, and especially Iran – managed to keep themselves sterile from the "Jewish virus." Now Eastern Europe has also fallen into the hands of the Zionists. Other countries, such as China and India, have still managed to withstand the Jewish onslaught, due to the non-existence of any significant Jewish community there.

In the Soviet Union, in Baku, I had an Armenian acquaintance. He was a very nice person and was one of the few people to whom I could confess about my efforts to escape from the Communist state. He once told me that he also wanted to emigrate to the West, to the United States. Besides that, he said that he intended to improve his public standing, but to accomplish this he had to marry a Jewish girl.

I asked, "Why have you decided this? What is so special about the Jews? You can marry an Armenian girl and try to move to Los Angeles with its huge Armenian community."

To this he said, "Armenians are not that important a people, but these Jews are very important people, and if I marry a Jewess it will help me improve my position in society and business."

The first Western city that I arrived in was Berlin. It might be thought that after Hitler, Germany was free of the Jewry, but not any longer. As I soon realized, the Jews today once again owned most of its antiquarian shops on Kurfurstendamm. Just a visual observation was enough to see that the Jews had once again taken control of all the antiquarian business in town. I went to Christie's and was confronted there by an attractive brunette, who was the manager of the auction house. She turned out to be a recently arrived Russian Jew. I assumed that she must have had an influential patron to get this job. It must be a very sought after position in Berlin, but of all the people in Berlin she, a Jewish Soviet émigré, took the job. Thus how influential the Jews must be in today's Berlin!

Years before this, I saw on Soviet television a KGB-sponsored documentary about a large group of Jewish immigrants from the USSR that moved to West Berlin and settled there. The documentary said that the Jews who arrived from Russia completely took over all the antiquarian businesses, and were heavily involved in the stolen art business. First, they started by selling smuggled Russian icons, and then they moved on to other art objects.

The filmmakers put the question of why the German authorities were allowing them to conduct their illegal business. Later, they suggested that these Jews were under the protection of the German intelligence agency. And as a reason for the German secret services protecting these Jews, they suggested that they were cooperating with them. Thus it was understood that the German authorities allowed them to do their shady business in Berlin, in exchange for their assistance in intelligence work against the Soviet Union, where these new arrivals had many contacts. However, what the filmmakers never said was that these Jewish art dealers had a very warm relationship with the KGB as well. Therefore, actually, these Jews allowed the Western intelligence agencies to maintain a liaison and contact between them and the KGB.

One of my Russian acquaintances in Berlin was a medical massage specialist. He made friends with Berlin's Russian émigrés. He earned himself quite a sum of money by rubbing the expensive backs and bottoms of the local Jews. He gave me his impressions, and told me about modern palaces and marbled drawing rooms with walls fully covered with smuggled paintings. These people had arrived in Germany just recently, some ten years before this, from the poverty-stricken Soviet Union, but by then they were living in fantastic luxury and had millionaires' lifestyles. The hard working Germans probably wondered how these Jews got so rich in such a short time. Unlike Germans, the Jews are very eager to display their prosperity.

Several months before the fall of the Soviet Union, I met a drunk in a hotel in Berlin, a weeping Jewish man. I found it somewhat unusual for a Jew, a former professor, to be in such a despicable condition, but he said that he had a good excuse for this. He told me that he arrived in Germany to ask for asylum. He had on his hands a sick wife who required constant attendance to survive. But, unfortunately, he was made to part with her by the German immigration authorities. They put her in a hotel in a different German city. According to him, she now had very little chance of surviving on her own. This man was blaming himself for the mistake he made by claiming asylum as an ordinary Soviet citizen, rather than as a Jew. In Russia, a Jewish lawyer had advised him to apply as a Jewish person escaping from anti-Semitic harassment. He said that he now understood that if he had used a Jewish application, they would have treated him differently, better, since "the Jews are a privileged people."

The next city I visited was Munich, and there I learned that every newly arriving Soviet Jew received an apartment as a gift from the German state.

The next European city that I visited was Nice. In this city, an old artist asked me whether I wanted him to give me some advice. I said, yes, and he told me that if I wanted to stay and live in Nice, then I had to make myself an acceptable person to the Jews, since the city was under their control. He said that if the Jews do not like you, they will make you leave. But later I learned that they controlled not just Nice, but Paris as well.

Then I went to Amsterdam and there I heard a complaint by a Dutchman, who told me that the city was no longer theirs, but belonged to the Jews. He said that Dutch people today go to Amsterdam as day visitors, as tourists, and return in the evening back to their cows in farms in the countryside. If this is true, the local Jews must be extremely rich people, since property in the city is fantastically expensive.

The city itself is the Sodom and Gomorrah of Europe. The central streets are lined with windows displaying naked prostitutes to the public, to pedestrians. The coffee shops sell hashish. Gay partners are everywhere. The streets are full of tourists who are attracted to the nightlife of Amsterdam and its openly gay culture. But the major attraction to tourists is the availability of drugs. Hashish cultivation has been made legal and it attracts young addicts from Europe and America. The local authorities have allowed the cultivation of hashish to enrich the coffers of the city. They claim that they allow the sale of only soft drugs, but I saw hundreds of drug pushers in the central square, blocking the passage of tourists and offering them hard drugs such as heroin and cocaine, while police officers stood nearby and looked the other way, pretending not to see anything. I read somewhere that Ecstasy tablets are produced in Holland, and it brings in billions of dollars of profits yearly.

Later, when I got to London, I saw that this city is also totally controlled by Jews. Hampstead and its surroundings, the nicest areas in town, are considered to be Jewish boroughs. In England, most supermarket chains, department stores, banks, and industries are Jewish-owned businesses as well.

At that time, the Conservative government was in 10, Downing Street. Jews headed most of its ministries, including the Foreign Office and the Home Office. The Defense Secretary at that time was Michael Portillo, who, I think, is a Jew as well – otherwise it does not make any sense to me that a Spanish man such as he would be allowed to head such an important ministry.

I have never been to the United States, but I know that the situation there is the same. The mighty United States is the second stronghold of Zionists after Israel.

Even in the countries with small Jewish communities, the Zionists can exert a decisive influence. One of their methods of taking control over the state is to take over its secret services. By getting a hold of these agencies, the Jews take charge of society.

Chapter Seven: Conspiracy Theory 141

The problem is not in the fact that a Jew is holding an important position in a Christian or Muslim country. The problem is the Jewish abuse of the positions they hold, and that they serve the interests of Israel rather than the country they are living in. But the interests of the majority, the interests of the entire world, should not be sacrificed for the interests of this ethnic minority or for the interests of Israel.

The organizational skills and the boundless ambition of Jews make them a very dangerous people. I would liken a Jew to a player who cannot take defeat, who likes to win by all means, by any means. It must be said that the Jews are not victims of Zionist ideology, but its beneficiaries. All of them have tremendously advanced their businesses and financial affairs under the banner of Zionism. Any Jew on any continent, in any corner of the world, has personally felt his or her fortunes improve with the advance of Zionism across the world. But there are losers. The losers are the rest of the world, non-Jews, the majority of the population of the planet.

In the past one hundred years, Muslims have been the most obvious victims of Zionism, the most oppressed people in the world, since the advance of the Jews was mostly at the expense of Muslims, and to a lesser extent at the expense of Christians. Today, it would be correct to call virtually every Jew a Zionist, since just about every Jew on the planet has benefited from this ideology and somehow is a part of this intrigue. So, henceforth, I will use these words alternatively, as synonyms. Thus any Jew, no matter where he or she lives, feels like a stranger or a foreigner. Today, it is to Israel that they owe their allegiance. A Jew thinks, "What is good for Israel is good for me." Besides, he or she thinks that what is good for Israel is good for the world. This type of mentality is a very sick and destructive mentality, which can bring grave consequences to the affairs and fortunes, not just of the Jews, but also of the whole of humanity. Thus to my mind, if there ever was a third world war, it would be the fault of Israel – the fault of the Zionists.

The mentality of Jews is like this: rather than let the Israeli Zionist regime fall, they would start a world war. What would remain after the end of this war, I cannot say. Whether this war would bring the end of everything, would bring the Judgment Day, I do not know.

Just think about it; the Israeli regime sits on a huge arsenal of nuclear weapons. They possess chemical and bacteriological weapons as well.

Israel is a client state of the Western powers, especially of the United States. As is known, the Americans have supported this Zionist regime for years by handing it a gift of three billion dollars annually. Israel is an illegal entity, established on the ethically-cleansed territories of Palestine, and can never survive economically without American help.

Very recently on a French TV channel, I saw a newswoman who brought up an interesting historical fact. She said that the leading theoretician of Zionism, Herzl, approached many world leaders early in the twentieth century and made a proposition that they accept the idea of a Zionist state; he offered to arm and equip Christendom with a new Zionist doctrine, with a new global plan and strategem. Later she made a significant remark, that "at first" they looked at this thought, this proposition, with skepticism. But, it seems, subsequently they accepted the idea, took it on, and made the Zionist creed the foundation of the modern political philosophy of the Occident.

Thus the Elders of Zion managed to frame an ideology which is the cornerstone of present-day Euro-American politics. According to it, the West and its freedoms are under a great threat from religious fundamentalism, and especially from the Muslims, from Islamists. It claims that Islam is the archenemy of the West, of its "democracy," the foe of "European civilization," and that Muslims represent in themselves a danger to the peace and well-being of the Occidental people, while Jewry, the State of Israel, should be used as the spearhead of this fight against the Islamic threat.

But in reality, Muslim countries are economically underdeveloped. They are technologically dependent on the West and militarily cannot represent any threat. Trade with the technologically advanced Western countries is vital for them. Besides, it would be impossible to convince any sane person that Muslim countries desire to invade the Christian world, to start a war against Christendom. However, the Jews – Zionists – want to use this imaginary "Islamic threat" as an excuse to show, to demonstrate, their own importance to the West, to the Christian world, in order to defend themselves from the Muslims.

The events of the twentieth century have proved that the Jews want to build their earthly paradise on the backs of Muslims – but not anymore. As I see it, the Jewish advance has reached its peak and has started a decline, which will eventually bring about the fall of Zionism. Although the inevitable collapse of the Israeli regime is obvious, still nobody can predict its day or hour. It could take several years to happen, or maybe just several months. It could collapse as soon as tomorrow. Nobody can give a specific date. Only God knows.

Chapter Seven: Conspiracy Theory

I will tell you that I will not regret the Israeli collapse, nor will any other Muslim. The same can be said about Christians and the representatives of other religions. The losers will just be the Zionists, the Jews. But the rest of the world will gain; the majority will be the beneficiaries. With the collapse of this racist Zionist state, the power base of Zionism will start to deteriorate and diminish.

The leader of the Iranian Islamic Revolution and founder of the Iranian Islamic state, Ayatollah Khomeini (may his soul rest in peace), called the United States the great Satan. I accept this statement with an addition, that we define the heart or brain of this Satan as Israel. Although Americans have advanced technology and military might, it seems that they have no brains for international politics. I would liken America to a huge machine without a driver, directed by remote control from a distance, from Israel. Americans do pride themselves in the marbled parliament building in Washington, but what is the use of it if their government is controlled by the Israeli parliament? In today's America, the decisions of the U.S. parliament must first be taken in Israel, in *its* parliament, its Knesset. Therefore, America could be likened to a giant, an athlete or a heavy-weight boxer, of whom the world is scared, but who himself is battered by his wife – by the pigmy state of Israel. As I feel it Israel will inevitably collapse, but it will drag the United States to destruction along with it. I do not know how, but I just feel now that the United States, by behaving as a bully, as a dumb giant, will end up badly.

They often show on TV a frail, gray-haired, bearded old man in a wheelchair, who spent ten or twenty years in an Israeli prison. This man, a sheikh, instigated the start of the Intifada uprising against the Zionist occupants. His religious bright mind made him decide to start this revolt, which was conducted by throwing stones. Remember the Bible story of David and Goliath, a giant warrior who was slain by David, a small youth, using a sling? Thus Palestinians empowered by religious wisdom will destroy this evil Israeli state by throwing stones at the Zionist soldiers armed with the latest, the most advanced, military technology. One has to be a very dumb person not to see the inevitable ruin of the regime.

But here it must be said that the events of the twentieth century taught lessons to the Muslims, made them realize the importance of religion on all social levels, to their self-preservation and livelihood.

Here I want to have an intermission and bring up a conversation I had, some twenty years ago, in Moscow's Friday mosque. I met there a Palestinian Muslim. After a short while, I saw that he was giving alms to a drunken woman. I brought it to his attention that she was not a Muslim, and that, more than that, she was a drunkard and was going to use this money to buy herself some wine. To which he said, "No, she is a Muslim and she is not drunk." He tried to ignore the obvious facts, but to see only what he wanted to see.

He also told me that he wished to see Palestine free from Jewish occupation, and that the Russians promised to help. That is why he loved Russians very much. He said that he arrived in snow-covered Moscow directly from the Middle East in his light clothes, but the generous Soviet people provided him, free-of-charge, a nice overcoat. He indicated the cheap overcoat that he was wearing. He said that if Palestinians would accept communism, then Russia would be on their side. I tried to explain to him that the Soviet leaders had an opportunistic interest in the Middle East, and that they do not love Muslims or Islam as they are atheists. His reply was that he and other Palestinians are disappointed with the Islamic religion, since it had not helped them overcome Israel. Thus now they want to embrace communism, which will help them to bring about a victory over the Jews.

Today, I am glad to see that the Palestinians are now using Islamic religious slogans to fight the Israelis. I am happy that Palestinians and Muslims elsewhere understand that their faith will save them. Upon the commencement of the twentieth century, the onslaught of the West with its advanced technology brought Muslims around the world into a state of shock. It scared them and they started to doubt the truth told in their holy book; they started to cool down to religion or altogether turn their backs on the faith. Now, after a century full of sufferings and humiliations, most Muslims understand the vital importance of Islam to their destiny in this life and in the hereafter.

For the benefit of the reader, to explain how the U.S. government operates, I will bring out here an episode about the workings of the White House reported in American newspapers. Several years ago, during Clinton's presidency, as he was vacationing at his official residence somewhere in America, the members of his administration were holding a meeting at the White House. The Secretary of State, Madeleine Albright, the Defense Secretary, Cohen (in Hebrew – a high priest) and a speechwriter (Eric Tarloff) came together to counsel. At the end of it, they decided to bomb several African Muslim countries. They found a phony excuse for this action, that they were doing it to destroy possible chemical weapon-making facilities in these poverty-stricken countries.

This political trio was Jewish, thus these three Zionists drew out an anti-Muslim plan, but to put it into action they needed approval, the

Chapter Seven: Conspiracy Theory

signature of the President. So they sent a helicopter after the President to bring him to Washington. As Bill Clinton was taken from his bed, he protested, "What was the urgency, why couldn't this affair wait for a couple of days?"

In the Oval Room, the Jews put in front of him on the desk a paper, urging to sign it. When he was informed about the contents of the paper, he started to strongly protest against these bombing raids. He was concerned about his image and reputation in the eyes the rest of the world, and of Muslims. But despite his doubts and protests, the Zionist troika insisted and made him sign it. As soon as he had done it, he was put back on the helicopter and was sent back to his residence to continue the vacation, and the U.S. Air Force attacked the African targets. Later, when independent European inspectors searched the ruins left after the bombings, they concluded that the factories destroyed in the raids produced nothing more dangerous than aspirin. But who cares!

As I see it, the Zionist objective in taking this action, bombing the territories of sovereign nations, was to get the public used to these kinds of military actions, to make it an acceptable, legitimate policy in the future. This incident is an example of the workings of the U.S. government. American political journalists themselves admit that all U.S. politics are cooked by the "Washington's Jewish Arabists."

But why are Muslims the prime target of the West and the Zionists? Has it something to do with oil? Oil has something to do with it, but it is only a partial reason. In reality, the Zionists are using the oil issue as an excuse. Israelis are trying to convince the American public that the existence of a friendly Jewish state in the heart of the Middle East, with its large oil reserves, is important for America to exert pressure on Muslim states, that the territory of Israel could be used to control the oil routes, to secure its safety. Fears about the possibility of the Arab states boycotting the oil sales to the West were sounded. But the question is how a prolonged embargo is possible, if Muslims states are very much economically dependent on the oil profits received through its imports. Thus it can be said that this anti-Muslim hostility has very little, if anything, to do with oil, but is a consequence of Zionist intrigues. What they are doing is taking control over every organization or institution around the globe, and replacing the agendas of these entities with their own Zionist agendas so that these structures will serve their own interest, the interests of Israel.

There is a test by psychologists. By giving a person a word, they ask him to bring all possible associations that this word springs to his mind. I will bring here a shorter list of my associations with the word "Zionism": Jew, Judas, Jesus Christ, Judaism, the Evil, the Devil, Satan, Palestine, Arabs, Muslims, Christians, Pharisees, A-bomb, H-bomb, Neutron-bomb, nuclear physicists, Leon Trotsky, Karl Marx, Hitler, Taliban, Wahhabis, Masonic Lodge, diamonds, jewelers, Sigmund Freud, psychoanalysis, Sylvester Stallone, the BBC, Hollywood, the French Revolution, Amnesty International, Marks & Spencer, Sainsbury's, the Bolsheviks, communism, immigration, globalization, internationalism, capital punishment, women's rights, gay rights, antiquarian shops, the mass media, etc…

To say it differently : today, in this new order of the world everything and every event, in one way or another, is influenced by the Jews, by Zionists.

One hundred years ago, in Baku there was a widely circulated saying that whatever happens in the world, it is the Englishman who is fingering it. But an alteration in this maxim would make it to sound more appropriate to our time, that whatever happens in the different quarters of the world – wars, assassinations, international conflicts, revolutions, coups d'etat, and terrorist acts – it is the Jew who is fingering it.

When I arrived on the English shores, I had very little knowledge of British history. At the time, I thought that Britain, unlike America, is a country of little importance in international politics. But later I found out the historic facts that, except for a few countries in northwest Africa whose Muslim kingdoms were established by the French, all other Muslim kingdoms – starting from Egypt to the East, as far as Indonesia – were creations of the British. Most of these kingdoms or states continue to be subject to the British, to its dictate and influence, while the Zionists, through the British institutions, control these so-called Islamic countries. Today, in our Zionist-controlled world, the Mecca and Medina of these Muslim monarchs is no more in the Arabian Desert, but in London, where they, with their foresight, purchased expensive residences. The city is ultimately going to be their last refuge.

It can be said that Jewish hostility to Arabs and Muslims in general is something opportunistic; there is nothing personal about it. As I explained in the previous chapters, the Jews as a minority group, as the representatives of Judaism, of this minority religion, have a greatly disadvantageous position in relation to other nations. For this reason, to fulfill the Jewish Dream of domination over others, they have to remove, to destroy, all the barriers rising in front of this goal. And the most fundamental barrier or obstacle is religion. The Jews presume that if religion goes, if it is made obsolete, then nobody can call them strangers, either in the West or in the East. Thus, according to Zionists, the old world order built on religious precepts and laws should go, to be replaced by the new world order without religions, without faith, which would be built on the materialistic values. Today, the Zionists are using religious slogans just for propaganda of Zionist ideology, as a smokescreen, while representing themselves as the archenemies of religion and the faith.

No matter where Jews are living, they still need the State of Israel to legitimize their Zionist Cause. Hence, a Jew in America, Russia, or Turkey thinks that by serving Israel he is serving his own interests as a Jew. However, Jews will never agree to come together and live in the Middle East, since by this they will lose their dominant positions in different parts of the world.

The majority of Zionists, if not all of them, are indifferent to religion. Thus Zionists by trying to destroy Islam, Christianity, Hinduism, or Buddhism are doing it not out of intent to replace it by Judaism, but to clear the way for the Jewish minority to facilitate their domination on the globe. If Zionism can be likened to Hydra, then this monster would have many millions of heads with different faces. It can be said that Zionism today is everywhere, without making any exaggerations. If I decide to use religious terminology, then I can call Zionists Satan's servants, as they see their fortunes and prosperity in the total elimination of religions. And the Devil chooses them as the best choice of servants available, due to their cunning mind and sophistication. But they like to call themselves the "chosen people," as if God chose the Jews for a special mission. Yet in reality, in the twentieth century they acted as if they were the Devil's chosen people, with a mission to eradicate religion from the face of the earth.

If the reader will take a look at a political map and find Iran on it, and try to imagine this country to be the last fortification on the surface of the earth still standing firm against the Zionist offensive, then he will get the picture. Today, the spiritual leaders of Iran – perhaps the only true Islamic state, which was built on the ruins of the pro-Western Shah's regime – are left with no other choice but to voice, almost daily, calls to their population to stand firm and not to give up and surrender to the siege of the Devil's army.

Once, in London I visited the office of a Tibetan organization struggling for the region's independence from China. An assistant – while she was trying to help me to find an address of a Buddhist charity that I was looking for – produced a large book, a directory of all registered British charities. She told me that the book contained the names of two hundred thousand organizations. Zionists control the totality of these charities, every one of them, without exception. If anybody tries to check, he can find out for himself that this statement is correct. If not all of them, most of them are headed by Jews. If, in the case of a non-Jew managing the organization, then it means that the true boss in the charity is another person who works in the office – a Jew.

Even this Tibetan charity was managed by Jews and used to promote the Zionist interest in the Far East. Not all charities in the directory were religious. In the case of a religious organization, I can't adequately explain the absurdity of the situation – when Christian, Muslim, or Buddhist organizations are supervised by Jewish people.

In Britain – as well as in other parts of Western Europe – all organizations are controlled by Zionists. There is no difference whether it is governmental or non-governmental. Usually, the mechanics of this control are maintained by the governmental body of the secret services. Some readers can say that it is not possible for the secret services to supervise and manage hundreds of thousands of charities. But they are wrong. Big Brother never sleeps. No charity stays away from its watchful eyes. This control is especially strong over religious charities, since Zionists consider religion as a highly sensitive area.

This is what the Zionist conspiracy is all about. The conspiracy was devised to help the Jews maintain control over the whole world. As faith and religion represent the prime obstacle to Zionist ambitions, their venom is targeted at the prime prey – the beliefs of the populace. This is the premier article of the Zionist doctrine – to liquidate faith and religion, to make the world spiritually sterile, free of all beliefs. But it is a futile goal. It is impossible to destroy faith unless humanity itself is wiped off the surface of the earth.

Recent history, our recent experience, has taught us lessons. We can see that Jews have managed to achieve certain tactical victories by shattering the positions of religion, but it is obvious that strategically the task is an impossible one. No matter how obstinate and determined Satan is, he can oppose people and God forever, but his fight is futile, since his positions are wrong and false. Likewise, the positions of Zionists, of this anti-religious lobby, and of all other godless circles, will crumble eventually.

One day, as I was crossing Hyde Park I noticed an unusually large group of people who had gathered at Speaker's Corner. This well-known place in London is a well-publicized item of the tourist sightseeing tours. I

Chapter Seven: Conspiracy Theory 149

was wondering who the speaker was that managed to attract such an audience. When I got closer, I noticed another unusual sign. I saw that near the speaker were stationed two mounted policemen. The speaker was somebody dressed as a Muslim priest in a turban and traditional garments. The middle-aged man was giving a sermon in a very agitated form and manner, while screaming so loud as if he wanted to be heard across the whole of London.

But why did this man choose this tourist attraction rather than a mosque to read his sermon? Later, as I listened to his speech, I understood who he really was. The man was calling the audience to take arms and to kill Christians, to burn churches and British government offices. Next to me was standing a pretty, young American girl with her boyfriend. Both were tourists. She was listening to the "mullah" with her mouth wide open. She seemed to be terrified. Except for two Arab businessmen and me, the audience was made up of American tourists. The Arabs, it seemed, were embarrassed and had a puzzled face expression on their faces. They had probably never heard this kind of a sermon from a Muslim priest in their entire lives. They were shocked and confused. It seems that nobody there besides me understood the intrigue.

The man was a Jew in disguise. The intent of this bogus show was to give Islam a bad name, a bad image. Even before this, I met in London numerous British men, some of them Jews, employed by the British secret services, which took Muslim pseudonyms, pretending that they were Islamic converts. They are usually used in different schemes against Muslims. In this particular case at Speaker's Corner, they probably had a minor objective, to test their agent, to give him field experience for the next more serious schemes or sabotage activities.

The agent provocateur continued to make calls to arms and bloodletting, while trying hard to suppress his urge to smile. The mounted policemen stood on alert without movement, protecting him. I thought that it would be a good idea to get closer and to punch his cheeky mug and run away before the policemen could intervene. But I just went away, since fighting and punching does not represent my mission in this world. I have more important things to do. After all, he was just an ordinary agent.

I remember another episode with a Pakistani Messiah. But this one was a heavier intrigue. I had some questions connected with television. While I was leafing through a guide of television companies, I found a TV station with a Muslim sounding name. I found it strange, since to my knowledge there was no Muslim television in Britain. I decided to go there and find out if they could answer my questions. I thought that since they were Muslims, it may be that they were friendlier and more willing to assist.

When I got there, I was let in and offered tea. There in the yard stood a huge satellite dish antenna. The room where I was sitting had walls covered with screens of monitors showing live religious programs. The people at the office were all males, wearing black business suits and ties. They told me that they represented the Pakistani sect of Ahmadiyya. Their TV channel was transmitting religious programs by satellite around the globe twenty-four hours a day, non-stop. They had a huge hall where hundreds of books produced by the sect's publishers were on display. I was told that they published the Koran even in Russian. In addition, I was informed that to spread their message they printed books translated into more than one hundred languages.

Gradually, I started to get suspicious about them. Who were their patrons who could provide them with such huge funds, logistics and organization? A senior Pakistani offered for me to go upstairs to see their spiritual leader, who according to him was no less but the Messiah himself, in person. He meant the Islamic Mahdi that was promised to come at the world's end. I turned down the offer, and left.

I had never before heard anything about this sect. All I heard sounded very much cultish. But the ominous feature was that the sect played so easily with such an important religious matter as the Messiah. It was obvious to me that the motive of the resourceful patrons of this nasty sect was to damage Islam, to confuse Muslims, and to create disturbances.

A week later, in an Islamic book store near Baker Street, I complained to the shop assistant about the scheming of the CIA in supporting of such a filthy, pseudo-religious group as the Ahmadiyya. But this young man turned out to be a well-informed person. He even corrected me by saying that this sect is supported by an intelligence service closer to home. He meant the British intelligence agency.

Later, after checking encyclopedias, I learned that right from its birth in 1889 in India, the sect received support and encouragement from the British authorities. Much later, the brazenness and impudence of the message of the sect caused disturbances in Pakistan; the entire Muslim community rejected and condemned it as un-Islamic movement. Thus the authorities decided to ban the disruptive activities of the Ahmadiyya, and deported them abroad. Today the British Empire is no more, but the sectarians have found new patrons – the Jews.

Chapter Seven: Conspiracy Theory

In 1996 in London, one could see small stickers on the walls with just four words printed on them – "The *khilafah* is coming." This mysterious advertisement aroused my curiosity, but I could not find an explanation to it. Later still, I did find an answer to all of this, but only after I bought a brochure from a man who was selling books outside of the London Central Mosque. The publication belonged to the same people, who announced on the stickers the coming of a caliphate (*khilafah*), of a worldwide Islamic state to be ruled by a spiritual and temporal leader of Islam, by a caliph.

I was interested to find out who these people were. I called them and made an appointment. They gave me an address in north London. On the London tube, while I was heading there, I read from the brochure. I liked it very much. They were advocating the idea of the establishment, or rather restoration, of a caliphate, where the true leader of all Muslims would rule according to the Sharia Islamic law.

The writing brought out a lot of Arabic quotations from the Koran. I liked the work for its excellent English and perfect logic, in the justification of the principles of the movement. I think they called their organization "Al-Muhajiroun."

When I got there, I saw a cameraman from a British TV channel preparing to make a film or rather a documentary about the movement. I met a middle-aged man who introduced himself and told me that he was the head of the organization. He said that he damaged his leg while fighting somewhere against the enemies of Islam. Now he has political ambitions only. He also boasted about his skills in addressing huge gatherings of people. He said that his last meeting took place at Wembley Stadium and he gathered ten thousand people. I found it strange that the British authorities allowed him to read his inflammatory speeches to the public in this famous sports arena, in which he called Muslims to stand up against the Saudi regime and to bring it down. Is not the Saudi Kingdom the state with the closest ties to the British?

Then I asked the lame warrior if they had a candidate to the caliphate's throne. He said that they had the candidate, but declined to name him. But as he claimed that he personally wrote the manifesto, I never believed him. He did not produce the impression of an intellectual, nor of someone with a good education. The language of the manifesto indicated that its author was a graduate of a prime British university. But the man that was sitting in front of me was a minor, insignificant person, lacking resources to organize such a movement.

A year or so later, I saw him appear on British television a couple of times. Thus the group received tremendous publicity in London. I must say, that in the six years of my stay in England, I had never seen any prominent Muslim religious figure invited to give an interview on British television. In these interviews he produced a negative and unfavorable impression, behaving on the TV show as a funny character, like a clown.

This was another example, another scheme of the British secret services and Zionist circles. The enemies of Islam and religion take a particular issue of faith, a holy, religious idea, and then organize a group around the cause. Later, they appoint an insignificant man, a stooge, a pygmy persona, as its leader, as an agent provocateur with the ultimate object to mar and undermine the original religious idea, religious tenet. Thus Zionists, while sitting in the vaults of the British intelligence headquarters drew a plan, possibly wrote the manifesto itself, to organize a movement with the objective of putting pressure on the Saudis, and to use it as political leverage in promoting their interests in the Middle East.

Similarly, in Germany there lived a Turk by the name of Kaplan who set up an organization to promote the idea of the restoration of the caliphate in Turkey. But this one was also a paid agent of the Western secret services.

In the modern world, it is impossible to find a single Muslim organization that is not a part or a component of the greater conspiracy of Zionists. My advice to Muslims is to keep a distance from all Islamic movements and organizations, and to ignore all calls to join them.

In the nineteenth century in Persia, the sect of the Babis appeared. The founder of the faith was a man, with the alias of Bab (in Arabic – "the Gate"). Later, the followers of this man altered his teaching, and it became better known under the other names – "Baha'ism," or the Baha'i Faith. These sectarians caused a lot of destruction and disturbance that brought about a civil war in the country. The teaching itself was intended to be in opposition to traditional Islam, to replace it with the new, the "purer," form of the religion. However, all Western encyclopedias, strangely, describe it as an Islamic movement.

The destructive activities of the movement were so great that there was a real threat, not just to the monarchy, but to traditional Islam in Persia and the neighboring states as well. Their insurgent activities frightened even the Russian Tsar, who ordered a historian, a Persian Christian convert, to write a history on the sect, so that the Russian authorities could benefit from it by drawing conclusions and making themselves prepared for the

Chapter Seven: Conspiracy Theory 153

possible spread of this heresy in Russia, to the Russian-controlled Muslim territories across the border from Persia. Also I read somewhere that in those times, there was a widespread conversion to Baha'ism of Persian Jews, who were attracted to its globalist philosophy.

Today, the sect's headquarters is located in Haifa, Israel. Also in this city, the sectarians built a huge hilltop shrine. So today, Baha'is are under the protection and support of the West and of Zionists.

I read a report about a delegation from England that was sent to Turkey to look into the grievances of a single Baha'i sectarian in this country with a population of sixty million. These English human rights supporters hypocritically shed tears for the imaginary plight of this cult follower. But they ignore the mistreatment of the majority of Muslims in this fiercely anti-religious, secular republic. They would say that their only concern is the condition of the minorities such as Jews, Armenians, and others.

When the Communists were still in power in Russia, my mother was in a group of Soviet tourists in India. Although the whole group was made up of Muslims, the KGB man, the tour guide, warned them about visiting any mosques. He said that visiting places of worship of Islam was strictly forbidden for them, and if anybody ignored his warning, the perpetrator would be punished. But the Soviet tourist authorities decided to add the Baha'i New Delhi temple to the tour's list of tourist sights. That is, paying homage to an anti-Islamic sect's temple was an alright thing to do.

It is also worth mentioning that Jews are controlling all human rights organizations around the world, to help them conduct the interests of Zionism. And the best known of them is Amnesty International, whose prime targets are always Muslim countries. This organization is never interested in the plight of inmates of the U.S. jails, about the inhumane conditions in there, or with the officially admitted torture practices in Israeli prisons. Amnesty's concern is the Muslim world.

Once in a library in London, I came upon an autobiography of a woman, the wife of the founder of Marks & Spencer. I read just a few opening lines in which she wrote that she spent her childhood in my hometown of Baku, when it still was under Tsar's rule. She said that her Jewish family lived there in the Caucasus, surrounded by wild Asian tribes. Then she continued by saying that fortunately they managed to escape to England.

I would like to ask her to which tribe she herself belongs? When industrial oil production started in Baku, many thousands of Ashkenazi Jews, including Alfred Nobel, arrived in the city seeking job opportunities, to make profits. They considered themselves Europeans, civilized people, since they had some European blood in their veins, while looking down at the local Asian Jews living in the region. Jews for many hundreds of years lived and prospered in the Muslim lands, and when they leave they show no gratitude toward their hospitable hosts, they express nothing but abuse and rudeness. They say, like father like son. It was her son who established and founded Amnesty International, this intensely Zionist organization. She should have given him a better upbringing.

On another occasion, I went to the London office of a leading British Muslim weekly, *Q-News*. I brought a caricature and was interested in seeing if they could use it in their magazine. I saw a white British man there, who stood akimbo in the center of the office giving orders around to the staff of Pakistanis. I witnessed there how he used an Asian editor of the weekly as an errand boy, who was running this, that and the other, at his service, like a puppy. This white man was the real boss in the office. But you cannot find his name among the editorial staff. In my opinion, he was a British intelligence officer. Thus the British authorities provided the funding for the publication, to allow them to "order the music."

One day I found an article in *Q-News*, written by a staff writer, in which he criticized a renowned Muslim scholar in an abusive manner. The scholar, sheikh Hamza Yusuf, is an American convert to Islam. He works as an imam in a mosque in Santa Clara, California, and is famous for his excellent sermons that bear a definite Sufi touch. The offended readers bombarded the magazine with letters defending the scholar. One reader wrote that the journalist's conduct was unacceptable, that he should not use such rude words as "lunatic" to describe a prominent Muslim theologian who had a good command of English. He wrote, that even though the Muslim world has many excellent theologians, they are writing in Arabic only and do not know English. Another reader warned that he would stop reading this magazine altogether. Although eventually the editor apologized, the harm was done. But was he not employed in this magazine for exactly this kind of work, in anti-Muslim activity to serve the interests of his Zionist masters?

Several years ago, there was an airplane disaster in Amsterdam, Holland, in which a cargo aircraft crashed into a huge housing block in the working class area of the city. It half-destroyed two buildings and caused many deaths and injuries to the tenants. It was discovered later that the airplane was carrying a load of forbidden chemical weapons from the United States to Israel, using the Dutch airport for refueling. The revelation that the shipment was a secret operation between America and Israel

Chapter Seven: Conspiracy Theory 155

brought about a major scandal. I do not know the end of the story, whether the Dutch families of the victims got any compensation or not. But this tragic accident once more revealed the hypocrisy and cynicism of Washington, when it declares itself as a defender of world peace, and as a watchdog of non-proliferation of weapons of mass destruction.

Years before, an Israeli man informed American newspapers about the Israeli secret nuclear weapons program. Israeli secret service men abducted him in the daytime on the streets of an Italian city, took him forcibly to the airport, and put him in a plane to Israel. After twenty years, he is still in prison serving a sentence for revealing state secrets, by exposing the truth about the Israeli stockpiling of nuclear bombs. He tried to contribute to world peace. However, no Western government, nor the United Nations Organization, nor the human rights organizations did anything to release this nice person from Israeli prison. Nor did the Italian authorities ever complain to the Israelis about this brazen abduction incident which took place on the Italian soil.

I read a book by a Norwegian journalist about another scandal involving a team of Israeli agents who assassinated and murdered a Palestinian immigrant in a small Norwegian town, in front of his pregnant wife, a native woman. This team of a dozen Israeli intelligence officers arrived to that country to kill an "important Palestinian political activist." After carrying out the murder, they left the country. Later, Norwegian journalists found out that the Arab was a victim of mistaken identity. He was a menial worker who was never involved in politics. But the Norwegian authorities took no action against Israel. Although the Israeli officials never admitted their blunder, very soon afterwards several top directors of the Israeli intelligence agency – Mossad – were forced to resign from their posts since their operation ended up in a scandal and bad press reports.

The Western press likes to praise the Israeli secret services very much, using such adjectives as "the most efficient," "legendary," "effective," etc. But it is easy for the Israeli agents to be effective, to conduct their illegal activities – like abductions, assassinations and so on – when the Western authorities are giving the green light and silent encouragement; when all Western intelligence agencies are assisting them.

There was another report in the press about a scandal involving Mossad agents. A group of former Mossad officers (two majors and a general) decided to enrich themselves through a kidnapping scheme. They conducted an elaborate operation to kidnap the granddaughter of the late Greek shipping magnate Onassis, who was an heiress to a three-billion-dollar fortune, with the object of receiving a ransom. But they failed and were caught by the Swiss police. This particular incident is not something accidental or irregular. The secret services recruit rascals and criminals to do various illegal tasks. When they lose their jobs, they continue to be involved in criminal activity, but now for their own financial benefit, on their own initiative.

One day on TV, a BBC presenter was reporting an unusual news item. It was a murder case of an Arab banker who was working for a Swiss bank in London. A British intelligence agent recruited a British woman to spy on this banker. After the passage of some time, the agent ordered her to kill him. The woman was later caught and imprisoned. But the agent, despite all his guilt and available evidence, was allowed to walk free from the courthouse. It was thought that the intelligence officer was a double agent, that besides the British, he worked for Mossad as well. The presenter continued by saying that it was thought that the agent received the orders from Israel. His task was to find the way to kill this banker. She said that the motive behind the murder was to liquidate this unusually bright banker so that the Arab world would be deprived of its star banking cadre. In the last shots of the newsreel, a TV reporter stopped the agent outside the courthouse to ask questions about how he managed to plot the murder and at the end go free. The Zionist agent just pointed his fingers to the TV cameras in the V sign.

In the twentieth century, the world witnessed the coming of a bogus messiah, a sham savior of mankind, of a fraudster and scoundrel – Sigmund Freud, who introduced to humanity the Freudian belief, an atheistic cult, a pseudo-scientific teaching.

There is a biographical book of Freud in which an American writer made fine research into the origin of his teaching. The biography described his state of mind and motivations cleverly, in fine literary style. He was a Czech Jew with great ambitions. In Austria, he managed to unite a group of some thirty Jewish psychologists around him. In this circle, they set the foundations of the Freudian doctrine. They regularly, secretly, came together as conspirators to devise a plan: to introduce to the world a new kind of belief, to destroy and shatter olden traditions, moral codes, and values.

In Freudian teaching, in its vision of the world and Man, there is no place for God, religion, or morality. All these things, according to it, should go, to clear the way for the patriarchal figure of Freud and his disciples, "apostles," who will explain to humankind who they really are. According to them, humanity during its history, was blind and ignorant, and worshiped the wrong gods, while this new messiah will enlighten and deliver them, will show them the right direction.

In short, the man was a total maniac, but despite it he wanted to cure humankind of its conceived insanity. According to this teaching, humanity – all of it – is made up of insane people with inborn dark desires to commit incest. In reality, Freud, from his early childhood, was possessed by an abnormal sexual desire toward his own mother. This sick mental condition shaped his soul, mind, and the world outlook. Even in adult life he never managed to overcome this dark craving, could not cure his illness. Instead, he came out with a teaching which states that every person has an inborn sexual desire for his (or her) parent. It is obvious that Freud, with his sick mind, produced this teaching to suit himself, to calm himself with a thought that his mental condition was a very ordinary, natural condition for every individual. A Russian physiologist, Pavlov, described Freudianism as a religion. By which he meant that, unlike science, this theory does not require any proof, but should be accepted on faith.

The fellow conspirators took the teaching to America and for many years continued to disorient its population, its intellectuals, with this false, ungodly ideology. In this way, several generations of Westerners subscribed to these sick ideas of Freud and his disciples. Previously, conventional psychiatry did not accept Freudianism as something scientific, but most recently, under pressure from the Zionist lobby, it was forced to resign itself to accepting it as a part of psychiatry, as a science.

According to the Islamic tradition and custom, a Muslim, at the beginning of any work, should clear his heart of notions related to self, and apply the work to serving God. Without this, any action and creativity is futile. Atheistic people cannot produce anything but that which is trivial, vain, and fruitless because their motivations are based on empty, futile values. But the foundation of a believer is strong and right. A nation whose creed and values are not based on faith is heading for Hell, and their only prospects are to be burned in the eternal fire.

As God says: "Surely (as for) those who disbelieve and act unjustly, Allah will not forgive them nor guide them to a path… Except the path of hell, to abide in it for ever, and this is easy to Allah (Koran, 4:168-169).

***

Once, as I walked in the South Kensington area of London, I noticed a small poster attached to a wall. In this part of town lived a significant number of Iranian immigrants. This poster bore the portrait of the deposed Shah of Iran, Mohammad Reza Pahlavi. It was blaming the British for bringing down the monarch. Besides this, the United Kingdom was described as a small island state and the Brits as a scheming people. The people who produced this poster were obviously Iranian monarchists, who after the fall of the Pahlavi regime were forced to escape, and to take refuge in England. They had bitter feelings toward the British government for its role in toppling the Iranian monarchic dynasty, for the loss of their motherland.

I read a book written by a Cambridge-educated Iranian, who worked as an adviser for the Shah. In one place in his book, he mentioned in passing that the Shah once made a speech on Iranian television in which he made declarations to change his policy toward Israel. The Shah said that Israel acted as a destructive power in the Middle East; therefore, he was going to take a hard stand toward the Israeli regime. The author did not put much significance to this statement. However, in reality, this decision of Shah to make such a kind of political declaration was a mistake; it was political suicide for him, since this made him an enemy in the eyes of Zionists.

Israel will not tolerate the existence of a powerful and hostile state in the Middle East. Thus the Zionists decided to dump the Pahlavi regime, by which they effectively put an end to the 2,500-year-long monarchic tradition on Iranian soil. In fact, the Shah's regime existed for just two months after this anti-Israeli speech. Besides Israel, the British participated in this destruction of the Iranian monarchy as well. It was the British who brought the Pahlavis to power in Iran and established the dynasty. For this reason, the Shah very much relied on the British monarchic state to support him. But this trust ruined him, since the most destructive attacks came from Britain, from the London-based Amnesty International organization, acting as an arm of the Zionist movement. The director of the organization received orders from Tel Aviv to start a campaign against the regime, which in the end finished the Iranian monarchy.

By saying this, I am not trying to belittle the role and will of the Iranian populace in its revolution against the dynasty, the repressive pro-Western regime. There always was an opposition in the country against his rule. But what I want to say is that his reign was much dependent on Western political support. When the Shah saw that the West was no longer backing his regime, he lost heart and resigned himself to defeat.

Once in Hampstead, I attended a lecture delivered by a Nobel Prize winner, a nuclear physicist, about the nonproliferation of weapons of mass destruction. He was awarded this prize for his scientific works in the U.S. nuclear arms project. But now he was on a pension and, it seems, he wanted to get the laurels for his stance of opposition to the arms race. He

Chapter Seven: Conspiracy Theory

had a German sounding name. But, in reality, he was a Jew. His speech and the heated remarks made by the members of audience made the gathering look like a Zionist convention – almost everybody in there was Jewish. The lecturer, at length, spoke criticizing Saddam Hussein as being a very dangerous man who wanted to make an A-bomb. Another man from the audience described the dictator as a maniac, a man who represented a threat to the world peace. It appeared to me that these people came together to promote Jewish interests, rather than being interested in stopping the buildup of nuclear armaments.

It sounded to me as a hypocrisy that the White House is trying to look for nuclear weapons in countries such as Iraq or Iran, in the places where there are no nuclear weapons, while Americans are not interested in looking for them in Israel, where they actually could be found. It is almost a funny thing that Jews themselves invented these horrible weapons, while blaming others. This Jewish scientist was calling Muslims dangerous people who were interested in building a nuclear weapons arsenal, while the bomb itself was their own, Jewish-made invention. Were not most of the scientists who developed tha A-bomb Jewish?

The physicist said that he and other American scientists attended international conventions of nuclear physicists, where he met his Soviet counterparts. According to him, the U.S military authorities were very negative about seeing them attend these forums. They were afraid that the Russians would learn U.S. A-bomb secrets through them. Then, he proudly related how he managed to reassure the American military authorities not to be afraid. He reassured them by saying that rather than giving away their secrets, he will get their secrets from the Russians. But as much as I know, the Soviets were cleverer than that, since they never sent the actual scientists to such scientific forums, but rather their impersonators, their doubles, KGB agents. It was against the Soviet regulations to allow Russian nuclear scientists to travel abroad. As usual, the KGB sent their agents to these conventions, who were trained to some extent in physics so it would be easier for them to convince the Western scientists that they were the real people. The agents took the names of famous Russian nuclear scientists, and helped the Soviets, in this way, to get the useful secret information. The KGB, much later, boasted how they helped Soviet nuclear programs, after extracting U.S. nuclear secrets from naïve American scientists.

Recently on Russian television, I saw a Jew who is currently the head of the Russian nuclear center. He was shedding tears about the fall of the Soviet regime. He said that the regime was very generous in its support of the center, while today the Kremlin disregards the needs of the nuclear scientists.

I remember also Andrei Sakharov – "the father of the Soviet hydrogen bomb." To my knowledge, this man also may have been a Jew. I heard on Soviet TV that his previous surname was Zuckerman, though some people dismiss it as slanderous. He received many awards for his contribution to the Soviet nuclear program. Later, he decided to declare himself as a fighter against the nuclear arms race and received the Nobel Peace Prize for this. But why then did he invent this bomb in the first place? Why didn't he use his scientific talent to produce something useful for people?

I remember how Sakharov wrote an open letter to Leonid Brezhnev, as if in opposition to the persecution of believers in the Soviet Union. In this letter he was saying that religion is a nonsense idea, a useless superstition, and called religious people humans with a feeble mind. He tried to defend religious people before the atheist regime by saying that the oppression of religion is a waste of time and resources, since he believed that this superstition in this scientific age would not survive for longer than twenty years. Fifteen years later Sakharov died. Thus now we can say that the nuclear physicist who predicted the end of religion and faith is himself dead, while religion will survive.

Today, in the Western countries and in Israel, they have started to use bizarre and ridiculous terms like "Muslim fascism," "Islamic fascism," and "Islamofascism." Nowadays, these completely misleading concepts are widely used in the Western circles holding a hostile attitude toward Islam and Muslims. Undeterred by the fact that these terms are considered offensive by Muslims, they are still adopted by many Jewish and Christian authors and newsmen, as well as by the American Christian Zionists. The term "Islamofacism" was even included in the *New Oxford American Dictionary,* defining it as "a controversial term equating some modern Islamic movements with the European fascist movements of the early 20th century."

As I see it, Christians and Jews who are using such pejorative terms against Islam and Muslims, act according to the theorem that the best defense is offense. By claiming that Muslims aim to destroy the Western world they want to cover up their own militarist, imperialistic, neocolonialist policies toward the Muslim world. As they call the Muslims names, in return I could call them names. I can coin here a new term – *Eurofascism*. I will define *Eurofascism* as – the hostility of the representatives of the European race towards Muslims as a religious, ethnic, or racial group.

Racism has always been present in Western countries and cultures. National chauvinism – doctrines based on a belief in the inherent superiority of the white race over other races, theories and policies that the white race should be supreme, should be a master race – are very typical to the psyche of all Christian nationalities of Europe. Europe is populated by fair-skinned people. By belonging to a white race, they assume that it is the God-given duty of this race to manage the affairs of the less developed non-white people, of the colored people. The birthplace of Fascism is Europe. In world history, the first Fascist governments came to power in Europe, initially in Italy, then in Germany, Spain, Portugal, Romania and so on; at the same time, Jews cherish the idea that they are the "chosen people," racially superior to others, they believe in Jewish predominance.

Contrary to this, the Islamic religion does not recognize racist theories; it rejects the idea of racial superiority and inferiority of ethnic groups. In Muslim countries, there are no Fascist movements or parties. To my knowledge, in the Arab world there exists just one far right nationalist movement, the Falange party. Ironically, this is a party of Lebanese Arab Christians.

It was the European mind that fostered such ideas as racial superiority, xenophobia, national chauvinism, the Aryan race, the Inquisition, pogrom, anti-Semitism, ethnic cleansing, apartheid, Zionism, Communism, Fascism, concentration camps, racial segregation, Francophobia, Anglophobia, and genocide.

By the way, I want to mention here the fact that Swedes are considered the most racist people on the continent. Some twenty years ago the Swedish government forcibly sterilized its entire Gypsy population. Swedes justified their actions by stating that gypsies are a useless, antisocial ethnic group, and they should be totally eliminated as a race.

No matter how strange it might sound, during World War II some pragmatic Muslims regarded the marching German army as the liberating force which could put an end to the occupation of their lands by the Western and the Eastern Christian imperialist powers.

It seems that Adolf Hitler was not as fanatical a leader as his detractors described him. During the war, he acted very diplomatically toward the Muslim world. Hitler, of cause, with his political ideology of dividing nations as racially superior and inferior, was not very fond of Muslims as the representatives of Asian and African races, but still he understood that they, as allies, could be useful to Germany in the fight against Britain and France, these great colonial powers, as well as against Marxist Russia.

To put the final touch to the picture, I would say that the Zionist circles have hugely benefited from the inherent racist sentiments and instincts of the Westerners, of the white men. By skillful manipulation, they made it serve their interests, achieve their own goals, and harm and damage Muslims and Islam.

Modern Western policy wishes to see the world divided in two parts: on one side, the masters, and on the other, the servants. They want to see the Western world as prosperous, blooming, successful, and fortunate, while the East and the South as another world, which would be economically underdeveloped, poor, wretched, and unfortunate. They want to build the prosperity of the West on the misery of the rest of the world. By employing religious slogans they are trying to play on the Christian sentiments of the people, to cover up the real causes, the real motivations, that stand behind these slogans. Today, various Western Christian preachers, the representatives of the Church, and even the secular leaders of the Western world are making anti-Muslim pronouncements, while using Christian religious rhetoric, pretending that they are standing in the defense of Faith. They interpret the Christian Holy Scriptures according to the current political trends, which proves them to be merely lackeys and servants of imperialism and Zionism. Today, the Church is subservient to the atheistic Western Establishment. Modern clerics of the Church consider this institution to be a business, a profit-making organization, rather than being interested in the strengthening of the spirituality of the congregation. They are after the contents of the pockets of believers, rather than their souls.

It seems that the Jews, the people that lost its way, are moving to Hell, but along with them, they are driving the flock of Christians there.

God Almighty and Glorious, has said: "And they say: None shall enter the garden (or paradise) except he who is a Jew or a Christian. These are their vain desires. Say: Bring your proof if you are truthful" (Koran, 2:111).

CHAPTER EIGHT:
WHY THE BBC HATES CHRISTMAS?

After several years of watching British television, I concluded that it hates religion, since it is obvious that its programming policy is definitely anti-clerical, has an anti-religious orientation, and serves immorality. A TV viewer has no chance of seeing a single religious feature film in the stretch of ten years. But if you ask them about it, the directors of British channels would deny it firmly. But one day I managed to catch them red-handed.

It was on Christmas day of 1997. On this holy day for all Christians, BBC 1 had a film scheduled to be shown that evening with the title – *Why I Hate Christmas?* Of course, this film was merely a comedy with contents that bore no malevolent intent toward the Christian faith.

Modern Western society, with its consumerist attitudes, tends to misuse all religious ideas to suit its materialistic requirements and tastes. The Roman Pope protested many times about the exploitation of this Christian holy day in the West for its own materialistic, consumerist purposes, while emptying it of its religious contents and meaning. However, unfortunately there is very little that he can do about it.

There was another film scheduled for that evening on BBC 2. It was a French film about the persecution of the Huguenots in sixteenth-century France. The film depicted the tragic events of the civil unrest and hostility that took place in that country between two Christian sects. The objective of the filmmakers was to produce in the audience a negative image of religion in general, and of the Catholic Church in particular. Definitely, it was the most violent film shown on British television in its entire history. It described, in an extremely naturalistic way, mass killings, tortures, executions, assassinations, gang rapes, etc. All this was portrayed in the most graphic, brutal fashion ever seen on TV screens.

While this particular instance of scheduling can serve as documental evidence and proof of ill intent, the regular programming policy also, on a regular basis, demonstrates the malicious, venomous attitude that the directors of the channel bear toward people's beliefs. The very timing of the airing of this film on Christmas day is indicative of the inherent hostility of the TV establishment toward believers. They do not care for the feelings of Christian viewers, for their religious sentiments. Their pathological hatred of religion kept them from showing any restraint, and they chose to insult Christians on the very day of religious festivity. They show, year-round, films, features, and programs of an immoral, unethical, and corrupt nature, full of obscenities; as if this is not enough, they cannot help but humiliate and abuse the Christian religious audience on their own national television on the most holy, sacred day of the calendar. What other proof is necessary to demonstrate the obvious, anti-clerical bias of these people?

British Channel Four is considered a channel with the most liberal attitudes towards sex, and especially to sexual abuses, with little moral or decency scruples. The channel has special days devoted to advertising homosexuality and drug use. They call it the "twenty-four-hour homosexuality marathon" or the "twenty-four-hour drug marathon." Thus, on one day, the channel had an around-the-clock demonstration of programs entirely devoted to promoting the gay lifestyle in society. On another day, it promoted, for twenty-four hours, features advocating the legalization of drugs.

But these types of programs and shows are not just the preserve of Channel 4. Other channels are doing the same. Every day on various British channels, you can find programs or films dedicated to the propaganda of the abnormal sexual practice of gay males and lesbian females.

The TV bosses defend themselves by claiming that they are merely trying to suit the viewers, trying to serve the tastes of the British audience by showing what they want to see. But to my mind, rather than serving the interests of the people, they are trying to form and mold their minds according to their own – the TV director's – immoral and atheistic agenda.

As I clarified in the previous chapter, there exists in the West an anti-religious lobby that is made up of Zionists, which has put deep roots into its establishment. And Jews are biased against religion because they want to live in a world which is free of religion, in a society without religious confessions, in which they could be equal, and not any longer an alien minority.

At that time, I made an enquiry and found out that all five British terrestrial channels have Jews as their top executives – all five of them! There were letters sent by viewers asking about reasons for the massive presence of Jews among the personnel of British television. A TV personality tried to deny it, and in a feeble attempt to explain it said that actually only a minority of the staff were Jewish. To which it could be said that if the managerial staff is made up of Jews, as is the case, then that is quite enough to describe British television as Jewish, as Zionist-controlled.

Chapter Eight: Why the BBC Hates Christmas?

These Jewish television executives usually deny their immoral attitude and anti-religious agenda, defending themselves by saying that they do not show any pornographic films. To which I could say that it was the children's and teenagers' programs and shows that I found the most offensive and harmful. Don't they continuously produce various children's shows that advertise promiscuity for eleven to fifteen year olds? I think that watching these shows is much more harmful than watching porn films.

British TV executives try to make us believe that their policies are to keep TV screens free of pornography, while wickedly producing shows with much more harmful and obscene contents than pornography itself. Hence, the British Zionist TV establishment attempts to shape the minds of the British audience, starting from an early stage, according to their own requirements, to lead them away from religious values, ultimately to keep them away from the Church with its uniting, organizing function.

Look what happened on a talk show. This show outwardly appeared very decent and nice. A TV talk show hostess, a Jewess, invited children and teenagers to her program who had decided to follow the latest American trend of setting up teenage abstinence groups. These groups make vows to abstain from having sex until they grow up and get married in a religious ceremony, in accordance with Christian mores. But it was not something that this Zionist woman, the talk show hostess, could stomach or accept. Thus she used all her adult intelligence and cunning to persuade these kids to change their minds, to break their abstinence vows to suit her Zionist agenda.

She used this kind of "logic" to persuade these youth to immorality. She said, "Let's say that in case you marry a virgin and consummate your relationship with her on your wedding night, won't she become thereafter a woman who is no linger a virgin?"

"That's true," a youth answered.

"So after this night she will no longer be a virgin and no longer good enough for you to have sex with."

"That's true. In that case she would no longer be a virgin, no longer a good woman. Now I understand how foolish this idea is. Now I will abandon this abstinence group membership. Now I see how silly it is."

This shameless middle-aged woman, by taking advantage of the naivety and mental infirmness of a child, tried to persuade him to start having sex at his age, before marriage. This thing, which I would describe as a criminal activity, was done in front of millions of the British TV audience.

I read about a case of a children's book produced by the British Ministry of Education, which appeared to promote homosexuality, to enforce and to impress this abnormality on the weak, childish mind. The picture book told a story of a kindergarten boy who came upon the scene of his father fondling of another man that was sitting in his lap:

"Who is this man, daddy?"

"It is my lover, my boy."

"But, daddy, he is a man, not a woman. How can he be your lover?" the child asked.

"You are wrong, my boy. Some men can love women, but some others can love men; they are both right."

Thus the ministry which made this publication justified itself by saying that it didn't want children to be traumatized by being raised in an abnormal atmosphere where they are made to think that only heterosexual love is the normal thing. They stated that a child should make a choice himself, and that society has no right to impose on children their ultimate value system. They stated that children should be allowed to experiment, to find for themselves what kind of sexual orientation suits them.

It is obvious to me that through the lips of these people, the Zionist atheistic lobby, Satan is speaking. They are trying to bring equality between right and wrong, normalcy and abnormality, health and disease. They hate to see parents raise their children according to their own religious beliefs, to have them grow up as Christians, Muslims, or Hindus. They want to take the parenting into their own hands and, ultimately, to raise immoral degenerates who will no longer be a part of any religious confession.

Some naïve readers could say that this is merely the work of a strong gay lobby in England, not of Zionists. But this is not a correct assumption. In reality, gay people in the West have powerful Zionist patrons to support them. Without this support, gay people could not achieve anything.

Mass media persuades the British to think that they, by being tolerant to homosexuality and other queer sexual practices, are a progressive people, that theirs is an advanced society. But to my mind a society that promotes abnormal sex is not advanced in any way, but is the unhealthy one – a degrading society. They want us to believe that their concern is for potentially gay young people who could be traumatized by the straight society mores that accept only heterosexual practices as standard and conventional. But it seems that they have no concern for the healthy

Chapter Eight: Why the BBC Hates Christmas? 167

normal youth that could be traumatized by being introduced to experiment in abnormal sexual practices. Is not homosexual activity something fruitless and therefore meaningless? On the contrary, heterosexual sex does facilitate the procreation and continuation of the race. Is not normal sex the foundation of family and society? Thus heterosexual sexual union was God's intention and is the norm for humans, while homosexual individuals are nature's mistakes and errors.

They can ask, "How can God make mistakes?" Homosexuality is something common to humans rather than to animals, to the animal world. Thus, in my opinion, because of the complexity of the human psyche and mind, it is much easier for nature to make mistakes in the production of humans. Therefore, nature's blunders and miscalculations happen, and it gives birth to individuals with homosexual orientation, confused types, males and females with a confused gender identity. But religious books, the holy books are guides given to people to take the right orientation – to health and normalcy.

I remember another bizarre case of an English gay schoolteacher who could not be persuaded to follow the school curriculum and take students to the theatre to watch Shakespeare's *Romeo and Juliet* play, because, according to her, it depicts heterosexual love in an unbalanced way. In her opinion, the playwright should have balanced the story with the scenes of gay love. Despite the protests of parents, the Ministry of Education was not able to do anything about this eccentric teacher.

It is noteworthy to say that in Muslim countries there are no gay rights activists, because there are no Zionist patrons to support them. In this part of the world the gay lifestyle is forced underground, where it should stay, by society and by the requirements of Islamic religious law.

A Christian author, Nikolai Berdyaev, wrote a clever book about the inequality of everything in life and in nature, as he tried to argue philosophically the laws of nature and the universe. He rejected the Western ideas of liberty, equality, fraternity, and democracy as not normal, as going in contradiction with God's dictum.

Here is one of Mulla Nasrudin's anecdotes:

Nasrudin once came upon three men arguing loudly. As they noticed him, they said, "Mulla, you are a godly man. Will you please help us to divide these walnuts among us justly?"

"Can you explain to me what is your problem?" Nasrudin said.

"We put together our money and bought a hundred walnuts. Now we have a difficulty in dividing it."

"All right, I will help you. But you must tell me what kind of justice you prefer, God's justice or Nasrudin's justice?"

"We want God's justice, certainly, since God's justice would be more just than yours."

"All right," said Nasrudin. He took the nuts and divided them like this – he gave one man eighty nuts, another man he gave twenty, and to the third man he gave nothing.

The third man started to protest loudly. He said, "What kind of justice is this? To this man you gave eighty and to this man twenty, and to me nothing at all. Is this God's justice?"

"Yes," said Nasrudin, "that is what I call dividing according to God's justice. Don't you see how wealth is distributed among people in the world? One is very rich; another has nothing at all. So, I divided the nuts as you wished in a godly fashion. But if you want I can divide them equally and it will be Nasrudin's justice."

Then Nasrudin divided nuts anew. He gave each man twenty-five walnuts and took himself twenty-five as fees for his judgment. The men accepted this division.

To put it in other words, it can be said that God did not create people and things as equal to each other. There are different creatures and people; some are low, and some are higher. The story tells us that inequality is an essential quality of nature.

All that was said in this chapter allows us to come to the logical conclusion that the Zionist circles endeavor to destroy humankind's spirituality with their anti-religious, godless propaganda. They discovered that indirect attacks on the belief systems could be more fruitful. Since public morals, morality laws, are closely related to religion, originating in religion, their major assault is on ethical values, moral values, and human virtues. They assume, very correctly, that by destroying morality they can destroy customs, traditions, and ultimately – religions. You can take into consideration films, novels, or the contents of television shows and you will see that the Zionist controlled mass media, book publishers, and filmmakers are charging at the religious commandments:

Thou shalt have no other gods before me.

Thou shalt not make unto thee any graven image.

Thou shalt not take the name of the Lord thy God in vain.

Remember the Sabbath day, to keep it holy.

Chapter Eight: Why the BBC Hates Christmas? 169

Honor thy father and thy mother.

Thou shalt not kill.

Thou shalt not commit adultery.

Thou shalt not steal.

Thou shalt not bear false witness against thy neighbor.

Thou shalt not covet thy neighbor's wife.

Zionists want us to believe that these religious commandments have no value anymore and have to be made obsolete. Hence, television around the clock is going to promote sexual promiscuity, gambling, greed, violence, corruption, and other kinds of vices. Similarly, Jews stole the human rights issue, and are going to use it to promote their own agenda. As religion says no to suicide, the Zionist lobby is going to promote euthanasia. Religion says that humans are not equal to beasts, while the Zionist lobby is going to support animal rights groups with their silly ideas about the equality of the rights of humans and animals. Religion is saying no to gambling, while they are going to popularize all forms of gambling. Religion wants to see the woman at home tending her children, but this Jewish lobby is going to promote feminism, career women, "liberated women," and so on. Religion stands firm on the necessity of capital punishment, while the Zionist lobby is going to advocate the opposite. It must be understood that all these human rights organizations are not unconnected entities, but coordinated bodies that are directed and supervised from the same center. Their ideology and creed is formed by precepts of the sages of Zionism.

In our modern age, there was Hitler's totalitarian propaganda machine. However, with the fall of the Third Reich, its propaganda machine was destroyed, and it was gone. Then, there was the Communist totalitarian propaganda and brainwashing machine. But with the fall of Communism its propaganda machine also vanished. Thus it appears that the world is now free of all totalitarian propaganda specters. To the contrary, there is another totalitarian propaganda machine, with a network that encircles the planet and which is much more technologically sophisticated than its previous variants. Thus the West, with its advanced technological capabilities, introduced to the world a network of broadcasting propaganda structures. While the bases of the former totalitarian propaganda were Fascism and Communism, the ideological base of the Western totalitarian propaganda is Zionism. The British Broadcasting Corporation is the best example of this modern totalitarian propaganda machine. Perhaps, it would be more appropriate to call it the "Zionist Broadcasting Corporation."

Let us take the case of Salman Rushdie. He wrote a book in which he spoke sacrilegious and defamatory things about the Muslim religion. By this he immediately became the darling, the hero, of the Zionist mass media. This forced Ayatollah Ruhollah Khomeini (may his soul rest in peace), the imam or religious leader of Iran, to exercise his religious duty and to issue a *fatwa*, a religious edict to Muslims, to execute the person that defamed the sanctity of Islam. This decree had merely symbolic significance; it was the legal opinion of a theologian, rather than a call for direct action. All this brought about an ideological war between the Muslim world on one side and the Zionist mass media on the other. Zionists put Salman Rushdie on a banner and charged on Islamic Iran, calling for the reinforcement of Western, mostly American, economic sanctions against this country. They call themselves the advocates of the freedom of speech, but they never will allow any authoritative representative of Islam to come on television to express his religious point of view. They claim that they are concerned about the life and well-being of this single person, but they do not care for the welfare of the tens of millions citizens of this Muslim country affected by the economic blockades. No, they do not care for freedom of speech; they do not care for human rights. All that they care for is the glory of the Zionist dream of world domination.

If you ask an average Englishman whether there is censorship in Britain, he will answer, with conviction, negatively. In the West, people are made to think that they are living in a free society in which there can be no censorship center authorized to examine printed material, radio, and television. It is wrong. If we take British television as an example, we will see that it has its censor's bureau. But in England they call it differently. It is called the Independent Television Commission. And this institution conducts the censorship of the ideological content of television channels.

Unlike other countries, in Britain they charge the citizens fees for watching television. This is done mainly to support the BBC, which does not use commercials, and so is reliant on subscription money. I read somewhere that the BBC's yearly turnover is three billion pounds. Thus one can see how much money it spends yearly on propaganda. How can other countries, especially the Third World countries, compete with this huge propaganda machine?

Other British TV channels are expensive as well. They are worth hundreds of millions of pounds. Television is big business, and the people who work there – besides having prestigious jobs – are earning a lot of money. But the destiny and fortunes of these people are dependent on the Independent Television Commission, which issues a license, permission to run a TV channel, and it can be withdrawn any minute. One can imagine

Chapter Eight: Why the BBC Hates Christmas? 171

how the TV broadcasters are terrified to do anything contrary to the conditions and demands of the Commission!

Simply by watching television one can get knowledge about its workings. I am not an outgoing person and prefer to know what is going on in the outside world, in society, by watching the box. The Soviet Union held the sixth part of the world and it was almost a continent, a very complex multinational society. Britain, on the other hand, is a very simple and easy place to understand. One can know Britain after living in this country for several months. Therefore, very soon, I understood the workings of the British TV. I noticed that the news footage on all five terrestrial channels is identical. But how can this be if they are considered to be businesses independent from each other, while every channel has its own camera crew, its own news reporters?

Even the home news footage made on London's streets is identical, despite the fact that you can see on the footage the presence of cameramen from other channels as well. Even more so, when I compared the news texts I noticed that the wording and comments were absolutely identical. Thus there can be no other explanation to it, but that the footage of the news bulletins and their commentaries passed through a certain censorship center before it was approved to go on the air. Hence, the ITC is the British censor's bureau that controls the contents of all the news bulletins – both visual contents and texts – to give the British public just one version of events, approved by the authorities, to manipulate the minds of the TV audience.

But why it is so important to use the same footage? A professional cameraman knows that the camera angles and position are very important. When an event is filmed from different angles or camera positions, it produces assorted impressions on the viewer and gives another version of event. I remember something that I heard from a Russian TV cameraman, who said that the Soviet authorities demanded all cameramen to follow the official rules for camera positions while filming Leonid Brezhnev. It was allowed to film him only from one side, the side on which he was most photogenic. Thus the ITC demands from the TV broadcasters to provide just one version of the news, which was initially authorized by them, or otherwise to go out of business.

I read in the newspapers about the cases of dismissals of the directors of several TV programs. They lost favor with the Commission, which insisted that they be removed from their posts, and the TV channels obeyed the orders.

Once, the British Customs reported that they found two hundred dead cockroaches in a parcel sent from Latin America to a private collector. These insects were probably a rare species. All five national TV channels broadcasted this report as the major news item. For many times during the day and until the next morning, they offered this news as the number one issue of the day. But how can this insignificant subject make the heads of the news departments of different channels decide, unanimously, to choose it as the major news item? Even the British love for animals cannot explain this, since these were insects – they do not bark or mew. The only sensible explanation is that there must be censors, a center which advises the broadcasters on the contents of news bulletins, what should be made the news of the day, or else, what information should be kept off the screens. I know about several wars that took place in various parts of the world with huge losses of life, which were never reported by the British news broadcasters. Thus the British censors, now and then, suppress various unwanted information from reaching the TV audience, hence feeding the people with disinformation.

The events of September 11 in New York brought about a period of several months when the BBC World Service radio started to transmit, unrestrictedly, hostile anti-Muslim programs. They interrupted the normal diversity of programming and replaced it completely by bilious, anti-Islamic propaganda. Thus the Corporation shed all its masks, disguises, and clearly demonstrated its true Zionist face. Their propaganda was so venomous and ludicrous that it forced me to stop listening to this station altogether. There was no longer a pretense of balanced opinion or sophistication, but the station reduced itself to the dumbest brainwashing of Yellow Press journalism. The reason for all this was in an urgent and most pressing matter – Zionist Israel is arriving, steadily, to its finish and it requires their brotherly help. After all, blood is thicker than water.

There was a time when I was considering my chances to set up an Islamic TV channel in Britain. I made inquiries to find out how realistic this idea was. Soon I read about a case of a Christian channel. The report disclosed that the ITC considered an application from a South African couple to set up a Christian satellite channel and, consequently, issued them with a license. The couple paid twenty-five thousand pounds as the license fees and soon put the channel to work. The strangeness of this case was in the known fact that this husband and wife were heroin addicts for twenty years. Probably, this fact made them, in the eyes of authorities, very appropriate types to run a religious channel!

Chapter Eight: Why the BBC Hates Christmas? 173

In my opinion, this couple was recruited by the British secret services, by its Zionist directors, to start a Christian station so it would be under their constant control and allow them to block the way to any true religious groups, the independent people. The ITC, henceforth, will get an excuse to turn down all other applications for a Christian channel, by arguing that there is no need for a second Christian channel. Similarly, if a Muslim group would apply for permission to start an Islamic TV channel, they will deny them permission by saying that a Muslim station already functions, the Ahmadiyya TV station. But this is a pseudo-Islamic sect, a harmful cult! To which they will answer, we are not specialists in religious matters; to us they are Muslims if they describe themselves as such. Thus the true Muslim people will be denied a license, while the Ahmadiyya sect, a child of the British intelligence agency, will continue their work in spreading their heresy to bring discord and confusion to people's minds.

I remember how, with the arrival of Gorbachev and his reforms, Soviet television was allowed to introduce short religious programs. What they did was invite to the TV studios different bohemian crowds – artists, sculptors, ballerinas, dancers etc., to discuss spirituality and faith and to read imitations of sermons. Today, mass media makes people see bohemian personalities as the heroes of our times. They are described as very intelligent individuals and, as a criterion, were usually brought on because of their financial success, their profits. Thus today in the West, one's intelligence is judged by the amount of money in one's bank account. But this kind of mercantile attitude was introduced to the world just recently. Previously, at all times, bohemians were nobodies; they were regarded as people of little intellect. They were considered immoral types who disregard the conventional standards of behavior.

It is obvious that by inviting this kind of people on television, the atheistic establishment prescribed religion to the Soviet audience, but in very limited quantities, drop by drop, or not at all. They were afraid to give the matters of faith to people to whom religion really belongs, to the clergymen, who are really qualified to read sermons, to discuss morality and religion. As I see it, the Jewish advisers of Gorbachev were afraid, unwilling to give religion real freedom, since it could ultimately bring about the demise of their control in the country. At that reformist period, the authorities felt very uncomfortable about the possibility of the arrival of celebrities of a new kind, of popular preachers with true religious credentials. Thus they merely tried to produce an appearance of religious freedom, rather than being interested in seeing a massive spiritual revival in society.

Today religion still makes its way onto television with difficulty in all former Soviet republics. A minute amount of spirituality here and there makes no difference to the overall immoral, materialistic, and corrupt contents of the box. Therefore, ten or twenty minutes per week of Christian programs on Russian national channels cannot make much difference to its otherwise pornographic contents.

Once in Nice I met a nice, well-educated, ethnic Frenchman. Soon I found out that he was a Muslim convert. Before this, I read statistical reports about the existence in France of a large group of Islamic converts. I was interested to see him explain himself, to find out his motives for changing his religion. Many Muslims consider themselves as such only because of their birth to Muslim parents. But converts are usually highly motivated people. This man also was like this. He told me about his problems as a Muslim in France. He was homeless, unemployed, and without any money. Besides, he was forced by the circumstances to live separately from his wife, who was an African Muslim. He told me that his brother was also an Islamic convert, an important Muslim scholar who worked in an Iranian university. He related to me his story, of his difficulties and problems with the French education authorities, which would not allow him to work as a teacher. He said, "Teaching is my only skill, but they will not allow me to practice this profession, as I am a Muslim."

The French law, or as they practice it, is fiercely secularist, and the authorities are especially biased against Islam and Muslims.

"But," he said, "I will continue my fight; I will continue to bombard the ministry with my plea letters, to make them allow me to work as a teacher."

The reason why I brought my memories up here is in his religious reflections about the Antichrist – or, according to Muslims, Dajal.

"I had a long meditation about Dajal and his appearance on the earth," he said. "At the end, I came to the conclusion that he will come into view on television. I see that television will be the media through which he will address the world."

His English was far from perfect; hence I could not learn from him what he meant; whether, he meant to say that television is a devilish design, or if its contents are Satanic, or he meant the physical, bodily manifestation of Dajal, the Antichrist, on the TV screens to address the humanity, to read his proclamation.

Chapter Eight: Why the BBC Hates Christmas?

But, today, I clearly see how television in the East and in the West is monopolized by Jews, where Satan appears daily, while wrapping himself in an Israeli, Zionist flag, to do his devilish murmurings. Nevertheless, even the great symbol on the flag known by the name of the *Seal of Solomon* would not deceive the people, would not protect him, nor would allow him to preserve his disguise. The Jews, of whom a large proportion are atheists, are proud of themselves; they like to describe themselves as the cleverest race, as superior and the most successful people. But by God, how can an atheist be a clever or superior person, or be described as a successful person?

The domination and rule of an atheistic people, by a people of ignoramuses, is the worst kind of oppression. How can atheistic justice and law be just? How can religious law be inhumane, oppressive or unjust; likewise the commandments that He decreed, since God is the Merciful and Compassionate? I hope that there will come a time when religion and faith will regain its lost position in the world and society, when the holy laws will rule once more and prevail everywhere.

Recently, on Russian television a Brazilian soap opera was shown. Many millions watched this expensive, lavish production. Unfortunately, they were hardly aware that by entertaining themselves with this serial, they subjected themselves to intense Zionist brainwashing. Thus even in a distant country like Brazil, the film industry fell under the control of Jews, of the local Diaspora. But unlike this simple-minded majority of TV viewers, a clever person could benefit from the serial by getting a full and detailed study of evil, wicked Jew-Masonic ideology. Actually, this Latin American soap opera was a virtual encyclopedia of Zionism.

The film was based on a story about a prostitute. Her disreputable profession allowed her and her mother, father, and child to live a comfortable life. Jewish producers of this serial worked over every detail in this well-thought up, sophisticated, and expensive production that was made to serve their own ethnic interests. However, the TV audience, in the majority, was heedless; they never perceived the vile intent of the filmmakers.

In this fictitious story, a prostitute was described as a positive character and placed in opposition to a moral, respectable, married woman who, on the contrary, was depicted as a negative character. The plot was designed so that the married woman gets to have an unfortunate life, as her husband prefers this high-class prostitute, who in the end achieves success and happiness and finds a loving man. The storyline was made to persuade many millions of Christians on the both side of the Atlantic, that Christian mores, moral values, are silly and ridiculous, that they are no longer relevant to modern man and society. Sadly, modern Christians and Muslims are subjected daily to similar films produced by numerous agents of Satan, who are feeding an unwitting audience with this poisonous medicine. V. I. Lenin described cinema as a tremendously powerful means of propaganda that should be used as an effective instrument to fight the religious sentiments of the masses.

We, good Muslims, God-abiding people, should put before ourselves the noble task of disarming the modern-day satanic powers, by boycotting Hollywood, and not watching its malevolent film productions.

Recently, a Russian national TV channel held a discussion among local intellectuals. A movie industry celebrity, who worked for some time in Hollywood, pronounced that he wanted to see the Christian world, Europeans, the civilized world, unite and defend itself against the threat coming from the Islamic world. He continued by suggesting that Russia should join other European countries and the United States in this fight. Then he finished with the remark that Russia was a key country to assist the West in finishing with the Islamic threat. It seems to me that this man was not a Jew, but still it could have been that he was a half-Jew. In one way or another, it is obvious that by this fervent defense of Zionist propaganda arguments he was seeking the favors of Hollywood and its Jewish establishment. All his assertions were nothing but mythology, fables that Zionist propaganda wordsmiths manufacture to feed the Western populace. First, today, there is no longer a Christian world, nor does there exist an Islamic world. In the modern age, the Christian states, as well as the Muslim states, are governed by anti-religious regimes. Therefore, describing them as Christian or Islamic was meant to disorient people. More than this, in reality, today, the Jews rule the Christian world. Thus these kinds of definitions are merely Zionist propaganda ploys. Second, they are trying to misuse the religious sentiments of people by mixing them with fundamentally unreligious ideas like nationalism, racism, and tribalism. Hence, when this film director said, "we should stand for European civilization," it is nothing but slightly disguised racism. What he meant to say was that we Westerners and Europeans – the Nordic races – are civilized, unlike those Asians, those barbarous, backward Muslims. He meant to say that his was the superior, rational race and therefore, by higher birth, have a natural right to govern, to rule over Muslims who are an underdeveloped, inferior race.

I want to make a remark here that ever since Tsar Nicholas II abdicated in 1917, under pressure from the revolutionaries, Russians no longer had a true Russian government. Starting from those troublesome times and right up until today the country is ruled by Jews.

But the last statement of the film director, about Russia representing a key country to help the West to neutralize the Islamic threat, was an allusion to Iran, to this ultimate Islamic regime. Islamic Iran depends on Russia economically and militarily, so the strategic military coalition of Russia with the West could deprive Iran's economy and army of crucial Russian supplies, and would isolate it completely. Moreover, the collapse of Islamic rule in Iran would allow Zionists to celebrate their final victory over Muslims. Does not the existence of the Islamic Republic of Iran represent a threat to Zionist Israel? As I see it, the Iranian Islamic revolution – this truly Islamic government in this large Muslim country – brought to power an authentic Islamic rule which is Islamic both in form and in contents. The Iranian revolution from its birth served as an example to all Muslim nations to use its experience and to revolt against their tyrannical, ungodly rulers, to restore in their countries the Islamic statehood in its entire splendor.

The only group on earth that has a potential to change this modern status quo in the world are the Muslim people, as they have a ready-made ideological base to withstand and oppose the rival Zionist philosophies. Thus in case any Muslim nation chooses to establish the Sharia state, with a genuine Islamic leadership, it will make a new bastion, a new defense line in front of the armies of Evil.

Surely, the Western leaders by making declarations of war against Islam are attempting to produce the wrong impression, that it is a religious war, a Crusade of the Christian West against Muslims. But certainly, a thoughtful observer will classify all this precisely, properly, by describing it as a war between the Western satanic dark powers on the one side and Faith on the other.

Jews describe themselves as the "chosen people," as if God brought them to this world with a mission. But if this is the truth, then why are they doing all these satanic things? If they are really God's favored people, they should stand along with religion rather than fight against it. Instead it, they are trying to do everything to suit Satan in his efforts to lead humankind away from religion, to disobey God's decrees.

God Most High has said: "And they say: Our hearts are uncircumcised. Nay, Allah has cursed them on account of their unbelief; so little it is that they believe" (Koran, 2:88).

CHAPTER NINE:
BYZANTINE INTRIGUES

While reading history books written by European authors, I often came across a mention of the Young Turks movement. This nineteenth-century Turkish secret society created a sensation in the West, and got much publicity as they started their political activities, agitating the public to stand against the Ottoman imperial rule, demanding the abolition of the Islamic caliphate, to replace it with a new kind of state which would be westernized and oriented toward Europe.

As I studied the political program of this society I found it most perplexing; something that was very difficult to understand was why Turks were involved in this political plotting activity against their own state, demanding Turkish withdrawal from Arab lands. I wondered at first, that if these people were Turks, then why did they seek for the abolition of the vast Turkish Ottoman Empire so intensely? Second, if they were Muslims, then why were they against the caliphate, this Islamic super state, and wished to see the withdrawal of the Turkish Islamic army from Palestine, Mecca, and Medina?

Thus to me the intentions of the Young Turks were very obscure, confusing, and incomprehensible. Their mind, their ideas, seemed to me as illogical and irrational. Who was this political program supposed to serve? I was in the dark about their motivations. They acted as if they were trying hard to help the adversaries, the enemies of Turks and Muslims, and to help the Western imperial powers, who could benefit exceedingly from the collapse of the Ottoman state, which would allow them to invade and capture the lands abandoned by the caliphate's troops.

It was much later when I was in England, that I understood it, and managed to find an answer to this question. I met in London an Englishman who, as I understood, worked for the British intelligence agency, while holding a position at a Muslim charity, pretending that he was an Islamic convert. Besides this, he told me that he was very much interested in Sufi philosophy, that he considered himself a Sufi. At that time, I met several Englishmen who made similar claims, that they were Muslim converts, and that they were Sufis. I never trusted these men, and understood that they were working for the British spy agencies. I understood also why they, all like one, claimed themselves to be Sufis. I think that it was in the spy schools that their instructors advised them to

Chapter Nine: Byzantine Intrigues 179

take on the disguise of Sufis, as their pretensions to be Islamic converts would require them to pray five times a day and to perform other Muslim rituals, which would be tedious work for them, too much hard work for them to bear. Calling themselves Sufis would allow them to skip performing required Muslim praying, since it is thought that they are less formalistic and more liberal toward the observation of the traditional Islamic rituals.

This man received good training at his spy school, learned Arabic, and bore an Arab alias. His employers send him to far-away places like South Africa and Australia to collect information on Muslim organizations, to spy on Muslims. He was a very busy man.

I was able to get from him information which solved the puzzling question of the Young Turks. He said to me that his history professor, in a conversation, related to him that the membership of this society was mainly made up of the Jewish subjects of the Ottomans! This explained everything to me. Later, I learned that all the theoreticians and ideologists of the Young Turks, and of the Pan-Turkist movement as well, were Turkish Jews.

The Jewish community in Turkey has an interesting history. In the 15th century, when the Christian Church was still very powerful and influential, the King of Spain ordered all of the Jewish population to be deported from his kingdom. The Turkish sultan, when he heard about this news, sent an invitation to Jews to come and to settle on the Ottoman territories. While trying to justify his edict, he said that the Jews were resourceful people, and therefore, they would help the Ottomans to strengthen their state. Thus Jews moved to the regions which today are parts of the Turkish Republic and Greece.

A large part of these Jews abandoned their old faith, and declared themselves as people who accepted Islam. In Turkey they were brought under a category of the population called *donmeh*, which is "defectors." Despite the fact that they changed their names to Muslim names and described themselves as Muslims, still they remained faithful to their old religion, secretly observed their religious rites, and continued to consider themselves as the Judaic people.

Much later, the Jews, in gratitude to the Turks for their hospitality, set up secret societies with the intention of destroying the Islamic caliphate and putting an end to the Muslim control of Palestine, of Jerusalem (in Arabic – Al-Quds), which they eventually intended to capture for themselves to build there their own Jewish state. Thus the destruction of the six-hundred-year-old Ottoman state was to a large extent the consequence of a Jewish plot.

At the end of World War I, when Mustafa Kemal (Ataturk) came to power, he introduced revolutionary reforms, borrowing the ideology and political program of the Young Turks, of whom he was a major exponent. The Ottoman state was brought to its end, to its destruction, not by the Western victorious armies, but rather by Ataturk, who abolished it and terminated the Islamic caliphate. After finishing with Islamic rule, with Islamic statehood, he replaced it with a secular Turkish Republic, which he governed with a dictatorial rule for twenty long years, as he continuously uprooted all the vestiges of Islamic heritage.

He introduced in the country a reform program which was based on the infidel ideas of the Young Turks. His reforms attacked the spiritual and religious foundations of Muslim society on every level.

He replaced the Islamic code of law with a secular legal system based on the Swiss Civil Code.

The traditional dress of the Muslim population was forbidden. There were cases when Muslim males and females were beaten up on the streets by gendarmes and imprisoned just because they were wearing un-European clothes.

The Western atheistic model of education replaced the traditional Muslim schools.

The Muslim calendar was set aside and replaced by the Christian one.

Traditional Muslim names were forced to be substituted with new un-Islamic surnames.

The Arabic alphabet – the alphabet of the Koran – was concealed, and instead of it, the Christian Latin alphabet was adopted.

Classical Turkish music was restricted. Instead, the dictator forcibly demanded civil servants to attend the concerts of classical European music.

His goal was to Westernize and to de-Islamize Turks; after the completion of the secularization of Turkey, he conceived to spread this anti-Islamic model to the Turkic-speaking people of Russia and China.

Ataturk also introduced a bizarre kind of language reform. The traditional classical Turkic language of the Ottomans, spoken by the population for six hundred years, was abandoned for replacement with a new Europeanized language of modern Turkey. As is known, ninety

Chapter Nine: Byzantine Intrigues 181

percent of the vocabulary of all Turkic languages is made up of Arabic and Persian words. Therefore, a good education required a good command of Arabic and Persian, to allow speaking properly in any Turkic language. But this was something that this atheistic leader could not stomach. He wanted to draw Turks as far as possible away from these two classical Muslim languages, and, ultimately, away from Islam. For this reason, he had a department set up to deal with language reform. His goal was to destroy the classical Ottoman language. All educated and cultured classes, scientists, and linguists refused to join this bizarre reform program. Therefore, he filled this department with different poorly educated, but cooperative individuals, those who supported his reforms. Historians say that all the language reform professors of Ataturk were made up of non-Muslims, non-Turks, of Christians and Jews. These pseudo-linguists concealed the Arabic and Persian layers of the language and replaced them with words borrowed from French, German and Italian. Otherwise, they invented all-new words, claiming that they introduced these words to restore the pre-historic Turkic language of the heathens.

When the Latin script was introduced in the country, people with an excellent Islamic education lost their jobs and positions and since that time have lived a miserable life, as they were never able to master the unfamiliar Latin script. It was said that one professor, an ethnic Armenian, invented ten to fifteen, all-new, artificially made words every day, which were introduced to the Turkish vocabulary. Thus it can be said that the Jewish and Armenian professors of Ataturk invented the new un-Islamic language for Turks and forced them to speak this weird tongue. Because of this malevolent reform, the modern Turks do not know their classical Ottoman language, do not know their classical literature, their history, their Islamic heritage, cannot read nor understand it.

Once, a Turkish president complained to journalists that he preferred to read the British newspaper, *The Times,* rather than Turkish newspapers because he found their modern Turkish language incomprehensible.

Arabic and Persian to the Turkic group of languages are the same as Latin and Greek are to English. As it is known, English would not be the excellent and sophisticated language it is today without the words borrowed from these two classical languages. It would be a useless and primitive language. For the British it would be difficult to imagine that their head of state would issue a decree in which their English would be banned and replaced by a different language, by a language that is unknown and incomprehensible to the population. But this is what happened in Turkey, owing to this infidel Kemal Ataturk.

In modern Turkey the personality cult of Ataturk still exists, enforced by its atheistic establishment, as well as by its Zionist circles. Turkish historians under threat of imprisonment are not allowed to write the truth about this man, his private life, or to criticize him. Therefore, anybody who wants to find out the facts about his biography has to consult the works of foreign authors and researchers. Here I want to bring out some facts which I took from non-Turkish sources, from the works of solid historians.

Ataturk's childhood and youth was passed in Salonika, a city that was populated mostly by Jews. Right from his youth he lived a very immoral life-style and had a corrupt personality. He most loved and craved three kinds of establishments – a gambling house, a wine shop, and a bordello. He died of cirrhosis of the liver at age 57. People who knew him in his young years related that he used to spend most of his time being entertained in these places. Some say he contracted syphilis in a bordello, and during his entire life he suffered from this disease, which was the cause of death of V.I. Lenin.

No wonder that when he became the head of state his initial decrees were to legalize casino gambling, whorehouses, and alcoholic drinking places in Turkey – which were forbidden under the Ottomans. In short, he built himself a godless state in which he could live his wicked and corrupt life freely.

He fell in love with a European opera singer, who was his partner for some period. Once, she said to him that she hated living among Turks, and she would rather go to live in Europe. Ataturk said, "Do not go. Wait. You will see that soon Turks will be indistinguishable from Europeans; in a couple of years, I will make all Anatolian villagers learn to speak French." However, despite all his pleas, she left him for Europe.

An English historian made a research work, checked the British, French, and German state archives and found there the official reports of their ambassadors of those times informing their foreign offices about the situation in Turkish capital city, Ankara. The reports described the loose lifestyle of Ataturk. The reports stated that he suffered from insomnia and stayed awake all night. Therefore, his official residence, until morning, was used to entertain him and his friends. They gambled and had orgies with invited prostitutes.

Ataturk considered the Soviet dictators – Lenin and Stalin – as his friends. When he traveled to Russia, at a meeting with Stalin, Ataturk criticized his host, saying that he had suppressed the Islamic Arabic script in Turkey, so "Why do you not do the same in Russia?" At the time Muslims were still allowed to use the Arabic script in the Soviet Union.

Stalin said, "I don't want to do it by the use of force. If the Muslim population of the Soviet Union prefers to keep their Islamic script there is nothing that I can do about it."

Ataturk repeatedly urged Stalin not to be soft with the local Muslims, but to Europeanize their language and scripts as soon as possible by forceful means. Thus even the Soviet "butcher" Stalin was less dictatorial and aggressive toward Muslims than his Turkish counterpart.

He also demanded that Muslim priests abandon using the Koran in the sacred Arabic, and wanted to force them, instead, to utilize the Turkish language translations. He also demanded that, henceforth, the traditional Arab language calls from minarets must be read in Turkish, which was something unprecedented in Islamic history and tradition.

He ordered all traditional Islamic seminaries to be closed down and replaced them with European-style universities, with religious faculties in which government-appointed theologians were employed as professors. Thus, recently, the Grand Mufti of Turkey, to suit the secular government, announced shamelessly that the Sharia code of law was not obligatory for Muslims. With this kind of statement it is clear what kind of theologians Ataturk's Turkey is producing – pseudo-theologians who speak against the sacred laws of Allah, who advocate the amoral, godless, infidel code of law of the West instead.

In addition to all this, Ataturk banned the activities of all the Turkish Sufi brotherhoods and closed down their monasteries, forbidding them to conduct their work.

Western historians wondered what was behind his animosity toward everything that was Turkish and Islamic. By trying to understand his motivations, they made the logical assumption that he was not of Turkish decent, but was, perhaps, a Yezidi Kurd – a sect who worship Satan. The fact that he was born in Adana, a city in the south of Turkey, which is populated mostly by Kurdish people, supported their suspicions.

However, I do not think that this is true. His ethnic origin has nothing to do with his hostility toward everything Turkish and Islamic. The true explanation for Ataturk's pathological hatred toward religion was in his psychology, in his typological traits. There is a particular psychological type in whom the animal nature, the hedonistic instinct, is the dominant factor of the personality. This type is a natural born atheist, for whom religion and morality are barriers, obstacles to the fulfillment of the requirements of his hedonistic self. If such a kind of person is an ordinary man, his loose way of life would not affect the lives of the public much. But in the case of him coming into a leadership position, then he can harm the whole nation, even people who live in other countries. Thus his anti-Islamic reforms harmed not just Turks, but the entire Muslim world, since the Turkish Ottoman caliphs were both the secular and spiritual leaders of the Sunni Muslim world.

His Turkish chauvinism should not be understood as a sign of his love of the Turks, but was merely his malicious trickery intended to confuse Turkish Muslims, to play on their nationalist sentiments, while turning them away from Islam and making them lose their Islamic identity.

I can foresee that the day will come when Turks will come to their senses, will remove the remains of this tyrant, of this evil man, from his grandiose mausoleum in Ankara, and will put the secularist accomplishments of the Turkish Republic on the ash heap of history.

Nowadays, the pro-Western regime of Turkey continues to hold its traditional hostile policy toward its Muslim neighbors. In contrast to them, Turkey has a very warm relationship with the Zionist Israeli regime, the country that is at war with all its Muslim neighbors. It is evident that Turkey's army generals count their American superiors in NATO as their masters, and are always on the ready to replace, at any moment, any elected Turkish government not favorable to the United States, if orders arrive from abroad.

Many years ago I saw a picture in a German magazine taken in a Turkish night-club, which was very symbolic of the realities of Ataturk's Turkey of today. In this photo, U.S. soldiers from an American military base were sitting with their feet propped up on the side of a stage on which a fat Turkish woman, a striptease dancer, was performing her show. I saw in it a symbolic sign, a proof of what Kemal Ataturk achieved in Turkey, in realization of his dreams and goals to destroy all Islamic values, by turning the country into one big bordello, which shattered the pride and dignity of its believers.

I can bring up here something that I heard on Turkish radio some thirty years ago. It seems that in Turkey, the whorehouses are under the supervision of the Ministry of Sports and Recreation. Its minister was once approached by journalists who asked him, why in Turkey, unlike in other countries, prostitution is legal?

His answer was, "By the legalization of prostitution we achieved two objectives. First, we provided jobs to Turkish women. Second, we provided Turkish males with the opportunity to entertain themselves."

The chief Madame of the red-light district of Istanbul was an Armenian woman – Margarita Manukian. Once, she made an interesting public statement to journalists: "Turkish people should pray to their Allah for me, asking to prolong my life, since with my bordellos I am the biggest tax-payer in town."

I ask the reader just to think about it: once, Constantinople (Istanbul) was a major city of both Christianity and Islam, but today both religions there are under the siege of the followers of Ataturk, who stand in the service of Zionists, and ultimately in the service of Satan.

The realities of modern Turkey are so that gendarmes can make raids on citizens' houses, and if they find copies of the Koran or other religious literature, then the members of the household would be dragged to the police station for questioning. The next day, on a prosecutor's orders, the police would release them, since there is no law in the Turkish penal code prohibiting the possession of the holy books. By this kind of harassment, the authorities are trying to send a message to the populace to keep away from religion.

Very recently, the godless regime's government introduced a new law that Turkish civil servants' wives would not be allowed to wear headscarves covering their hair, with the object of fighting any religious leanings among their personnel. According to the regulations, in the case of their wives being seen in public wearing headscarves, their husbands would automatically lose their jobs.

I saw on Turkish television footage of a scene where a civil servant that recently lost his job approached his minister in sobs, begging him to reconsider his case. According to him he was a victim of slander, since his wife never covers her head.

It is interesting to know that when Ataturk came to power, he started a propaganda campaign in which he urged the Muslim people to turn their backs on Islam, as it was an alien faith, a religion of Arabs. He announced that Turks in the ancient times, as they roamed the Mongolian steppes, worshiped wolves. Thus according to Ataturk, Turks should worship wolves rather than God (Allah), and return to their pagan roots. The agitators of the regime continue to promote this bizarre campaign even today, long after the death of the dictator. More than this, they are trying to spread this idea to other Turkic-speaking Muslim nations to encourage them to move away from Islam.

Nowadays, some ethnically Jewish Turkish generals, when they hold speeches in front of their troops, often urge soldiers to keep distance from religion. Besides this, these generals, on a regular basis, talk abusively about Arabs, calling them a smelly, dirty ethnicity, and describe Islam as a religion of these smelly people.

It is interesting that all Turkish television stations prefer to employ blond presenters, who look un-Turkish, like the Northern Europeans. Once I saw a blonde talk show hostess of a Turkish TV channel say that only Europeans have culture, while Asians have no culture. I will not comment on this.

When I was in Istanbul as a tourist, I went to a bookshop to find out whether dervish circles still existed in town. The bookseller advised me to go to the Imperial Fatih Mosque, where he said lectures are regularly held on Sufism.

That evening the weather was very cold and damp, so at the last minute I decided against going there. The next day, I read in the newspapers that the previous evening, the police conducted the largest ever operation, involving not less than two thousand officers. They raided the mosque and arrested a number of theologians and believers who gathered there to listen to talks on religious matters. Several hundred people were brought to the police stations, but later most of them were released. This episode demonstrates very well that today in Turkey, believers are treated as criminals, as law-breakers. It is noteworthy to say that, while corruption and other criminality are endemic in the country, the police are harassing pious, God-fearing people.

I will note that the mosque is one of the most venerated by Turks, since it bears the name of the conqueror of Constantinople, Fatih Sultan Mehmet, and is the site of his mausoleum. This sultan, with a religious fervor, called on the Muslim troops to go and capture this city from the Christians, to realize the predictions of the Prophet (peace be on him) about the eventual fall and surrender of this greatest bastion of Christianity to Muslims. Thus the secular regime's police force committed this sacrilegious act in the country, where the majority of population is Muslim. To whom does modern Turkey belong?

It would be wrong to perceive the Turkish Republic as an independent state, as a free state. Actually, it is a colony, a "client state" of the West. Therefore, as I see it, the only possibility for the liberation of Turkish

Muslims is in an Islamic revolution. Then, the Islamic government would be a true guarantor, defender of the rights and interests of the Muslim majority, as well as the rights of other religious communities. The imperialist powers, the Western states are not friends, but enemies of Turkish Muslims. They want to see the Muslims forever remain as the most oppressed and poor community in the world. The Western policy is to do everything possible to keep Turkey an economically backward, weak state, with the population living in poverty and need, who will look to the Westerners as their benefactors, as their alms-givers. This Western policy toward Turkey was generated out of the fear that Turks may decide to return to their Islamic roots, to restore the lost position of Islam in this country and in the Muslim world. This prospect seemed to be the most unfavorable for the West, since Turkey with its huge human resources and economic potential could easily attain a leadership position in the Muslim world. Turkey, at all times, was one of the major powerbases of Islam. Hence, if Turkey is kept sterile of Islam, then the Muslim world will remain weak and impotent.

Recently, it became habitual for the Turkish journalists to ask their citizens questions like, "Aren't you afraid of Western influences, of the Western way of life and values spreading in our society?" And to others like, "Aren't you afraid that eventually the moral code of the Turks will be replaced by the Western one?"

I see in this hypocrisy, intended to confuse people, since there is no such thing as Turkish morality, Arab morality, English or French morality. Therefore, the journalists should put the questions differently, more accurately as, "Aren't you afraid of the spread of Western secularist values among Muslims?" Certainly, there is no morality besides religious morality. Indeed, all moral codes were introduced to the world by religions, by its prophets. These religious moral codes were not their personal inventions, but something decreed by God. Thus the Islamic code of law is not Arabic, nor was it Mohammad's personal invention, nor his whimsical ideas. Similarly, the Commandments of Moses and Jesus are not their inventions, but are of heavenly origin. These journalists are trying to confuse people by suggesting that there can be morality outside of faith and religion, like in the case of Muslims outside of the Islamic legal code.

Journalists often divide different nations, artificially, along religious lines; they divide the world into Christian, Islamic, and Buddhist parts. For example, they say that in the world one billion Muslims are living. But how many of them are true Muslims? Normally, priests, if they are sincere, should accept as true Christians, Muslims, or Buddhist only those people who fulfill all the requirements of the Canonical Law. In the case of Muslims, the majority live in secular countries under the secular legal code. Therefore, how many true Muslims are there on the earth?

In the modern age, they classify people as Christians or Muslims according to the religion of their parents or grandparents. Today, in the West, the Christians who ignore all Christian ethics and mores are hypocritically considered as the people of the Christian faith. It should be understood that in the West, the ruling class, the establishment, do not want to see the Christian Church as a vital and influential institution. The Western pharaohs of our times want the religious commandments and laws to be on paper only. They want to see the activities of priests restricted to the walls of the church, rather than allow them to go out and participate in social life.

Today, Turkish secularists are employing slogans of pan-Turkism, as if they wish to unite the different Turkic-speaking tribes to create a Turkish super state, but while they are doing it their true objective is to neutralize the pan-Islamic sentiments of Turks.

Thus while Islam unites different Muslim tribes and races, nationalist propaganda divides and separates them. To oppose these nationalistic slogans, the Muslims should consider the Islamic heritage, the Arabic language of the Holy Koran as their own, and unite under the Islamic banner.

Somebody with a humorous character could answer these journalists with their phony questions by saying, "It's true that I live an immoral lifestyle, not suitable for a good Muslim, but we are not living in an Islamic state, in the Sharia state." He could continue by saying, "I gamble, I drink alcohol, I seduce married women. All this is lawful under our secular code of law. Our secular laws allow us to live in sin."

Muslims do not require the Swiss Civil Code to make them happy or prosperous. They do not need these atheistic, godless laws, which are captivating them, enslaving them in their own lands by living life according to the rules set for them by strangers, by infidels.

They say, "We stand for human rights, for the personal freedoms of an individual to live his life as it suits him." They say, "We stand for the freedom of conscience." They state that their citizens are free to conduct their worship or to be atheistic. Actually, on paper, they allow religious freedom, but in practice the secular laws and regulations do not allow a believer to live his life in accord with his religious code of law. At the same time, godless people are free to live their immoral life, to live in sin, unrestrictedly.

What they call liberation and freedom in reality is the enslavement of the individual by his "lower self," by his animal instincts, and ultimately is the enslavement of Man by the Devil. The religious mind teaches us that true liberation and freedom for Man, for a believer, is in freeing himself from the shackles of materialism, in not sinning, since the perfectly conducted servitude to God ultimately leads him to true freedom and true liberation.

The divine religions of Islam, Christianity, and Buddhism, with their religious codes of law, allow their followers to escape the blind alley of individualism. Any sensible man can see that we cannot expect religion to be an integral part of society unless its ordinances and commandments are enforced on people, unless a community expects every individual to observe the sacred decrees of religion and God. Yet, they would call it religious fundamentalism, as something dangerous, as something outdated and not answering the requirements of modern society. Definitely, "fundamentalists," believers, who desire to see religion once more as an important institution, as the foundation of the social structure, represent a real danger to the secularist establishment.

Once, on a Turkish TV channel I saw a program, a discussion hosted by a local television celebrity, an old, bald, pot-bellied man. This was at the commencement of the most recent invasion of Iraq by Americans and the British. He, in tirade after tirade, impudently expressed abuses against the Kurdish people, calling them the most treacherous types, people who were repeatedly unfaithful and unreliable to all sides, who abandoned the battlefields, left the ranks of their friends and allies. This disgusting, malicious man, a propagandist of secularism, while using Nazi rhetoric, tried, hypocritically, to describe himself as a defender of ethnic Turks, as a Turkish patriot. Actually he behaved as an enemy, as an Israeli agent, as an agent of the enemies of Islam.

Ironically, this television channel describes itself as a religious channel, while promoting various pseudo-religious cults and sects that are not traditional Islam, broadcasts their messages by satellite to all parts of the world, to bring discord and confusion, to baffle and to muddle the minds of Muslims.

In answer to this television agitator, I would say that as a Muslim, I do not have any racist sentiments, therefore for me a Turk, a Kurd, an Arab, or a Persian makes no difference, as long as the person is of Muslim faith.

Being a Muslim for me is not something ethnic or racial, but something transnational, surpassing the boundaries of tribalism and nationalism. As we know from history, Kurds were always a very militant people. Unlike what this man said, they were independence loving, brave highlanders. It is a well-known fact that the legendary Muslim commander, the terror of the Crusaders, the sultan of Egypt and Syria, Saladin, was an ethnic Kurd. Did he not crush and defeat the armies of the Western Crusaders and return the control over Jerusalem (Al-Quds) to the Muslims? Although he was a Kurd, he was not a Kurdish tribal ruler, a tribal warrior, but an Islamic ruler. His Muslim faith made him what he was – a great warrior of faith.

This fat Turk continued to abuse the Kurds by saying that Kurds are not good enough, clever enough to run a country. He said, "They never in history had a state of their own, unlike us Turks." But I will reject all his sarcastic statements, with the thought that the majority of Turkish Ottoman sultans were of obscure ethnic origin, since the rulers of the empire had heirs mostly from European and Christian wives. These sultans had more English, French, and Russian blood in their veins than Turkish.

Besides, the Ottoman Empire was a caliphate, which united under its roof not just Turks, but also Arabs, Kurds, and other Muslim ethnicities. It was not a Turkish empire or Turkish state, nor a colonial power, but a pan-Islamic caliphate, a theocratic state. These sultans or caliphs were not Turkish rulers, but leaders of the Sunni caliphate, and the contents of their veins, their blood, had no relevance to their Muslim subjects. If they would have been non-Islamic, pagan rulers, like the Pharaohs, or like the Persian emperors, we could describe them unfavorably as tyrants, self-indulgent, arrogant despots. But what made them acceptable heads of state, as good rulers, was the fact that they served Islam, were Islamic leaders, and hence the defenders of faith.

The bald man held the debate, while a huge portrait of Ataturk, the founder of the Turkish Republic, hung over his head on the wall, as a reminder that he was upholding the line of the dictator, the tyrant that dared to dismantle the caliphate, the last genuinely Islamic Sunni state in the world.

During recent political developments, voices were heard claiming that Turkey needs the United States as a friend and partner. But in reality it is not Turkey that needs America, but America that needs Turkey. The United States needs Turkey to advance its interests in the Middle East, the Caucasus, and in Central Asia. As I see it, this relationship is totally one-sided, benefiting just one side, only America, but in no way Turkey. For many years, the Turkish economy suffered because of the intervention of the Western neo-colonialist powers. Is not Turkey the poorest country in Europe? Is it not true that the Turkish population has the lowest income in the whole of Europe? Is this not the result of Western economic dominance in the Turkish economy?

The U.S. military industry benefited from Turkey's membership in NATO, from the huge military orders coming from Turkey. Indeed, Turkey is losing economically and politically, as it is exploited to promote American and Israeli objections in the region. But there were times when Turks were the governors of the Middle East!

But the Turkish secular establishment and its Zionist masters want to use Turkey as a doormat for U.S. soldiers at the entrance of the Middle East, so that they can wipe their feet on it, in army boots and, at leisure, step beyond the Turkish borders inside Arab lands, especially inside the Islamic Republic of Iran. Is this not the ultimate objective and aspiration of the Jews?

An American researcher (Shaul Bakhash), in his book about Iran, claimed that the Islamic revolution in this country is not something exportable, as it is a unique development for Iran, for Iran's particular social structure and situation. So far, this statement proved accurate, because Iran is a Shiite state, has a Shiite brand of Islam, which is a minority sect, while its religious leaders, its clergy have little influence on the rest of the Muslim world and cannot extend their authority to the majority of Muslims, to the Sunnite world.

To my mind, the greed of the U.S government was one of the major factors that brought down the Pahlavi regime in Iran. The final years of the Shah's rule were the most profitable for the U.S. arms manufacturers. The U.S. president of those times, at an economic crisis period, urged Mohammad Reza Pahlavi, King of the Kings, to purchase a record amount, tens of billions of dollars worth of American armaments to the satisfaction of its arms barons. Thus the Americans put too great a load on the back of the donkey of the Pahlavi regime, much heavier than it could bear, which made it collapse under its load, and in the end damaged their interests in the country.

A similar kind of thing can happen in Turkey. As I see it, the U.S. government today is putting on the Turkish secularist regime loads and loads of burdens, to promote American and Israeli interests in the region, which, in the end, will break the back of the godless Turkish regime, with similar consequences and a dramatic chain of events as happened in Iran. This kind of development is a very probable perspective in the case of the

Americans showing its favors to the Kurdish nationalists, by allowing them to build their independent Kurdish state. In this case, while the Western states and Israel would get a new Kurdish allied state in the center of the Middle East, this would be of little advantage to them, since in comparison to it they are going to lose their important ally, the Turkish Republic.

The appearance on the political map of the world of a Kurdish state would trigger a possible Kurdish uprising in the neighboring state, Turkey, which would bring civil unrest, then a civil war. Then the fighting will cross over the border and would bring about a war between the Kurdish state and Turkey. This development would likely lead to American and Israeli involvement on the side of their new ally, the Kurdish state, and will end up in military confrontation between them and Turkey. As the result of this development, Turkey, possibly, would terminate its membership in NATO.

All these events, amid general anti-American feelings among Turks, can lead to a Muslim uprising, which, eventually will assist the coming to power in Turkey of a theocratic, Islamic government. This kind of Islamic revolution in Turkey would bring to power a genuinely Muslim government, a Sunni Shariah regime. The Sunni Hanafi branch of Islam of the Turks is the traditional orthodox branch (or school) of Islam, unlike the marginal, heretical sect that rules in Saudi Arabia and the other Persian Gulf states.

The emergence of Turkey as a Sunni Islamic state would be a major disaster for the Western political objectives in this strategic region, as well as in the entire Muslim world – a much bigger disaster than the emergence of Islamic Iran, as Turkey henceforth could serve as a model to all Sunni Muslims around the world. Besides this, an Islamic Turkey could serve as an exemplary regime for other numerous Turkic-speaking countries that emerged after the fall of the USSR, to follow suit and to establish their own theocratic states of government.

More than this, the Turkish Islamic state could eventually claim back all the lost territories of the Ottoman Empire, including Jerusalem (Al-Quds), Mecca, and Medina. The appearance of the new Islamic Turkey would lead to the annihilation of all the advances of the Western neo-colonialist powers in the Muslim world achieved in the past century. This development would certainly bring about the collapse of Zionist Israel and, eventually, would hit a severe blow to the Jewish Diaspora, to its established positions in Western countries.

The possibility of these kinds of political developments, the prospect of the unfolding of this kind of scenario, makes the secular Turkish regime very important for the West and for Israel. To them this fiercely secularist regime is a major guarantor against the risks of the appearance of powerful, united, pan-Islamic state in the region, capable of putting an end to Zionist Israel. Besides this, this development would bring about the cessation of Western influence over the Arabs, of its control over their oil fields.

Therefore, all these considerations make me think that it is the Turks, not the Iranians, who hold the keys to the deliverance of Muslims, to the Islamic revival, to the emergence of new, genuinely Islamic states. To my mind, in the other Muslim countries other than Turkey, there exists very little possibility of the advent of true Islamic regimes.

I should admit that Muslims, usually, are a disorganized people. There is no unity among them. They are not capable of organizing themselves so that they act together against their oppressors. The Muslim people can be likened to a flock of sheep, which with a good shepherd will be safe and secure, will avoid becoming the victims of wolves. Similarly, if genuine Islamic leaders were to rule the Muslim populace, then they would be safe and prosperous.

Thus my personal opinion is that our expectations of an Islamic revival or of a worldwide Islamic revolution would be fulfilled, not by any organized Islamic activities, but rather because of unpredictable events, different elemental influences, or climatic changes.

Despite everything that was said above about the Jews, no matter how strange it may sound, still, they can bring an apology in their defense, a justification to all their evil deeds. Thus they can say in their defense, that "although we committed a lot of criminal acts against great religions of the world, we did it because we had no other choice or option, since we are a small tribe. We committed and continue to commit evil crimes just to survive in this world." This is feeble, but still an excuse. On the other hand, the number of the Christians is large. They are the representatives of the largest religious community in the world. The Christian world is strong from all points of view, be it military, economic, or political. In the case of Christians, their hostility and treachery toward faith and religion could not be considered as a means of self-defense. There was no threat to them. Rulers and leaders of the Christian world sold their faith and religion to the Zionists. They did it to keep the full power in their own hands, so as not to share it with the Church. That is why the Christians can bring no argument for self-justification. They have no excuse. They are even guiltier than the Jews, twice more. They are multiple times guiltier.

Today, the apostate Christian nations, with an intention to destroy the Islamic faith, came to an agreement to enter into a covenant with the Devil, and declared a war against the Muslim world.

God Most High in His Book says, "O you who believe! Do not take the Jews and the Christians for friends; they are friends of each other; and whoever amongst you takes them for a friend, then surely he is one of them; surely Allah does not guide the unjust people" (Koran, 5:51).

CHAPTER TEN:
NEO-NAZIS, SKINHEADS, AND OTHERS

With the fall of the Soviet Union, when Marxists with their internationalist propaganda left the scene, in the new capitalist Russia, various right-wing radicals, neo-Nazis, and skinhead youth gangs gradually started to appear and organize themselves.

At first, I was surprised and taken aback by this phenomenon. How could it be, since the Soviet people in the Second World War fought against Nazi Germany and regarded Fascists as their mortal enemies? But today, a large number of Russian nationalists consider themselves followers of the ideological program of Adolf Hitler. Nevertheless, it seems that there is a good explanation for all this. It should be stated here that racial prejudice, extreme nationalism, is a characteristic feature of all European people, including the East Europeans and Russians. Back in the Soviet times, the authorities suppressed Russian nationalism and chauvinism and any propaganda of racism; the law forbade ideas of the racial supremacy of the white race.

In modern-day Russia, the press often writes that for unknown reasons, the local law-enforcement bodies are closing their eyes to the activities of the neo-Nazis, and even denying the mere fact of their existence in the country. They ignore all complaints concerning this matter.

Journalists are writing that many incidents of violence, of beatings, murders of the representatives of colored races, of inhabitants from the Caucasus region, pogroms in the market places, should not be classified merely as criminal incidents, but as offences committed on nationalistic grounds by loose gangs of nationalists. But despite the complaints of the victims and protests of the Russian human rights activists, the police continue to turn a blind eye, and describe these incidents as unconnected with racial motives.

All this reminded me of something I saw and heard before when I lived in Western European countries – in Germany, France, and England. As in Russia, the police in these lands try to ignore the crimes committed by neo-Nazis and skinhead gangs, especially when they are directed against Asians and Africans. Everywhere in Western Europe for decades, a multitude of right-wing radical movements operated organizations and parties. As I understand it, all these youth groups and parties are under the strict supervision of the local state security agencies, while their heads and leaders are state operatives and agent provocateurs. In the West, this state of affairs has continued for a long time and is the rule of the game. However in modern Russia, ultra-right nationalism and Nazism is a new, uncustomary phenomenon. Therefore the new authorities in their country are adopting Western political technologies, tested by time and experience.

In today's Russia, as in the West, the authorities use these groups in their political games. As a rule, the main targets of these attacks, of physical violence committed by these racists are the dark-skinned people from the Caucasus, the central Asians, and non-European foreigners. It appears that this state of affairs suits the authorities. It is not a matter of their concern; neither do they express any objection. As I see it, nowadays in Russia the people from the Caucasus region are in great demand. In this country, they play the role of scapegoats or of the "lightning rod." By using them, the authorities manage to redirect the social resentment and anger of the masses, away from themselves into a safe harbor.

Today in Russia, oligarchs are in charge – the representatives of big business. The country is controlled by a handful of people. A great many of these oligarchs are Jewish. Thus, as a striking example, I could bring up the billionaire, Mr. Roman Abramovitch, who in this wretched and poor Russia is bathing in money, spending hundreds of millions of dollars to satisfy his extravagant personal requirements. This filthy rich man sits like this, and looks at the Russian common man. He sees that inside this man everything boils and seethes. He sees that both class and racial hatred overwhelms him. All this gives him the shivers. He starts to shake and tremble with fear. He is afraid that the anger and hatred which fills the chest of the Russian man can overflow and burn him – a Jew. However, by no means can he allow this to happen. Exactly, for this reason he needs a certain "magical stick," a certain "lightning rod," a scapegoat, that will deflect the strike from him. The natives of the Caucasus play this role of a "lightning rod."

Today, in capitalist Russia these Abramovitches, and Vexelbergs, and others are the lords, the true governors, the true faces of the government, while the Russian secret services, in trying to suit this Jew-Masonic establishment, to secure its peace, solve the problem by their own means. I see it like this ... The Russian state security agencies make a contact, enter into a dialogue with the heads, with the leaders of different right-wing radical groups, explaining to them the political situation, and give them lessons on political education. Then they draw out for them the frameworks in which they can continue their activities, "If you touch the Jews or attack the Jewish establishments, we will break all your fingers!

Chapter Ten: Neo-Nazis, Skinheads, and Others

You're allowed to hit only the Caucasians, the colored people. That's all right!"

The authorities, by acting like this, allow the Russians to let off steam and to calm down. At the end, the wolves are fed and the sheep are safe. More than that, all this contributes to the fact that the Russian nationalists will get an illusion – "Since they allow us to beat up these dark-skinned Azeri vendors in the markets, then that means that at last, once more, our people are ruling!"

In the West there are no Caucasians, but there are non-European foreigners who become the prime target of the violence by neo-Nazis and gangs of skinheads.

I remember how many years ago, in Moscow, I met a Soviet historian, who specialized in the politics of West Germany. In a candid conversation, he tried to convince me that he knew the secrets of the German state security agencies. One of the secrets he knew was that these agencies were covert patrons of different extremist organizations, on one side the right-wing radicals, and on the other the left-wing anarchists. According to him, the German authorities were using these radical movements and groups to allow them to manipulate the political situation in the country.

To prove the authenticity of this information, I can retell here the content of an article that I read in an American magazine, which told the story of the activities of a notorious German left-wing group that carried out the assassinations of famous personalities and politicians in West Germany. According to this article, the head of this insurgent group was on the federal warrant list. The authorities described him as a very dangerous murderer and terrorist. However, for many years he was kept under surveillance by the German secret services, while they filmed all his movements. The author of the article, while trying to clarify the situation to the readers of this respectable political edition, between the lines hinted that this anarchist was actually a secret agent of the government. All this continued for a long time, until a German police officer managed to put an end to the terrorist career of this man.

Once, as this agent provocateur peacefully sat and dined in a restaurant, he was recognized by two policemen who were also eating in there. Then, there started a shoot-out between them in which he was killed. In this way, the police unwittingly killed a valuable agent, an operative working for the German government.

Years later, they arrested another member of this group. Soon after, she was found hanged in her prison cell. It is possible that the authorities staged this suicide. It is likely that they eliminated her because she knew too much, so that the close links of this terrorist group with the German secret services would never surface.

When I lived in Germany, in a small town, as I was walking on the street, I saw further ahead of me an entrance of a house which was guarded by two policemen, armed with small submachine guns. When I got closer, I saw that it was the Jewish Museum. I had already been living in this country for some time. I had been to its various parts, but I do not recall any instance when any site there was guarded by people armed with submachine guns. In those times, out of sheer curiosity, no less than ten times, I passed by the sentry boxes of the American army bases and barracks without permission, in and out without any interference, and nobody ever stopped me. This proves that the safety of the American army personnel, of the American soldiers, was not a priority matter, while this Jewish museum contained inside it nothing more valuable than exhibited photographs and posters, was guarded with all seriousness and earnestness. Similar things can be seen in all European cities, where Jewish organizations, Jewish sites, are guarded, as the pupil of one's eye, as the most important sites.

I remember another incident that took place in another German city, in the eastern part of the country, where there was high unemployment among the population and great social tension. In this town, the local skinheads, a group of one hundred people, surrounded a hostel where Vietnamese people lived. They nailed-up the entrance doors from the outside and put the ground floor on fire. The Vietnamese, without a route of escape, were forced to gather on the roof of this multi-story building and cry for help from there.

This siege lasted for five long hours, as all German national TV channels transmitted live pictures from the site. I saw all this live on television. While I sat there in front of a TV set, I could not believe my eyes. It looked more like a surrealist movie, rather than something happening in the real life. The local Germans who lived in the surrounding houses watched the developments from their windows and balconies. I especially recall a picture imprinted in my memory of an elderly German woman who stood on her balcony, appealing to these skinheads, to the hooligans, screaming encouraging words like, "Good boys, give these foreigners some heat," and clapped her hands.

Fortunately, there were no victims; nobody got hurt. After these events, the Vietnamese told the reporters that they managed to make a call to the police station, but the police ignored all their pleas for help. The German

Chapter Ten: Neo-Nazis, Skinheads, and Others 199

police are usually very efficient and uncompromising in fighting crime, while in this case they did nothing, demonstrated total indifference. For me it was all too clear that the state security agencies notified the police in advance, and instructed them not to interfere in the case, which was in their own jurisdiction and under their control.

Very recently in three German cities, several houses in which German citizens of Turkish descent were living simultaneously burned. Whole families died there. These incidents shocked and agitated the local Turkish diaspora, while Turkey expressed its concern. But the German government showed no desire to see any criminal intent, or premeditated arson attacks, despite the fact that witnesses of the incidents claimed that they saw young German men running from the scenes and screaming anti-Turkish expressions.

As I see it, in the European "democracies," the authorities demonstrate very liberal attitudes toward the right-wing radicals, and do not interfere in their activities, as long as they do not trespass certain boundaries. In other words, as long as they leave the Jews in peace. On the other hand, violence against colored people and Muslims is tolerated and receives no objections from the authorities.

Today in Britain, there officially functions a party of neo-Nazis – The British National Party. For its long history it did not manifest itself in any way. Tall and strong young men, members of the party, from time to time, amuse themselves by scratching swastikas on gravestones in Jewish cemeteries. It appears that the desecration of the gravesites is permitted for them, tolerated by the British authorities, and within the allowed boundaries of hostility toward the Jews.

Once, an English TV channel showed a film about local ultra-right political movements. In this documentary, besides other things, they showed former members of the British neo-Nazi party, a splinter group made up of young men and women. These people made an announcement (the film was made by a hidden camera) that they left the ranks of this party when it became clear that its leaders were "sold" to the authorities, collaborated with the British secret services. At the end, they said that, henceforth, this group will go underground and will continue their fight from there.

Another time, I saw on a television documentary footage about how, in an English town, the local hooligans surrounded the house of a Pakistani, on the ground floor of which there was his corner shop. Then they started to throw in its windows bottles filled with gasoline. All these bacchanalia, this orgy, continued for hours. The Pakistani and his wife, who was British, called the police and asked for help. The police station was within two hundred yards of the house. Nevertheless, nobody was interested; nobody came to their rescue.

In the last few years, I have heard about thousands of attacks on colored people and on Muslims in Western Europe and Russia, and only a few cases of attacks on Jewish sites. As I see it, all this is a result of the workings of the local secret services, who supervise the activities of the right-wing organizations and parties. While there were rare singular incidents of attacks on Jews, or on Jewish establishments, even if they took place, these actions were the consequence of the activities of unorganized individuals, who were not under the control of the state security agencies. In this way, the authorities all around Europe, including Russia, are using non-white people as the scapegoats, as sacrificial lambs.

In our times, Zionist ideology stands at the foundation of the political philosophy of the capitalist world, where the Jewry are treated as the most important people, as the untouchable people, and remain under the protection of governments and law-enforcement bodies.

CHAPTER ELEVEN:
THE ELITE SPEAKS RUSSIAN

Nowadays, many years since the collapse of the USSR, the political leaders of the Muslim republics of the former Union, in their speeches before of the people, like to state that they themselves, in a hard struggle, earned their sovereignty, their freedom. But in reality, Moscow itself granted them their independence. This independence was forced upon them, rather than them achieving it by their own effort. These Russified Muslim ethnic groups, the ordinary Soviet populace, with its mediocre mentality, lacking any initiative, were not ready for self-government.

One peculiarity of the Soviet Union was that there existed discrimination against the Muslim part of population, who got the treatment of second-class citizens. The USSR was organized like this. Initially, it was a union of the three Slavic nationalities or republics – Russian, Ukrainian and Belarusian. Next to this troika, to this main cell, two Eastern Orthodox ethnicities or republics – Georgian and Armenian – were amalgamated, turning it into a union of five Eastern Orthodox ethnic groups. Subsequent to this union of five, the remaining Christian nations, the Baltic republics and Moldavia, were molded, while the outer circle of the Soviet Union – which was the most neglected portion – was composed from six Muslim republics.

For this reason, today, the Russian leaders who have a nationalistic agenda, who cherish the idea and draw the plans for re-establishing the empire, should first restore its original cell and reconstruct its original foundation; that is, to unite in a single state the three Slavic nationalities. Therefore today, if Moscow proposed, let say, to unite Kyrgyzstan with Russia, then objections would be raised. They can bring up the argument: why should we Kyrgyz people join Russia when the brotherly peoples of Russia, Ukraine and Byelorussia, have no desire to do it?

That's why Moscow's attempts today to draw closer and to unite together in a single union the lands of Russia, Ukraine, and Byelorussia, might be seen as the signs, the indications, that it is trying, in any form or format, to restore the Russian empire, to reunite its lost territories.

Moreover, in the Soviet Union, the Russification program existed. This program was vigorously and harshly conducted in the Muslim lands. The aim of this program was to unite and cement together the population of the union. They especially encouraged inter-ethnic, inter-confessional marriages between Muslim men and non-Muslim women. Their target was to achieve, in the end, the complete elimination of all Muslim minorities in the masses of the Russian population.

Many years ago, in Baku, in Parapet Square, I saw a group of men, all three of whom were ethnic Armenians. I recognized one of them as my acquaintance. I approached them, stood by them, and started to listen to their talk.

One of them said: "I work in the KGB. That's why I know a lot. I know things that ordinary people are not aware of. For example, I know that in the Central Committee (of the Communist Party of the Soviet Union) there is an unwritten law that anyone who desires to get a promotion first has to prove his reliability and loyalty to the Soviet State. Thus in the case of him being a Muslim male, he must prove that he is not a nationalist. For this reason, he must create a Russian-speaking family. He must marry a non-Muslim woman – Russian, Ukrainian, Armenian or Jewish. He must send his children to a Russian language school. But if a Muslim male marries a Muslim woman like himself, enrolls his children in an ethnic language school, he falls under the suspicion that he is a nationalist. In that case, he gets no promotion; he can't rise up the departmental ladder. He won't get a chance to get a high-position job."

However, the Kremlin's policy toward its Christian subjects was entirely different. They were given a lot of leeway. In the Christian republics it was permitted to openly conduct nationalistic policy. In the Caucasus, the Kremlin especially pampered and spoiled the Georgians and Armenians. They were allowed to employ ethnic cleansing programs against the Muslim population on their territories, as well as to carry out mass deportations. The final goal and objective of the mass deportations of Muslim ethnic groups to Siberia and Soviet Central Asia was to make the Christian population of the Caucasus predominant.

Once during the Soviet times, I visited a bookshop in the main city of Georgia. As I could not find Russian-language books there, I asked the shop assistant about where in town one could find them. The shop assistant said, "Not just in our shop, but in the whole city, in the whole of the Soviet Georgian Republic you can't find books in the Russian language. In Georgia, we're not allowed to sell books in this language. We read books only in our native Georgian language."

All this was despite the fact that Russian was the only official language of the Soviet Union. In the Muslim republics, the situation was entirely different. Thus I remember how the bookshops in Baku were packed to full

Chapter Eleven: The Elite Speaks Russian

capacity with books in the Russian language. Russian tourists from other parts of the Soviet Union were amazed when they saw in Baku's bookshops shelves crammed with scarce publications which were impossible to find in the other parts of the country. The authorities deliberately overflowed the book outlets of the Muslim republics with Russian language literature, so that people, by reading these books, would gradually forget their own ethnic languages, so as to Russify them.

The situation today has hardly improved. Similarly, as in the Soviet times, bookshops in Baku are crammed with the Russian publications. They sell very well. The Russian-speaking part of the population lives in prosperity. They can afford to spend money on books. On the other hand, books in the national, official language – even when they are published – sell poorly. The Muslim majority cannot afford to spend money on books, on food for thought. So the publishing houses that print books in the official Azeri Turkic language go out of business; they get closed due to making a loss.

Today, the Western and Russian mass media, as it speaks about the situation in these newly independent Muslim states, demonstrate either hypocrisy or a lack of understanding. They forget to mention the most important thing; and the most important thing, the main peculiarity of these states, is that the Russian-speaking elite rule there. They created these elite on purpose, artificially, so that it would provide a guarantee for Moscow's control of these territories. As yesterday, as today, all members of the government, all ministers of these Muslim republics are Russian-speakers who do not speak the native, now official, languages.

Today, this is the state of affairs in these countries. The Russian language dominates there. The program of Russification of Muslims has not stopped; to the contrary, it has been intensified. The explanation for this is that the Russian-speaking elite understand that the high status of the language assures and secures their hold on power. On the other side, the strengthening of the status of the native languages of Muslims inevitably will bring about their loss of power, the loss of privileges.

Nowadays, the leaders of these republics from time to time are decorated with Russian orders and medals for their merits to Russia, for keeping and preserving, as before, the high status of the Russian language. In these republics, the Russian language remains a compulsory subject in all local schools and universities. This elite, this social stratum, sees in the Muslims their enemies, while they regard Islam as a hostile ideology.

Currently in Baku, in the classified pages of newspapers, one can find columns of advertisements offering good jobs to Russian-speakers, jobs with huge wages by local standards – from six hundred to a thousand U.S. dollars per month. Also, in these newspapers, one can find jobs ear-marked for the other category of the population, for the non-Russian-speakers, such as jobs for unskilled workers on building sites.

These positions don't necessarily require good knowledge of the Russian language. It is just discrimination against the part of population that prefers to speak their Muslim native tongues. In these Muslim republics, all high-paid jobs are preserved for the Russian-speakers. Likewise today, as in the Soviet times, it is the responsibility of the government to provide this privileged class with nice apartments and good, prestigious positions. This previous social structure, which is discriminative towards Muslims, is kept intact by the local authorities.

As an example to all I said above, I can bring out here a characteristic case where a Russian-speaking girl got a job as a presenter on a TV station in Baku. She was supposed to read the news, to speak in the local Turkic dialect. The fact that she could not speak this language was of no importance to her employers. It seems that the management of the station thought that all she has to do was to read from a paper. While she could master the newly introduced Latin alphabet easily, nothing resulted from it. For several days she sat in front of the cameras while she was on the air, and could not manage to read from the paper. They had to dismiss her, but maybe moved her on to another prestigious position.

Also in the newspapers in Baku, one can find many job offers from parents seeking Russian-speaking governesses. In Tsarist Russia, in the aristocratic circles, it was considered as a matter of prestige for parents to employ a French governess. In those times, the petty-bourgeoisie was fond of speaking French, so that with this they could pass themselves off as members of the aristocracy. Likewise, today in Baku, the lower classes, trying to pretend that they are representatives of the ruling class, try hard to speak Russian.

These days in Baku, more and more new expensive shops and boutiques have opened, such as Escada, Calvin Klein, Hugo Boss, United Colors of Benetton, Dolce & Gabbana, Versace, and Gucci. All the shop assistants that are employed in these shops are exclusively Russian speakers, so that they can give good service to the Russian-speaking clients, who can afford to shop in such establishments.

As I walk the streets of Baku, I see that the faces of the Russian-speaking people are shining with joy and happiness, while the faces of the non-Russian-speaking part of the population are grim and unhappy. As I see it, as long as the power and control remain in the hands of the Russian-speaking elite in these Muslim states, it is too early to speak about independence or freedom in that part of the world. Only when the truly patriotic circles come to power there – which, in my opinion, can be only the Islamists – will the Muslim majority in these states obtain true independence and freedom.

APPENDIX I:
A DERVISH'S LETTER TO TURKMENBASHI

In the name of God, the Merciful, the Compassionate!

Dear Sir,

I am a citizen of the Azerbaijan Republic. I am a believer, a practicing Muslim, and a Sufi. I have a great respect for the Islamic scholars (*ulama*), who have received the traditional religious education, but my true specialization is in Muslim mysticism (*Tasawwuf*). During the Soviet period, it was impossible to conduct any real religious activity in Baku. Today, the situation is not much different. The atheist establishment considers religion its rival, and treats it with suspicion.

Before, I unsuccessfully tried to find a place where I could conduct my Sufi activities without interference from the state and the local authorities. But in modern times it is difficult to find any country with a friendly regime, where one can set up an independent religious charity. The unsavory truth is that in all modern states, religion is under the inhibitive, restrictive control of the government, the police, and state security agencies.

Therefore, Sufis (*ahli tasawwuf*), as independent-minded people, find it problematic and arduous to conduct their traditional activities in such an atmosphere.

Thus, in my opinion, the only country that could be favorable for a work in the revival of Sufi tradition is Turkmenistan. The information that I received makes me think that your leadership style, your person, Sir, is my only hope to find a suitable place for my religious work.

Therefore, I want to make an appeal to you, Sir, to allow me to come to Turkmenistan and to set up a Sufi study center (*khanaka*) there.

Thus the project can be either the revival or reactivation of an old historic Turkmen Sufi study center, or the building of an all-new one. Naturally, I do not mean the academic, the secular, approach to study, but creating a traditional Sufi institution.

There exists a lot of hostile propaganda criticizing your leadership style. It claims that it is not democratic enough, not liberal enough, that it is an authoritarian rule. To all this unfair propaganda I will say that on my travels abroad I could never find any democratic or free country in the East or in the West. It is true that in the West there is economic prosperity. But, in my opinion, all this was achieved by the exploitation of the raw materials and the natural resources of the Third World countries. Therefore, the Western regimes are as undemocratic, unjust, and oppressing as any brutal, ancient tyrannies of the past. All the rest is merely Radio Liberty propaganda and misinformation.

What the world and mankind need is not an immoral libertine society, not the chaos of a multi-party system, not the "human rights" demagogy, but a party that will speak for the people, stand for their rights and needs, for the justice and peace of the majority. Society needs leadership that will be representative of the nation (*millat*), of the majority of the population, but not of the temporary settlers, or of the migrating, cosmopolitan minorities.

As an ordinary man, as a fair person, I dislike the bureaucracy, this self-serving, corrupt, faceless, and egoistic class. I do not trust them. To organize the work properly, I will need special conditions. No modern bureaucratic authority can provide or grant me these special conditions since it would be against their practices and rules.

For this reason, I am making this appeal to you, Sir, to a powerful leader, to Turkmenbashi, the father figure for all Turkmen people. I am asking you, to issue an exceptional permission, a document giving the special status of a holy place to this Sufi study center, so that its normal work could be conducted without any interference from the local authorities, police, or the state security agencies.

As I see it, there is no way that Sufis can organize any true Sufi work, such as a study group (*halqa*), the setting up of a society, unless the leader, the head of state, issues a certain kind of paper, an exceptional protection document that will allow them to conduct, in peace, useful spiritual activity within the center. It can be some kind of a license or a special privilege document.

The document, as much as I care, can be a symbolical one. What we need is for the authorities to respect the society, the study group, not to harass it in any way, not to conduct any forceful entries into its premises under any pretext, and thus not desecrate the site of this holy institution. The holy place, at any price, should remain as such. The authorities should treat the religious community with due respect.

Of course I cannot demand that any institution extend a holy status to my person. Respect toward a religious teacher, to a religious public figure, is a matter of personal faith and individual commitment. In case you, Sir, will issue such kind of special status document to our center, you will be free to revoke it any time Your Highness pleases.

In case anybody asks me about my nationality, I will answer that I am a Muslim and this is my identity, rather than my Azeri, Turkic identity. My slogan is – happy is he who says, I am a Muslim. Today I have no partners or followers. I am not connected to any group or organization. Thus, the center (*khanaka*) will remain in Turkmenistan and will belong to the local Muslims.

Nobody can organize a Sufi work unless he has the God-given talent, which is a rare gift. Very few individuals have such talent. Today, in the world it is very difficult to find a true Sufi Master (*murshid*), or any genuine Sufi institution. There are a lot of charlatans and imposters, a lot of phony, false Sufi centers, but very few, if any, real, true ones.

Nobody can conduct this job of spiritual leadership by mere appointment of the authorities, or by choice of the people. This kind of person must be a man chosen by God only. This man himself should appoint his deputies or heirs. The leadership of a Sufi center is not a worldly secular position; it is subject to otherworldly rules and demands.

Besides, if the center were to be established, I would like the site to be given to me as a permanent endowment, so that after me, possibly my family member, my descendent, would inherit the center from me. Otherwise, it will look strange if some stranger – especially some useless person – would benefit from it all; get control of the institution that was created by my mind and thought.

Who is going to finance this project? It is possible to do it in three ways. First, money brought from abroad can finance it; second, by the people through contributions; third, the Turkmen state can do it. I know a couple of sultans who might be interested in financing such projects. I think that the financial matters would be the easiest side of the project.

If the Turkmen people will let me set up the center, I can promise that in the future our spiritual institution will produce holy people (*awliya*) of the Najm ad-Din Kubra and Abu Said al-Mayhani caliber. These men were, and still are, the leading spiritual thinkers of all ages. Does Turkmenistan today have the spiritual leaders of such prominence as them? If the Turkmen people will allow me to set up a Sufi center on their territory, they will soon acquire the leading spiritual giants of modern times.

It can be that the Turkmen state has no money for the construction of the center (*khanaka*), while foreigners will turn down our requests to provide the funds. In that case, within the country, people offering their skills as builders, engineers and painters to work free of charge for the project will rise up. There will be people who will offer their old books for the library of the center, manuscripts in Arabic and Persian.

Many years ago, I saw a Turkmen who was boasting by saying that he, in his yurt, in this remote nomadic settlement, organized a public cinema, where on a home video, nomads could see American-made porno-films. At the time, I saw in it an omen that the days of the Soviet Communist regime were counted. As Muslims, as God-fearing people, we are not against Western technology. But we oppose, we cannot accept, materialistic, secularist, wicked ideology, and the ways of life of the West.

Many years ago, I wrote a play about Mulla Nasrudin. I think it was the most complete and authentic play ever written about our sage, who was, a Sufi thinker and a holy man. I offered the play to a theatre director in Ashkhabad. I think that his name was Alo Alolovitch. But unfortunately, nothing came out of it. Then, later I lost the other copy in my possession.

In an Indian book it was written that clever men would never make a home in the land where scientists (*alims*) are not respected. Probably, it was for this reason that Tamerlane invited Nasrudin to his capital and offered him a position at his palace.

Several years ago, when I was staying in England, I found out that Turkmenistan had no embassy in London, in this important capital city. Therefore, I decided to offer my services, as a go-between, to the Turkmen state to find an official residential house for its ambassador. I went to the top houses, and, at last found the best one, the most suitable house in town. It was a wonderful property located in the most exclusive area of London, near the London Central Mosque in Regents Park, next to the residence of the United States ambassador.

I met the director general of the Crown properties, who supervised the entire estate of the Queen, to discuss the matter, whether they were willing to sell it to Turkmens. I thought at the time that by securing the property for us, by flying our Muslim flag in front of the Americans, we …how can I say it, could help to put Turkmenistan on the map, and rub the Americans' noses. These arrogant Americans are used to looking down at us Muslims.

I tried to send a letter, to make contact with Ashgabat, offering my services as an estate agent, but my faxes never went through and so nothing came out of it.

I hope that this time this Sufi center project will be more successful, and will be accepted by the Turkmen government; by You, Sir, and as an outcome of it, Turkmens will get in their possession a unique spiritual center.

It should be mentioned here, that these days the Islamic world has no true Sufi masters, but mostly shallow pretenders only. In the Arab lands if I will tell there that I am a Sufi teacher, a religious worker, Arabs will not accept it. They will say that they are better specialists in religious matters, since their Arabic is better, their pronunciation is better; their knowledge of the sacred language of Islam is more superior. So they think that only an Arab can understand properly the Koran and Islam.

In case of Iranians, every Iranian I met told me that I never could know Sufism better than him, since Persian is his mother tongue. So, these days every Iranian is trying to pass himself off as a Sufi or even as a Sufi master, because he read several Persian poems. Today, the mystical verses are a part of the school curriculum in Iran, as it always was. But it can never make every Iranian a mystic or mysticism specialist. So, what I mean is that it is impossible to teach an ignorant one, who thinks that he is a man of knowledge, a scientist (*alim*). The world is full with people who want to teach, but there are very few people who want to learn. Besides, they think that it is impossible that somebody from the former Soviet republic, the land of infidels (*kafir*), knows religion better than them. Additionally, in these countries religion is a commonplace thing, the ordinary thing, while in the former Soviet lands it is something exotic and exciting. Here, they have a religious thirst, which is an essential factor.

On my first visit to Ashkhabad, in the Soviet era, I at first wondered where the ethnic Turkmens were, the Muslim population. It was impossible to find them anywhere in the town center. But at last, I found them at the marketplace, selling countryside products to the Russian-speaking city dwellers. The bus terminal was built, conveniently, next to the market, so that buses could bring Muslim peasants, in the early morning, to the city to sell their produce, and take them away by the evening.

I found Ashkhabad city dwellers to be unsympathetic, snobbish people. I do not think that they would like the idea of building a Sufi center. But I want to establish this center not for these cosmopolitans, for these strangers, but for those poor Muslim people, the true Turkmens.

A.Mirza-Beg
Baku, Azerbaijan
April 16, 2001

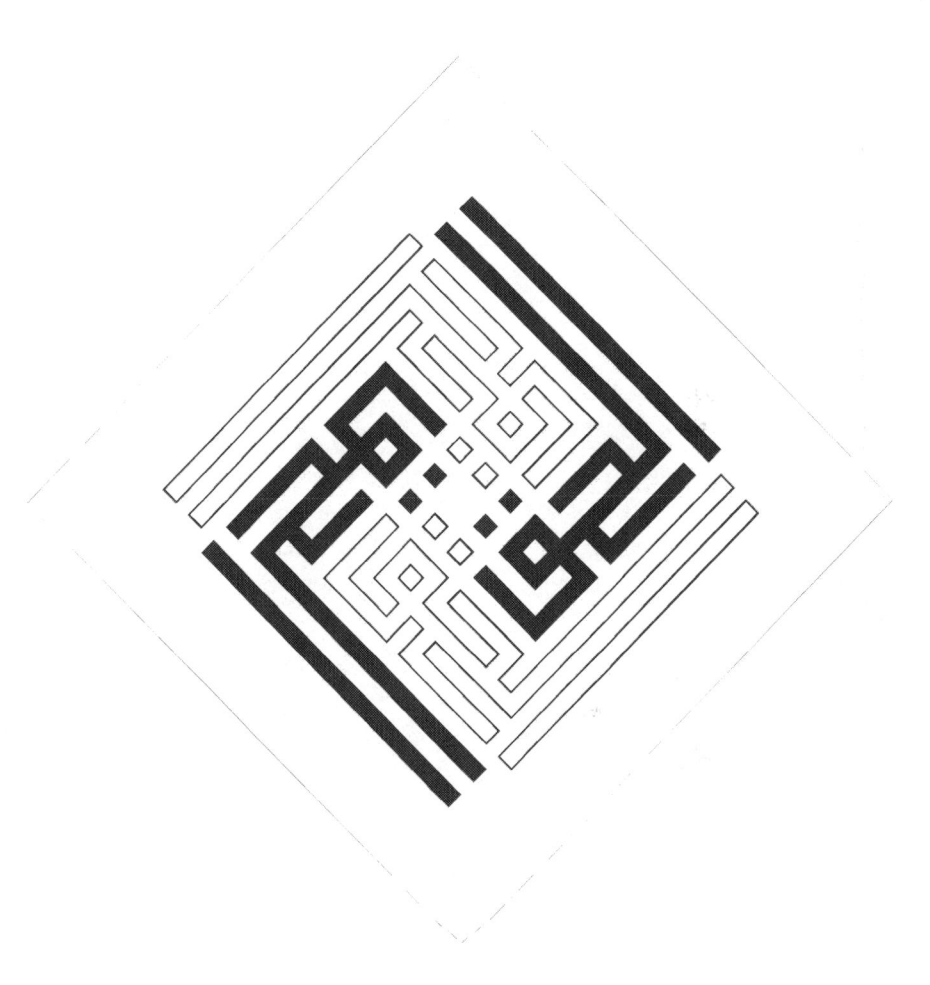

Made in the USA
Lexington, KY
09 July 2017